Positive Psychology for Teachers

Practical, actionable information about the positive behavioural approach to education is in desperately short supply, and yet when implemented properly the impact on school behaviour and achievement can be enormous.

Positive Psychology for Teachers aims to address this gap. Written by experienced practitioners, it gives teachers simple and direct advice on how they can use the positive behavioural approach for the benefit of their pupils and schools.

Based on the authors' own experiences of intervention in school settings and evidence of its effectiveness, this practical guide includes a number of vignettes and case studies illustrating how the behavioural approach has been used by teachers in a wide variety of classrooms to make their teaching more effective. Each case study will be followed by a number of suggested practical activities for classroom implementation. Throughout the book, background theory is explained in a concise and easily digestible manner and activities are clearly explained, with benefits and end goals clearly signposted.

Areas covered include:

- Whole school interventions, turning around under-performance
- Reducing disruptive behaviour in the classroom
- Improving creative writing and increasing reading attainment
- Improving pupils' self-concepts
- SEN interventions including autism, children with challenging behaviour and those classified as having social, emotional and behavioural difficulties
- The difference between teachers' treatment of boys and of girls
- Strategies for turning around the behaviour of very difficult pupils

This practical user-friendly text is aimed directly at trainee and practising teachers but would also be very relevant to those working with trainee teachers in university departments and to educational psychologists.

Jeremy Swinson is Principal Educational Psychologist for the Witherslack Group of Schools.

Alex Harrop is Emeritus Professor in Psychology at Liverpool John Moores University, UK.

Positive Psychology
for Teachers

Jeremy Swinson and Alex Harrop

Routledge
Taylor & Francis Group

LONDON AND NEW YORK

First published 2012
by Routledge
2 Park Square, Milton Park, Abingdon, Oxon OX14 4RN

Simultaneously published in the USA and Canada
by Routledge
711 Third Avenue, New York, NY 10017

Routledge is an imprint of the Taylor & Francis Group, an informa business

British Library Cataloguing in Publication Data
A catalogue record for this book is available from the British Library

Library of Congress Cataloging in Publication Data
  1. Educational psychology. 2. Classroom management.   3. Behavior
  modification. I. Harrop, Alex. II. Title.
  LB1051.S94 2012
  370.15—dc23   2011049346

ISBN: 978–0–415–68676–1 (hbk)
ISBN: 978–0–415–68677–8 (pbk)
ISBN: 978–0–203–80006–5 (ebk)

Typeset in Bembo
by RefineCatch Limited, Bungay, Suffolk

MIX
Paper from
responsible sources
FSC FSC® C004839
www.fsc.org

Printed and bound in Great Britain by
TJ International Ltd, Padstow, Cornwall

This book is dedicated to Michael Harrop and Andrew Swinson, both of whom died too young to show the world what might have been.

Contents

Figures

Tables

Acknowledgements

In writing this book, we have been influenced by many friends and colleagues who have shaped our thinking and been critical judges of our various endeavours. We would especially like to thank Mike Cording and Richard Melling who were instrumental in developing 'Four Essential Steps' and Brian Parsons who read the initial drafts of this book and gave us some thought-provoking feedback from a teacher's perspective. We would also like to thank the teachers and pupils who over the past 30 years have allowed us to observe them in their classrooms.

Finally, thanks are due to our respective partners, Sally and Lynne, without whose tolerance, good humour and cups of tea this book would not have been completed.

Preface

The term 'positive psychology' is comparatively recent. It derives from an address made by Martin Seligman to the American Psychological Society in 1998 in which he made the point that, during much of the last half century, psychology has been concerned with mental illness and with alleviating disorders to such an extent that it has turned attention away from any consideration of what makes life worth living. While accepting that psychology has been successful in helping individuals with disorders, he maintained that psychologists should also be thinking positively, not exclusively negatively. Positive psychology, in Seligman's view, should be concerned with 'happiness' and 'well-being'.

Seligman's address was particularly aimed at clinical psychologists and those working in psychiatry whose job often entails giving an explanation for some unusual types of behaviour and helping to devise a treatment plan for individuals who have mental health problems. His criticism, however, is equally relevant to educational psychologists who work in schools. Educational psychologists are usually asked to see those pupils who have problems with their learning or their behaviour or else they may be consulted for advice on how to help schools improve some aspect of their overall functioning such as how to increase their attendance figures or reduce their number of exclusions. Never, in our experience, has an educational psychologist been asked to look at pupils who are coping well and see how they could gain more from their time in school. As a consequence, educational psychologists have tended to become problem solvers when things go wrong or are in need of improvement.

In education, the notion of positive psychology has gained some credence. In 2005 the British government introduced SEAL (Social and Emotional Aspects of Learning) to all primary and secondary schools in England and Wales, an initiative aimed at enhancing pupils' 'emotional well-being'. The ideas behind the programme came from writers such as Goleman (2005), who developed the concept of 'emotional intelligence'. Goleman argued that emotional intelligence, which included the elements of empathy, happiness, social understanding and resilience, is just as important in determining successful outcomes for children as is their cognitive intelligence. The SEAL programme, which comprised weekly lessons aimed at enhancing emotional intelligence, was received enthusiastically by many teachers. Evaluation of the programme has, however, proved to be difficult, as has any evaluation of effects the programme may have on other aspects of children's learning.

While Seligman's address gave a strong impetus to psychologists to concern themselves with the more positive side of individuals there were, of course, a number of applications of positive psychology at work before that address. In educational psychology, we have known for some time now that positive approaches, be they in the form of reward systems in schools or positive encouragement from teachers, are the key to successful learning and well-behaved classes. The earliest account we could find in the research literature dates from the time of the Great War, when Gilchrist (1916) reported improvements in pupils' test performance as a result of praise from teachers.

The value of taking a positive approach towards pupils was brought home to us early in our careers. As an example, when one of us was asked to help with a very difficult class, described by a teacher as the 'class from hell', we followed the class around for a day observing both pupils and their teachers. There was no doubt that they were really hard work for their teachers but, by the same token, there was not a great deal of hard work being done by the pupils themselves in lessons. At the end of the morning the class was scheduled for a CDT (craft, design and technology) lesson. This took place in an old factory-like building across the schoolyard. As soon as the lesson began we became aware that the pupils behaved very differently for this particular teacher than they had for any others. He spoke in a quiet voice, was extremely courteous and was unfailingly positive in his remarks to the pupils, not only about their work but also about their behaviour. We counted his positive remarks over a 50-minute lesson and there were over 70 of them. He only had to 'tell off' one pupil and that was because she was so involved in her work that she didn't heed a request to come and see a demonstration.

After the class we asked the teacher where he had learned his technique. He seemed quite bemused by the question but after some thought told us that his original teaching was with apprentices in a factory. 'You quickly learn that telling them off doesn't work,' he said. 'The only approach that works with these difficult-to-teach kids and indeed with everyone is to be positive.'

The teacher's technique certainly worked and our observations of the pupils showed their involvement with the lesson, as measured by their 'on-task' rate (the time they spent doing what they were supposed to be doing), was virtually 100 per cent. When we asked the pupils why they were so much better behaved in this particular lesson than in others and why they seemed so involved they gave us many appreciative comments, e.g.: 'We all know what we are supposed to do.' 'He is so encouraging.' 'We all find his lessons so much fun.' 'We all feel we have achieved something at the end.'

A further example came to light when one of us was teaching in a non-selective secondary school in a deprived part of Liverpool. The school operated a house points system in which the pupils could earn points by good work and good behaviour in class. At the end of each week the winning house was announced with some enthusiasm by the head teacher in the school assembly and this was apparently appreciated by some of the younger pupils, the older pupils showing little interest and in some cases looking quite unhappy.

After some staffroom debate on the apparent ineffectiveness of the house points system, a new system was introduced through which the pupils in the winning house were to be allowed to leave school 15 minutes early on a Friday evening. This had an immediate effect. Pupils of all ages began to work and behave well in order to accumulate points and, for their part, the teachers were naturally very pleased with the success of the new system. Whether the system would have been effective in the long term, however, is not known, since the local education authority put a stop to the scheme as soon as it heard about it on the grounds that should any harm come to a pupil in the 15 minutes of free time, the authority would be responsible.

In retrospect, the giving of points to the pupils for good work and behaviour was having little effect because it was not linked to a reward the pupils valued. When it *was* linked to something the pupils valued it became effective.

Although the authors have had very different careers, one as an educational psychologist working in schools, the other teaching educational psychology to students and working with student teachers on teaching practice, we both began our working lives as teachers and we have both been trained as psychologists. A continual interest in the process of teaching and, in particular, in how we can help teachers to be more effective has shaped our professional lives. We have carried out extensive research, both separately and together, into the practice of teaching and in helping teachers to improve the behaviour and learning of their pupils. Moreover, our training in psychology has enabled us to apply scientific principles in measuring the effectiveness of any intervention (treatment) used.

Our aim in this book is to impart the general principles of the positive approach and to demonstrate a wide variety of techniques that we have used or those that we know others have used successfully to improve the learning experiences of young people from the ages of three to 18. The techniques and strategies we use have been subject to rigorous scientific evaluation and, as a consequence, we are not recommending certain strategies because we like them or think they work; any recommendations are based on proven effectiveness, because they do work.

Some of the interventions we describe are directed at specific aspects of children's behaviour, while others are directed at children's learning. In order for teachers to teach and pupils to learn, a degree of order is needed with pupil engagement, motivation and enthusiasm. The approach we take is aimed at achieving such situations. Well-run classes, good behaviour and enthusiastic, engaged learners are the essence of good teaching. In more general terms, the text contains a good deal of information about applications of the positive approach in a wide variety of classrooms and it is hoped that reading about investigations in classrooms will both inform the readers about what has been done and challenge them to try something out for themselves.

Chapter 1

Emergence of the positive approach

Background

If we look at accounts of teaching in the nineteenth century, we find they are peppered with references to unwilling pupils being punished by their teachers. Schools are not described as having been happy places. The literature is replete with stories of children being beaten. Schools are generally described as punitive institutions, and we get the impression that they were run completely on the basis of punishment and fear engendered in their pupils. Stories of such institutions are firmly embedded in our culture. In fact, Charles Dickens was so concerned at the state of what were called 'Yorkshire schools', schools to which unwanted children were sent and sometimes died at the hands of their carers, that he wrote his second campaigning novel, *Nicholas Nickleby*, on the subject.

If we look deeper, however, we find that some schools also included a measure of reward for their pupils. Practices that existed included awarding certificates to pupils who never missed attending, were always punctual, passed tests, etc. These certificates were taken home and often received with great pride by parents. In some schools, pupils would be shown magic lantern slides at playtime, or a class might be given extra playtime for doing well during an inspection. We hear little about such practices probably because they were few and far between and at least partly because they don't contribute as well to novels as do tales of brutal, sadistic schoolmasters.

Although there appear not to have been any systematic surveys undertaken in the early part of the twentieth century, much of the teaching in schools seems to have been authoritarian with severe consequences for pupils who broke the rules and not a great deal of reward or praise given for good behaviour. Sarcasm and ridicule ruled the day. Moreover, breaking the rules was often accompanied by corporal punishment. Put bluntly, pain was deliberately inflicted on the pupils by the use of the ruler, the cane, the strap and the *tawse* (in Scotland). The old saying, often used to justify a beating, 'spare the rod, spoil the child', comes to mind.

The first major source of evidence on the use of punishment and rewards in schools is found in one section of the report of a large-scale investigation that took place in the 1970s into the effectiveness of 12 inner-city London secondary schools (Rutter, *et al.* 1979). The team of investigators followed over 2000 pupils throughout their years of secondary schooling, and collected data on attendance, exam results and behaviour. Among the numerous findings, it was noted that while the particular kinds of reward and punishment employed varied considerably between schools, observations showed that, on average, punishments occurred twice as often as rewards. It was also observed that the average number of positive comments across all the schools was as few as three or four instances per lesson. Significantly, the use of punishment was found to be generally unrelated to pupil behaviour while the use of rewards was generally associated with better behaviour.

Punishments included teacher disapproval, detention, writing lines, being sent to the head teacher and corporal punishment, while rewards included teacher approval, public praise for good work, comments on individual pupils in assemblies and putting pupils' work on classroom walls.

The report concluded that while some sanctions are clearly necessary in secondary schools, the results of the investigation indicated that some schools were too negative in their approach. That section of the report ended by emphasising the value of a positive approach to teaching based on reward systems rather than a negative approach based on punishments.

The secondary school investigation was followed in the 1980s by a similar one undertaken in 50 junior schools in the London area (Mortimore et al. 1988). Some 2000 pupils were observed over four years. Among the findings, it was noted that the quantity of teachers' critical comments was related negatively to pupils' progress in a number of areas, while the quantity of teachers' positive and neutral comments was related positively to pupil progress. It was emphasised that teachers' praise and approval should be given as direct and immediate feedback to pupils for it to have maximum effect. It was also noted that teachers' criticism exceeded, on average, teachers' positive comments. Among the conclusions of the investigation was the recommendation that student teachers be made aware of the value of praise and the limitations of being negative towards their pupils.

Around the middle of the twentieth century public opinion began to change and the use of physical punishment began to be questioned, but it was only as late as 1987 that corporal punishment was banned in state schools and 1999 when it was banned in private schools. Teaching was becoming less negative. An important benefit to education, which appears not to have been noticed by many, was that the removal of corporal punishment forced those teachers who relied on physical punishment to look for other ways of keeping order in their classrooms.

First beginnings of the positive approach

Although many had doubts about the wisdom of the generally punitive methods used in teaching in the nineteenth century and in the early parts of the twentieth century, there was little evidence on which to base their doubts. It was only in the 1960s that any form of systematic investigation into the relative value of reward and punishment in schools took place. At that time, teachers and educational psychologists were becoming aware of research in human learning that demonstrated that children's behaviour was strongly influenced (reinforced) by adults' use of social rewards (praise, approval, smiles, nods, attention, proximity). As a consequence, a number of related investigations were conducted in the mid- to late 1960s in the USA to investigate the extent to which teachers could change their pupils' behaviour by their use of social reinforcement. They were aimed at making the teachers more effective in their teaching by encouraging pupils to become more engaged in their lessons and by generally making classrooms happier places through the application of the principles of human learning.

An underlying assumption of the investigations, albeit one not specifically stated, was that pupils in classrooms tend to behave in ways that have been learned as a result of the way they have been managed by their teachers. Consequently, the investigations were concerned with examining the effects of the use by teachers of positive comments, praise and/or approval, of negative comments, telling off and/or disapproval and of the rules that teachers imposed on their classes. These investigations were characterised by careful attention to defining behaviours to be observed and by seeking to ensure that observers' records were accurate representations of what took place in classrooms. The results of the investigations showed that, in general, the problem behaviour of pupils could be reduced by changes in teachers' behaviour.

In the 1970s one of the writers, a former schoolteacher, then involved in teacher training, read reports of the American studies with some scepticism but, seeing the potential value of their findings, decided to put his scepticism to the test in a British context. After some discussion with a Liverpool education authority senior educational psychologist, who was equally interested in setting up an investigation, the aid of three teachers in Liverpool primary schools was enlisted. These were teachers who were known to the educational psychologist as being experienced and confident in their abilities. They were all willing to try out what was described to them as a new method of improving pupil behaviour. Initially, each teacher selected one pupil in their class whose behaviour was a cause for some concern and left room for some improvement. From that point on the three cases followed the same general procedure, as typified by the case conducted with the pupil we called Victor.

Preliminary investigations

Victor

Victor was nine years old, of average ability, in a state primary school situated in the inner city in what was then designated an educational priority area. His teacher was a woman who had some ten years' teaching experience. Victor showed little interest in his lessons and spent much of his time talking to other pupils and walking about the classroom. He was learning little and disrupting the work of other pupils. He would settle down to work for short periods when reprimanded but rapidly returned to inappropriate behaviour when other pupils required his teacher's attention.

The teacher's permission was obtained for an observer, a trainee-teacher, to be present in the classroom for two or three lessons per week and it was explained to the teacher that the observer would be recording Victor's inappropriate behaviour and that this was to get an estimate of the extent of that behaviour before any attempt was to be made to bring about an improvement. In other words, it was to be a baseline against which any improvement could be measured.

The observer was informed that the recordings were to be made of Victor's inappropriate behaviour, i.e. talking or walking around the classroom when not allowed, and that it was important that recordings should be as accurate as possible. It was also emphasised that the observer should be unobtrusive in the classroom. That wasn't too difficult at the time since the school regularly had student teachers in the classrooms and the observer was introduced to the class as a student teacher who would be watching lessons during the next few weeks.

In the first, preliminary week, the observer sat in the classroom at the back and recorded Victor's behaviour during three lessons, while seemingly being engaged in watching the teacher and the class in general. The recording was done by dividing the observation time into 20-second intervals and checking an interval when an observed behaviour occurred, so that for example, after 30 minutes' recording, 90 intervals would have been observed and the observer would have noted in how many of these intervals Victor had been engaged in each of the two behaviours. After each lesson the results were discussed with the teacher and any necessary adjustments were made to the observer's understanding of what was to be observed.

Following that preliminary week the observer recorded Victor's behaviour for two lessons a week for one month. By the end of that month it was considered that a good baseline estimate of the extent of Victor's inappropriate behaviour had been obtained.

The investigators looked at the results of the baseline with the teacher and then outlined what they had read about the success of the American studies, in particular explaining that in those studies pupils' behaviour had been improved by the use of praise/approval/attention for appropriate behaviour, the ignoring of inappropriate behaviour and the statement of classroom rules. The teacher professed to find the technique of approval, ignoring and statement of rules very interesting but wasn't totally convinced that such techniques would improve Victor's behaviour. As a compromise, ignoring inappropriate behaviour was changed to 'minimising attention to inappropriate behaviour' The teacher then agreed to do the following with the whole class as a treatment (intervention) aimed at improving Victor's behaviour:

1   Make the class aware of the classroom rules and repeat the rules when necessary. Include in the rules that pupils should not talk to others when they are working and that they are expected to remain in their places and not wander about the classroom.
2   Give praise/attention/approval to Victor and to other pupils for behaviour that facilitates learning. Tell the pupils why they are receiving this positive feedback and try to give positive feedback to behaviours that are incompatible with Victor's behaviour that is not permitted, i.e. working quietly and staying in his seat.
3   Minimise attention to Victor when he does indulge in the unpermitted behaviours.

The teacher implemented the package of rules, praise and ignoring for a month and the observer continued to record during two lessons per week. By the end of the month the observer's recordings showed a considerable improvement in Victor's behaviour from the baseline recording levels to the end of the intervention, both unwanted talking and wandering about the classroom having been reduced to around two-thirds of their baseline levels. The teacher agreed that Victor had improved and felt that the observer's recordings were a true reflection of what had occurred.

Ted and Mavis

For the other two teachers, both of whom also worked in inner-city state schools, the investigation with their pupils followed the same format, albeit with some differences in the inappropriate behaviours of the pupils. For example, for Ted, giving other children 'nudges and kicks' was included, while for Mavis, 'shouting out' was included in the observed inappropriate behaviours. For both of these teachers, the recordings showed considerable improvement in the behaviour of the pupils after the month of intervention and the teachers agreed that improvement had occurred. Interestingly, for Mavis, the inappropriate behaviour became worse for the first week of the treatment before it subsequently reduced.

Research note

That all three pupils improved both in terms of the recordings and in the teachers' views was good evidence that the techniques could be implemented successfully in a British context. There were, however, at that time, some misgivings about whether it was the treatment given to the pupils, or some other feature of the investigation that had produced the improvement.

When the investigators thought of possible alternative explanations for the results, two that came to mind were concerned with the observers: one concerned the observers' presence in the classrooms, the other concerned the observers' expectations.

That the observers' presence in the classrooms might have changed the behaviour of the pupils was one possibility, but when we examined the recordings day by day there was no evidence of a reduction in the pupils' inappropriate behaviour during the one month of baseline recordings. Since it was only when the teachers changed *their* behaviour that the improvements began to occur then it was very unlikely that the observers' presence had caused the change.

That the results had been caused by the observers 'expecting' an improvement when they knew the teachers were changing their behaviour to the pupils and unknowingly making their recordings agree with what they expected was an alternative explanation that we couldn't rule out initially. We were able to rule out that explanation later by conducting an investigation that involved using two independent observers in classrooms and not telling one from each pair when the teachers changed their behaviour. The results showed no difference between the recordings of those observers who were told of the change and those who were not (Harrop, 1978).

Another concern that these results raised was that we had no measure of the effects of improving the selected pupils' behaviour on the rest of the class. That was thought to be such an important consideration that another investigation was devised in which the effects on other pupils was measured while the behaviour of one pupil was treated and improved. The results showed that the behaviour of the other pupils improved but not as much as did the behaviour of the selected pupil (Harrop, 1978).

Having ruled out those possible alternative explanations for the results of the preliminary investigation we were able to conclude that the improvement obtained with all three pupils was brought about when the three teachers changed their behaviour by emphasising classroom rules, by giving praise (approval and/or attention) when the pupils were behaving appropriately and by reducing attention to inappropriate behaviour. It appears that previously the teachers had concentrated their attention on the pupils when they had been behaving inappropriately and that the pupils may not have been clear about the classroom rules.

In practice

In a busy classroom, a pupil who misbehaves continually attracts the teacher's attention. The teacher has to attend to that pupil and one way or another seeks to get him or her back to behaving appropriately and becoming fully engaged in the lesson. Once the pupil is working appropriately, the teacher breathes a sigh of relief and feels free to turn his or her attention back to the rest of the class, feeling perhaps a little guilty about having to spend so much time on that inappropriately behaving pupil while neglecting the other appropriately working pupils. At that point, the teacher's attention is removed from the previously misbehaving pupil and continues to be removed while the teacher interacts with the rest of the class. If the pupil requires the teacher's attention, the way to get it back may be by misbehaving again. In other words, it is the teacher's attention that serves to maintain the pupil's behaviour.

The implication is that pupils who misbehave need praise and attention when they are behaving appropriately, not just attention when they are behaving inappropriately. That isn't easy for a teacher to do when the rest of the class also need attention. Moreover, from our experience of working with teachers, we know that some understandably object to doing that, on the grounds that they shouldn't be praising pupils who are doing exactly what they are supposed to be doing. They may think that way, but, by the same token, if they want the pupils to behave in the same way as the rest of the class then they need to give them attention when they work in the same way as the rest. We will explore that issue in subsequent chapters. That pupils who show a good deal of inappropriate behaviour need more attention than the others when they are working appropriately is likely to be a legacy of the way they have learned to attract teachers' attention during their earlier schooling. They need to learn that the way to gain attention is to work appropriately. The results obtained with Mavis, whose behaviour became worse initially when treatment was introduced, illustrates that point. When her teacher changed his behaviour and withdrew attention from her inappropriate behaviour, Mavis seems to have redoubled her efforts to gain the teacher's attention before discovering that behaving appropriately was the key to gaining that attention.

It needs to be emphasised at this point that, as was mentioned earlier, the teachers who were involved in the preliminary investigation were experienced and confident in their abilities. They were good teachers. That was an important feature of their success in improving their pupils' behaviour. Their attention was important to the pupils. Over many years of conducting research along the lines just described we have noted what appears to be almost a paradox, in that good teachers achieve the most improvement. One reason is that they are the primary source of attention for the pupils in their classrooms. In a classroom in which there is little order, misbehaviour by pupils is likely to be reinforced by the attention paid to it by other pupils.

The value of stating classroom rules lies in the fact that they emphasise the boundaries of pupil behaviour. Subsequent work with teachers has found that very often pupils in classrooms have only very hazy notions of what they are allowed and not allowed to do in class. The added advantage of stating rules in the preliminary investigation was that it included the opportunity of emphasising the inappropriateness of some of the behaviour of the pupils whose behaviour was to be improved. Generally, the number of classroom rules needs to be kept to a minimum. Most experts suggest around five (Canter and Canter, 1992; Rodgers, 1998). The rules need to cover key areas of classroom behaviour such as communication between teacher and pupil, e.g. the need to raise the hand, noise level while working, conduct while working and relationship between pupils. It is important to remember that rules, unlike the 'ten commandments', are not written in stone, and can, therefore, be changed or adapted to suit the needs of each lesson or class. One teacher we worked with had a particular problem with pupils wandering around the class so she had to introduce a separate rule for that behaviour, one that she used for half a term until the problem had been sorted out.

Comment/activity

At this stage, it is worth reflecting on your own classroom practice. If you want to be more active, you could, for example, ask the pupils to each write down what they think they are allowed and not allowed to do in the classrooms, prior to devoting some time to discussing the classroom rules with the pupils. Teachers who have done this have usually found it an interesting, valuable, and often amusing, exercise.

Teacher investigations

After the preliminary investigations, a number of in-service courses were conducted with teachers during which each teacher selected one pupil in their class whose behaviour was of some concern to them. The teachers were asked to give a 'pen portrait' of the pupils and then to convert the central issues of the pen portrait into observable categories of behaviour. Sometimes that was an easy task, when, for example, a pupil was described as interrupting the teacher or as talking when she should have been working. On other occasions it was not so easy; for example, when a pupil was described as lacking in concentration and daydreaming. In such cases, asking what it was that the pupil did (or didn't do) to enable the teacher to make such a judgement usually helped translate the concerns of the teacher into behavioural categories. Since the teachers on the in-service courses came from a variety of schools with pupils ranging from infants, through juniors to secondary levels, a wide variety of cases emerged.

After defining the pupils' behaviour in measurable terms, the teachers made baseline observations of the pupils' behaviour for a period of two weeks. The observations were usually made by the teachers themselves. After baseline observations, the teachers, with the help of the two course leaders, devised a strategy to use with the pupils.

The strategies used by the teachers all followed the same guidelines, based on the results of previous research and on our preliminary investigations. These were to reinforce the pupils' appropriate behaviour by paying attention to them and giving approval where possible, to seek to minimise attention to the pupils' inappropriate behaviour and to give prominence to the classroom rules. The teachers were urged to devote a lesson to a discussion of the classroom rules with their classes. A particularly valuable approach some took was to commence by asking the pupils to list the rules of the classroom before a discussion. Frequent misunderstandings were noted.

The initial 'pen portraits' of the pupils for whom the teachers showed concern covered a large range on a number of dimensions. Three examples (with fictitious names) are included here to illustrate the ways in which strategies can be applied.

Alan, a junior school pupil

Alan was an eight-year-old primary school pupil described by his teacher, who had some 20 years' primary school experience, as being above average in ability but doing little work. He would interrupt the others when they were working, by talking or pulling funny faces. He continually managed to lose pencils and books and tended to check continually with the teacher and with the other pupils to find out what work he was supposed to be doing.

In conducting her treatment of Alan, the teacher's first step was to obtain a baseline estimate of the severity of the problem. She decided to observe Alan for 10 minutes each day when these inappropriate behaviours were most likely to occur. For 10 days she noted down the number of times each of these behaviours occurred.

She followed that by a lesson on the classroom rules in which she managed to emphasise 'not interrupting other working pupils', 'not losing pencils and books' and 'paying attention to instructions before beginning work'. Subsequently, she concentrated on trying to pay attention to Alan when he was following the rules and trying to ignore him when he was not obeying the rules. She continued to do that for four weeks. She recorded his behaviour for 10 minutes each day as she had done during the baseline.

The results showed that while Alan's inappropriate behaviour increased a little during the first week of treatment, it eventually reduced to around a quarter of its original level, i.e. from around five or six instances per 10-minute observation to one or two instances. The teacher also felt that Alan had begun taking more interest in his work as well as improving his behaviour.

That brief outline of the work done with Alan in the preceding paragraphs may give the impression that the teacher's role was virtually effortless. That is far from the case. After obtaining the baseline estimate of the severity of the problem, she had to make a marked change in her behaviour towards Alan. She didn't find it easy at first either to find times when he was working appropriately in order to give him attention or to remove her attention when he infringed rules. It was also particularly difficult for her to persevere with her changed behaviour since Alan's inappropriate behaviour increased a little before beginning to decline. Nevertheless, she remained consistent and at the end of the four weeks she was pleased with the results.

Tom, an infant school pupil

Tom was in an infant school. He was bigger and physically more mature than most of the others in his class and was generally well-behaved, apart from the fact that he used his physique more forcibly than he should at times. The teacher was particularly concerned at his inability to queue properly. Whenever the class was asked to 'line up', Tom would push into the front, often jostling the smaller members of the class.

Tom's inability to queue concerned his teacher. Apart from the fact that queuing appropriately is important in school, Tom's behaviour was physically dangerous to the other pupils. This was particularly worrying for the teacher in PE lessons when he would excitedly push his way to the front of the queue. Talking to him or 'telling him off' had no effect. The teacher wanted to try the positive approach to eliminate, or at least reduce, that behaviour, but while she could see that discussing rules with the class and emphasising queuing properly and paying attention to Tom when he was queuing properly could both be easily achieved, she realised that she couldn't remove her attention from him when he pushed into a queue. Fortunately, since the teacher was on an in-service course, she was able to call on a number of experienced teachers and two course leaders to reflect on the problem and help her develop a strategy.

After some reflection, it was appreciated that rather than concentrate on Tom's inappropriate queuing behaviour, it was better to focus on setting up appropriate queuing behaviour. A good way of achieving that was for the teacher to be in close proximity to Tom when he queued, so that when the class were being lined up she would engage Tom in conversation about his work, putting a restraining hand on his shoulder and easing him into the line. The teacher did that and in a lesson on classroom rules she included comments about how pupils should line up.

The PE lessons presented more difficulty since the pupils often used apparatus in turns and any pushing into a line could result in an injury to a pupil. To try to stop Tom pushing into the line, the teacher began by stringing out the apparatus so that no pupils arrived back at the start before the last one left. She waited at the start and as Tom arrived back she greeted him and made positive comments about his performance, easing him to the back of the line. He quickly became used to this routine. After a number of such greetings, she then reduced the range of apparatus to be used so that Tom arrived at the start with one or two pupils in front of him. She continued as before, greeting him and commenting on his performance. Tom didn't push other pupils out of the line, he slowed down and waited for the teacher's comments. After a while, the teacher had Tom behaving normally in these PE lessons. At this point, the teacher forgot once or twice to greet Tom, yet he continued to behave appropriately.

Bob, a comprehensive school pupil

Bob was a 13-year-old comprehensive school pupil of above average intelligence who had arrived in the school with a record of behaviour problems in three primary schools. His behaviour in the comprehensive school was such that he had been placed in a classroom together with five other pupils who were not behaving appropriately in normal classrooms. His teacher, who was in his second year of teaching, said Bob had become the class leader. He would frequently make provocative comments and from time to time would roam restlessly about the room.

Bob was clearly beyond the point at which the teacher's attention to his appropriate behaviour combined with a discussion of rules and removing attention from his inappropriate behaviour would have a beneficial effect. Like a number of such pupils, Bob didn't seem to find the teacher's attention reinforcing. What he did seem to find rewarding was the attention he received from the other pupils when he misbehaved. That left the teacher with a problem. In order to apply the positive approach to Bob, he had first to identify what would reward Bob's appropriate behaviour.

After much thought and discussion, it was decided to enlist the help of the school's deputy headmaster, a man for whom Bob had great respect, mainly because of his sporting prowess. To obtain a baseline estimate of Bob's inappropriate behaviour the teacher observed him unobtrusively for 15 minutes a day, when the class was meant to be working, for three weeks. At the end of the three weeks the deputy head came into the class and announced, for all to hear, that the head teacher and some important people were very interested in the progress of the pupils in this unusual class. He produced a logbook in which he said he wanted recordings to be made of everyday events in the class. He gave the logbook to Bob, explaining privately to him that he had been selected to keep the log because of his high intelligence. He added that Bob could only fill in the log if he behaved well himself. Bob was to take the logbook to him at lunch time and at the end of the day.

Immediately after the deputy head left the class, Bob's teacher spoke privately with Bob. He outlined the purpose of the class, pointing out that disruptive behaviour and provocative comments didn't help and were against the classroom rules. He added that, in his opinion, Bob was not likely to behave well enough to be allowed to write up the logbook. Bob, for his part, maintained that he could behave well. Eventually, a compromise was agreed. For every 10 consecutive minutes that Bob worked appropriately the teacher would initial his exercise book. When four such signatures had been accumulated, Bob could fill in the logbook.

When Bob accumulated his first four signatures, he filled in the log and took it at the end of the session to the deputy head. For his part, the deputy head found the log very interesting and talked with Bob about the contents. Judging from Bob's subsequent behaviour he found talking with the deputy head very reinforcing. His inappropriate behaviour, as measured by the teacher, began to fall significantly and rapidly fell to less than once per observation session, from its original mean of four. After less than three weeks of log keeping, the teacher decided that observing Bob was no longer necessary. He agreed with Bob that the signatures were a waste of time and allowed Bob to keep the log, provided he behaved well. Generally, the whole class improved without having Bob as a catalyst. Bob began to make good academic progress and, towards the end of the year, he was able to return to a normal class.

Some general comments on the three cases

All three of these teachers, who were undertaking in-service courses, said that their normal method of teaching couldn't reduce the inappropriate behaviour and that the learning of the pupil and that of the others was suffering as a consequence. When they tried the positive approach they were, however, successful in reducing their pupils' inappropriate behaviour. The cases may seem very different along a number of dimensions but each has been selected here to illustrate certain features of the application of the positive approach.

The junior school case of Alan shows a relatively straightforward application of the procedures used in the preliminary investigation, i.e. attending to appropriate behaviour, minimising attention to inappropriate behaviour and giving prominence to the classroom rules. For a very large number of pupils, particularly of primary school age, this is all that is needed. For the other two pupils, a certain amount of ingenuity was required in identifying how to apply that strategy. In the case of Tom, minimising attention to the inappropriate behaviour was not a safe option, while for Bob, the problem was finding an appropriate reinforcer. Common to all three cases, however, was a careful consideration of how to reinforce appropriate behaviour and how to avoid reinforcement being given to inappropriate behaviour, together with the emphasising of classroom rules.

In describing the case of Alan, it was mentioned that his inappropriate behaviour increased when the teacher first put the strategy in place. That is not an uncommon phenomenon and a teacher has to be aware of the possibility. When teachers' behaviour changes to giving attention to appropriate behaviour rather than to inappropriate behaviour, pupils may well vary their behaviour in efforts to obtain the teachers' attention. Put simply, they haven't learned that behaving appropriately is the key to obtaining teacher attention. This phenomenon has sometimes been known as 'the storm before the calm'.

In the case of Tom, it was mentioned that the teacher occasionally forgot to catch him at the back of the queue and yet he continued to line up properly. That illustrates an important principle of human learning, which tells us that once a behaviour has been learned by continual reinforcement it becomes stronger if it is only reinforced intermittently. That is one of the main reasons why inappropriate behaviour is difficult to eradicate: it only needs occasional reinforcing for it to continue indefinitely. On the other hand, that principle helps the teacher who is trying to get a pupil to behave appropriately, since after continually reinforcing the behaviour the teacher can move to intermittent reinforcement without the behaviour reverting.

All three cases show teachers changing their behaviour towards their pupils in order to bring about an increase in their appropriate behaviour. The ultimate aim, however, must be that the pupil behaves in the same way as the other pupils without having to be given special treatment. As a consequence, the special treatment needs to be removed at some point and that is usually achieved by fading it out. In practice, that usually means moving to intermittent reinforcement and then to occasional reinforcement. Often that process occurs naturally when the teacher perceives that less frequent reinforcement is needed. Moreover, usually this process is aided by the fact that during the treatment pupils' academic work improves and they begin to be reinforced for good work as well as for appropriate behaviour.

Comment/activity

You might like to reflect on the cases described and think about whether one of your pupils shows behaviour that is inappropriate to his or her learning. You could set up your own study to see whether applying the positive approach can bring about an improvement in the pupil's classroom behaviour.

Other, related practices

For many years, teachers in primary schools have realised the benefits of giving stars and/or certificates to pupils for various reasons, such as very high levels of attendance, consistent punctuality and working well in class. These are all marks of approval. In secondary schools, house points are often used in a similar way. Canter and Canter (1992) suggest a technique called 'marbles in a jar' for primary aged pupils. In this technique, the teacher drops a marble in a jar, strategically placed so that all the pupils can see it, whenever they wish to reward a pupil or the whole class for appropriate behaviour or work. At secondary level, the Canters recommend ticks on a board. Both marbles and ticks can be converted later into more tangible rewards such as 'free choice time', 'extra break time' or perhaps having background music in the classroom. There is more discussion on such matters in Chapter 4.

The stars or house points used in schools often act as a reward in themselves and sometimes they bring with them other rewards; for example, when primary school pupils take their certificates home, these are usually received with some pleasure by the parents. The stars, certificates or house points may be seen as tokens of teacher approval.

A brief historical digression

It may come as a surprise to learn that the use of tokens goes back at least to the fifth century BC. They were used to increase attendance at the General Assembly in Greece, where citizens gathered to discuss issues and vote on them. The Greeks who attended the assembly had to take a day off work, so a small payment was made as compensation. After the Peloponnesian War, the state became impoverished and the payment, which was made at the start of the day, became low. In the mornings attendance was high but it rapidly dropped off during the day. Since the assembly was held in the open air and was surrounded by vegetation and rocks it was apparently easy to slip out unnoticed. By voting time only a few of the morning attendees remained. To try to stem this pattern it was decided to pay for attendance only at the end of the day. That, unfortunately, produced the opposite situation, with citizens appearing towards the end of the day, many voting on issues without having heard the prior discussions.

With characteristic inventiveness, the Greeks decided to make tokens that were tablets of baked clay. These were given to the citizens when they arrived at the assembly and were handed over for payment at the end of the day. Apparently this system worked well until the Romans conquered Greece in the middle of the second century BC.

Moving closer to the present, Malmonides, a Jewish scholar in the twelfth century, advised teachers of Bible studies to encourage their pupils to learn by giving them 'age-appropriate rewards,' such such as nuts, figs or a piece of sugar. He added that as children matured, things previously regarded as important would seem trivial and that different things would appear valuable, so that shoes, clothes, etc., could be used to encourage learning. Later, he advocated that money could be used. Money is itself a token, of course, one that can be cashed in later for something desirable. Moreover, Malmonides did not advise any negative consequences to encourage learning. He emphasised positive consequences for pupils so that they could be helped to learn important skills and knowledge. Mere advice, he said, was ineffective unless it was accompanied by current rewards.

If we reflect on those two historical accounts, we can see that there were some interesting precursors to the recent investigations in schools discussed earlier in the chapter. Yet, intriguingly, they occurred against a background in which the Egyptians, the Greeks and the Romans all used whips on their students. Not for nothing does a medieval sculpture depict a carpenter with his hammer and a schoolmaster with his cane.

In modern times, in some schools for pupils judged to have social, emotional and behavioural difficulties (SEBD), the use of tokens is taken a step further so that the term 'token economy' best describes the situation. These tokens are given by members of staff to pupils for their appropriate behaviour. The tokens can be exchanged at the end of the day for a choice of small rewards or, alternatively, the tokens can be accumulated and saved for a larger reward. The rewards exchangeable for the tokens might include such items as coloured pencils, a drawing book, extra time in the art room, etc. Chelfam Mill School in North Devon, founded by Dr Roger Burland, has been using the token economy approach for over 40 years and has been extremely successful in turning around some young people who had difficulties in the normal school system.

Further comments

There are a number of features associated with the positive approach that we would like to emphasise here.

The curriculum

Up to this point, no mention has been made of the curriculum. Yet it is obvious that if all the pupils in a class found the curriculum enjoyable, and therefore reinforcing, there would be little inappropriate behaviour. The difficulty for teachers, however, is that their first priority is that the curriculum must meet the learning requirements of the pupils. There is also the crucial dilemma for all teachers of discerning the appropriate level of difficulty for any learning task. If the work is either too difficult or too easy it becomes likely that pupils will become disengaged and open to inappropriate behaviour. Making school work both educationally valuable and enjoyable for all the pupils is an extremely difficult task when we consider that teachers are confronted with a class of pupils of varying abilities and differing previous classroom experiences. Nevertheless, when teachers want to increase the appropriate behaviour of one or more of their pupils, they should first consider whether their curriculum presentation could be improved. Using the positive approach to 'prop up' an inadequately presented curriculum would be a perversion of the approach.

Inappropriate behaviour

Deciding what constitutes inappropriate behaviour is usually relatively simple for a teacher. Such behaviour may best be considered as something pupils do that interferes with their own learning and/or with the learning of the other pupils. The cases previously outlined illustrate that definition. Occasionally, however, inappropriate behaviour can be something pupils do not do. There are a few pupils who shrink from activities, who do not volunteer answers, who try to avoid conversing with the teachers and with other pupils. Such pupils can easily go unnoticed in classrooms because their lack of appropriate behaviour doesn't affect the learning of other pupils, yet they need help to learn to interact more. For pupils like that, teachers need to seek to find opportunities to reinforce them for appropriately interacting.

Appropriate behaviour

After identifying a pupil's inappropriate behaviour it is usually relatively easy for the teacher to identify the corresponding appropriate behaviour. Appropriate behaviour is generally behaviour that is incompatible with inappropriate behaviour. For many pupils, just getting on with their classroom work would be the desired appropriate behaviour. Occasionally there might be some variation, as, for example, in the case of 'Tom' the infant school pupil who didn't queue properly. The appropriate behaviour for him was queuing in a proper manner. Praising and/or acknowledging the appropriate behaviour of other pupils, particularly those in close proximity to the pupil concerned, can also have a beneficial effect on the pupil.

Observing pupils

The brief accounts of investigations undertaken have all included reference to a pupil's inappropriate behaviour being defined in behavioural terms and baseline observations made. How observations are made depends on such considerations as how frequently the behaviour occurs and when it occurs. For a teacher, if, for example, it occurs very infrequently then a simple count of how many times it occurs in a lesson or in a day would suffice. If it occurs frequently, for example when the pupil is supposed to be working, then a time sample at pre-set intervals should be made, perhaps during a 20-minute interval while work is supposed to be being done by the pupil. If the teacher is able to employ someone else to observe then more complex observation could be employed as described in Chapter 9, which deals with research in more detail.

Baselines

Baseline observations are important since they show the extent of the pupil's inappropriate behaviour and act as a measure against which the effects of treating the pupil can be measured. They can be brief, as little as three sessions of observations, provided the level of the inappropriate behaviour is relatively consistent, but need to be rather longer if the behaviour is very varied from one session to another.

Intervention

In deciding on what intervention (treatment) to apply teachers need to use their professional judgement of the dynamics of the classroom and how these relate to their own knowledge of the pupil's characteristics and previous history. It may be that a simple application of reinforcing appropriate behaviour and reducing attention given to inappropriate behaviour, combined with an emphasis on classroom rules, is the obvious strategy to adopt. If, however, that strategy is deemed insufficient for the pupil a more artificial strategy may be needed. The brief accounts of the work done with 'Tom' in the infant school and 'Bob' in the comprehensive school offer particular examples and further examples are provided in later chapters.

Fading out of any intervention

Whenever teachers decide that a pupil's inappropriate behaviour needs to be improved by applying the positive approach, they need to include in their thinking the fact that the pupil is only temporarily in their care. They should therefore aim not only to improve the pupil's functioning in their classroom but also, if possible, to end with the pupil showing improved functioning without receiving any special treatment, i.e. under the same conditions as the other pupils in the classroom. It is important to appreciate that once a behaviour has become established it can be maintained by occasional reinforcement in the form of teacher feedback. That is why inappropriate behaviours tend to be intractable. There is a clear message here. As soon as the pupil is behaving appropriately with consistent reinforcement, the teacher should begin to reduce the frequency of the reinforcement. The teacher's aim should be that by the end of the treatment the pupil will behave in the same way as the rest of the pupils under the influence of the same reinforcement. Although that aim may not always be achieved it should be a final goal.

Concluding comments

In the opening paragraphs, we discussed the harsh punishments inflicted on children in schools up to and into the twentieth century. More recently, however, society itself has become more positive and less negative, so that, for example, measures have been taken through the Human Rights Act 1998 and the European Court of Human Rights to prevent individuals from being treated unfairly. In 2005, following considerable pressure, a law was passed to prevent smacking of children by parents (and others) that left any visible mark. Since 2005 there has been continual debate about the adequacy of the law, many feeling that any form of physical chastisement should be unlawful. It is also no coincidence that there has been in recent years a spate of television programmes in which parents have been shown the benefits of adopting a positive approach in order to handle 'difficult' children. It follows, therefore, that the emergence of the positive approach in education mirrors changes in society.

The emphasis in this opening chapter has been on showing ways in which the positive approach has been used to decrease individual pupils' inappropriate behaviour, with consequent increases in their appropriate behaviour, and the examples outlined may have given the impression that the positive approach is a kind of prescription applied in a mechanical manner. The reality is very different. What is true is that the teachers concerned have had to be very consistent in their approach. But it is also true that none of the cases outlined would have been undertaken had the teachers not been concerned about their pupils' inappropriate behaviour. Moreover, although the same basic principles are evident in each case, the way in which the principles have been applied shows considerable variation, that variation having been a consequence of the teachers' knowledge of their pupils.

Subsequent chapters

In subsequent chapters, we aim to show ways in which the positive approach has been applied. It has been applied to classes, to individuals and to whole schools. It has been applied with pupils who display inappropriate behaviour in ordinary class-rooms and with pupils who display behaviour that is more difficult to treat. It has been applied to pupils' classroom behaviour, to helping teachers realise their learning objectives and to seeking to improve the well-being of pupils. Our aim is to give you some appreciation of that breadth of application in the following chapters and to equip you with the relevant skills to undertake your own investigations. If you wish to involve yourself further than just reading the text, we have included at strategic points some suggestions for involvement, headed 'Comment/activity', two of which you have already come across in this chapter.

In Chapter 2, which delves into the relationships between teacher feedback and their pupils' academic and social behaviour, we move from considering individual pupils to work undertaken with classes of pupils. The chapter concludes with a brief discussion of the results of research, following on from our own, undertaken by 71 educational psychologists in classes in England and Wales. Chapter 3 gives details of a half-day training course using positive psychology, which we gave to a group of teachers from infant, junior and secondary schools. Following the course, changes were seen both in the teachers' use of positive feedback to their classes and in the pupils' behaviour. The teachers became more positive and the pupils became more engaged in their work. In Chapter 4, we examine the use of the approach with particular groups of pupils, i.e. pupils of different ability levels, race and gender, and pupils who are badly behaved.

Chapter 5 broadens the scope further, from classes in schools to the whole school. Most of the chapter is devoted to an account of work with one school. The focus is on a three-stage process that was adopted, i.e. assessment of current practice, planning for change and implementation, and evaluation. In Chapter 6, we switch attention away from pupils' behaviour, to work aimed at achieving teachers' academic objectives, specifically in English and mathematics. In Chapter 7, we look at work aimed at promoting pupils' well-being and at some of the effects of teachers' expectations.

Chapters 8 and 9 are concerned with more theoretical and research issues, respectively. The aim is to give the readers a deeper understanding of the applications of positive psychology and the investigative methods available.

Chapter 10, the concluding chapter, discusses some of the problems raised by teachers, together with a brief reiteration of the principles and practices involved in positive psychology.

Chapter 2

Teacher feedback and pupil behaviour

This chapter has at its core the account of two investigations together with discussions of the implications of their findings.

Background to the investigations

As we saw in the previous chapter, there has been in recent times a realisation that there is a complex relationship between teachers' verbal behaviour and the behaviour of their pupils. One of the early attempts to look at this whole area is seen in the work of White (1975), in the USA, who carried out an analysis of 16 separate classroom observation studies. She found those teachers of the youngest children, Grades 1 and 2, equivalent to infant children in the UK, gave more approval to their pupils than disapproval, while the opposite appeared to be the case for teachers of older pupils, i.e. teachers of junior and secondary pupils. When the teachers' behaviour was analysed in terms of whether approval was given to what she called instructional and managerial behaviour, known by subsequent investigators as academic and social behaviours respectively, she found that teachers gave high rates of approval for instructional behaviour, while for managerial behaviour the rate of approval was so low that White described it as 'almost non-existent'.

Other investigations followed, yielding similar results, particularly noteworthy being the work of Rutter et al. (1979) in the UK, based on observations in 12 secondary schools in London, involving 402 different lessons. They reported that reprimands occurred approximately twice as often as did teacher praise.

White's findings remained unchallenged for the rest of the 1970s, although later studies did however produce different results. Wyatt and Hawkins (1987), for example, found like White that mean rates of both approval and disapproval were highest in classrooms for the youngest pupils, but they also found that in all age groups approval was more common than disapproval. In addition, they also examined whether or not teachers used a description of the work or behaviour as part of the feedback. They found that approval with description, e.g. 'Well done Billy, for writing so neatly', was twice as frequent as approval without description, e.g. 'Well done Billy.' Disapproval with description was five times more frequent than disapproval without a description. Wyatt and Hawkins pointed out that the use of description is very sound educational practice as pupils need to know exactly what behaviour or aspect of their work they are being either praised or admonished for. That might not always be apparent to them in the absence of any description.

Brophy (1981) reviewed a series of six studies she conducted with colleagues between 1973 and 1980 with both primary and secondary aged pupils in the USA. Generally, she reported that teachers showed more approval than disapproval, were more likely to approve of academic behaviour than disapprove of it, frequently disapproved of social behaviour and were least likely to approve of social behaviour. Brophy made the further point that it is important to make a distinction between teachers' use of praise and criticism and simple feedback statements. This is a central issue. Brophy argues that in her view, feedback is virtually never harmful whereas praise may be. She also concedes that the distinction between the two may be difficult to decide, 'when for instance, a teacher says "Correct" whether it includes an evaluative component or is pure feedback' (p.116). Brophy's point is a very important one. She argues that it is feedback that influences pupil behaviour not merely praise or disapproval. She also makes the point that variations in reported rates of teacher feedback of both a positive or negative type may be as a result of different methodologies used by different researchers, but most crucially centre around the definitions used by researchers as to what constitutes the categories of feedback.

British studies

In addition to the work of Rutter *et al.* (1979) previously discussed, a major study reported by Galton *et al.* (1980) was carried out in the 1970s into junior classroom practice, which took as one of its foci teachers' use of language and its relationship to pupils' learning. Their observations recorded only teacher praise and criticism rather than broader criteria of positive and negative feedback. They reported rates of teacher praise to be around half those for statements of what they called 'critical control', a category that appears primarily to be concerned with feedback about behaviour and did not include any comments teachers may have made about the pupils' work. The definitions used in this study are not precise, so their results should be treated with some caution.

Merrett and Wheldall (1986) developed an observation system known as observing pupils and teachers in classrooms (OPTIC). The system recorded teacher approvals and disapprovals but the observers also recorded any non-verbal behaviour by the teacher that could be interpreted as a positive or negative event, such as smiling or frowning at a pupil. The OPTIC system allows the observer to look at two aspects of classroom behaviour, the behaviour of the teachers and the behaviour of the pupils, specifically their *on-task behaviour.* The schedule is in two halves. In a typical observation session, three minutes is spent recording the teachers' positive and negative responses to the pupils and classified according to whether these responses were directed to the pupils' academic or social behaviours. The following three minutes is concerned with observing pupil behaviour in which the observer estimates the student's on-task behaviour by observing each pupil in turn. This pattern was then repeated until the end of the lesson. The observers in much of Merrett and Wheldall's early work were teachers who were taking part in a series of workshops on pupil behaviour. They were all trained to use OPTIC as part of the course. When independent observers used OPTIC, their level of agreement averaged out at over 90 per cent., i.e. the level of inter-observer agreement of this schedule is reported as averaging over 90 per cent (Merrett and Wheldall, 1986, 1987).

Merrett and Wheldall (1987) used their OPTIC schedule to examine the rates of teacher approval and disapproval in British primary and middle schools. In total, 128 teachers took part in the research. It was found that, in general, teachers gave more approval than disapproval, but that the majority of this approval was directed towards work rather than behaviour. Conversely, more disapproval was directed towards behaviour than work.

The OPTIC schedule also allowed Merrett and Wheldall to examine the relationship between the teachers' use of feedback and the behaviour of the pupils. Small relationships were found. There was a very small negative relationship between disapproval to academic behaviour and on-task behaviour and a larger negative relationship between teachers' disapproval to social behaviour and on-task behaviour. Their results were very much in line with Brophy's (1981) stance that teachers' verbal praise cannot be equated with reinforcement.

Merrett and Wheldall also pointed out that it appeared to be the case that 'teachers were very quick to notice social behaviour of which they disapprove and continually nag children about it . . . but they hardly ever approve of desirable social behaviour'. In other words, children are expected to behave well and are 'continually reprimanded if they do not' (p.100). They suggested that the relationships they reported are as a result of teachers responding to children's behaviour rather than teachers acting in a proactive manner.

In a second study, also using the OPTIC schedule and using teacher observers, they looked at teacher and pupil behaviour in 130 secondary schools (Wheldall *et al.* 1989a). They found a similar pattern of teacher verbal behaviour to that which they had reported earlier in primary schools. In terms of the rates of approval and disapproval they did, however, find some differences with primary/middle school-teachers giving considerably more feedback to the pupils than secondary schoolteachers.

Further studies

A number of other studies that also used the OPTIC schedule developed by Merrett and Wheldall (1986) have been reported from schools across the English-speaking world. Winter (1990), for example, observed 86 secondary teachers and their classes in Hong Kong. He reported very similar results to those reported by Wheldall *et al.* (1989a) in terms of the proportions of verbal feedback given by teachers. He also found a strong relationship between teacher approval and on-task behaviour and a strong negative relationship between disapproval and on-task behaviour.

One study that does not fit this pattern was that reported by Charlton, Lovemore, Essex and Crowie (1995). This research was carried out on the island of St Helena in the South Atlantic with a sample of junior school aged children (seven to 10 years old) and their teachers. Again they used the OPTIC schedule. Charlton *et al.* reported high approval rates directed towards both behaviour and learning. In particular for the younger children, more teacher responses were directed to social behaviours (57.4 per cent) than to academic behaviours (42.6 per cent). This appears to be the only study to find that approval rates for both social and academic behaviours exceeded disapproval rates. It is true that the population and culture in St Helena may be very different from that of the rest of the world; for instance, at the time of the study there was no television on the island. It is also possible that these pupils differed markedly in other characteristics from populations previously studied. It is noticeable that the vast majority of other studies have been carried out in schools in essentially urban areas. St Helena, in contrast, is essentially an isolated rural environment. What is clear, however, is that the teachers in that particular school appear to have been on the right track as far as classroom management is concerned, since on-task rates of 96 per cent were reported for the younger children in their sample and 92 per cent for the older children. As Beauman and Wheldall (2000: p.442) noted, 'the behaviour of the pupils and the responses of the St Helena teachers suggest that the classrooms of St Helena could be exemplars of effective classroom behaviour management.'

The first investigation

In designing the first investigation reported here, the authors were aware that studies previously quoted in this chapter could have their methodology improved. In particular, what was observed in many investigations was not clearly defined, so we were careful to give considerable detail on our observed categories. Also, the Wheldall and Merrett studies and the others that used the OPTIC schedule for assessing pupil and teacher behaviour were not, in fact, recording pupil and teacher behaviour simultaneously, but at separate times, albeit in the same lessons. They were also restricted in what they were able to record in terms of both what the teacher actually said and also in the types of pupil behaviour they could record. To get over these problems, we decided to use a more detailed method of recording pupil behaviour, the Pupil Behaviour Schedule (Jolly and McNamara, 1992), and to use a small tape-recording device to record everything the teacher said over the period of observation. The advantage of this approach was not only in terms of simultaneously recording both teacher and pupil behaviour but also of our being able to analyse what the teacher actually said in some detail. These results are published in Harrop and Swinson (2000).

In this study, 50 teachers from a variety of schools were observed. Their natural rate of verbal feedback in their classrooms was recorded on audiotape while they taught a class of pupils. At the same time, observations of the behaviour of the pupils they were teaching were also recorded.

It was explained to the teachers that the investigators wanted to make an audio-record of teachers' verbal behaviour for analysis, and that while this recording was taking place, the pupils in the class would be observed using a simple recording sheet. The teachers who agreed to participate each wore a simple radio microphone while teaching one lesson to their class. The device was discreet and simple to wear and did not affect their mobility. All teachers seemed at ease with the equipment and no teacher withdrew consent to participate in the research as a result. A variety of lessons were observed. In the primary schools, infant and junior schools, literacy and numeracy sessions were excluded. In secondary schools, most lessons observed were classroom based, but did include a PE lesson in a games hall, science in a laboratory and two craft lessons. Each period of observation lasted approximately 30 minutes.

Observations of pupil behaviour were made using the Pupil Behavioural Schedule, which allows the observer to record whether a pupil is 'on-task' and if they are 'off-task' exactly what they are doing.

The categories of off-task behaviour are:

1   Inappropriate in-seat behaviour (IS), e.g. in-seat fidgeting, turning round, leaning back in chair, sitting out of position, rocking, playing with items.
2   Out-of-seat behaviour (OS), e.g. walking around the classroom, leaving class, changing place, climbing on/under/around furniture.
3   Shouting out (S), e.g. to attract attention of another pupil, shouting out answers inappropriately, e.g. without raising hand, or making a joke or wisecrack.
4   Inappropriate talking (T), e.g. social conversations.
5   Disturbing other pupils (DOP), e.g. interfering with or damaging possessions/work/ person; taking, 'borrowing', or throwing property/equipment; making demeaning/ disapproving comments about others; singing/chanting or non-verbal noises including whistling and humming.
6   Arguing with/challenging teacher (A), e.g. backchat, refusing to follow instructions, disregarding/ignoring specific teacher instructions, prevarication and petulant behaviour, commenting inappropriately to teacher about work.
7   Distracting teacher (DT), e.g. engaging teacher inappropriately, non-task-related conversation, making personal comments to teacher about dress/ appearance.
8   Inattentive to task (IN), e.g. daydreaming, attending to other pupils' behaviour.

The tapes were analysed in great detail, by two researchers who listened to the tapes independently and recorded from an agreed version of exactly what was said. They recorded:

•   *Teachers' approval*. Any response that indicated praise or satisfaction with the behaviour of one or more pupils. That included such comments as 'Excellent', 'Well done', 'Good girl/boy', 'Yes'. It also included the rather less effusive statements 'That's right' or 'That's what I was looking for' and the repetition of a pupil's answer in a positive or neutral but non-querulous tone.
•   *Teachers' disapproval*. Any response to one or more pupils that was a rebuke or that indicated disapproval. Common examples included 'Stop that', 'Be quiet', 'No, Pat', 'Now is not the time to be doing that'. This category included the teacher repeating a pupil's response in a querulous or questioning manner, together with comments implying negative consequences, e.g. 'I won't tell you again' and saying 'No' in response to an incorrect answer. It also included directions given with intonations implying teachers' intentions to reduce behaviours, e.g. 'Now I want you to listen quietly', and teachers' use of questions to which there is no answer, e.g. 'How many times do I have to tell you all to be quiet?'
•   *Individual pupil*. Any response given to a single pupil following the pupil's behaviour.
•   *Group*. Any teacher response given to more than one pupil following their behaviour, e.g. 'That's good Chris and Alex', 'You lot ought to sit still' and 'That's what I like to see, a nice quiet class'.

- *Academic behaviour.* These were the normal curriculum behaviours, such as reading, writing, listening, answering questions, i.e. performing prescribed activities.
- *Social behaviours.* These were behaviours indicative of classroom manners, following class rules and routines, e.g. settling down to work quietly, remaining seated when appropriate, putting hands up to answer questions, lining up in an orderly manner when requested. They also included the converse behaviours of not settling down to work when asked, not working quietly, not remaining seated when appropriate, etc.
- *Description.* Teacher response that described the pupil behaviour for which approval or disapproval was given. For social behaviours, this category is relatively obvious, so that, as in the previous example, 'That's what I like to see, a nice quiet class', the behaviour of the group is described, as well as being given approval. For academic behaviour, an approving or disapproving comment followed by description is also relatively obvious, e.g. 'Yes that was a quick calculation' (approval plus description), 'No you appear to have made a mistake in the units column' (disapproval followed by a description of the error). For academic behaviours in which the teacher repeats the pupil's response, it was decided that if the correct answer was repeated and then commented on, it would be categorised as approval with description, e.g. 'Sixty eight, yes that's right Val.' In like manner, an incorrect pupil response that was repeated and then commented on was categorised as disapproval with description.
- *Redirection.* Teacher's response following disapproval that describes an approved behaviour, e.g. 'Don't do that Viv, I want you to work in silence.' For pupil answers to teachers' questions, redirection could take the form of rephrasing a question, e.g. 'No Sam, it isn't a simple addition; look more carefully at the wording of the question.'

Two independent observers were used in scoring some of the audiotapes and in observing some of the lessons so that inter-observer agreement levels could be calculated. These calculations yielded satisfactory levels of agreement. (For details of how that was done see Chapter 9.)

After a close examination of both the tapes and the observational schedule we found, as Table 2.1 shows, that the percentage of feedback directed to pupils in terms of their work and behaviour was similar to that reported by both Wheldall and Merrett (1987) and Wheldall *et al.* (1989a) in that the majority of feedback was of a positive nature and directed in response to pupils' work. Most negative feedback was, by way of contrast, directed towards pupils' behaviour. Very little positive feedback was directed towards pupil social behaviour.

When the feedback was subdivided there appeared to be little variation between teachers of different age groups, as Table 2.2 illustrates.

Table 2.1 Mean percentages of types of feedback by all teachers (*n* = 50)

Feedback	Academic behaviour	Social behaviour	Total
Positive	57.30	3.85	61.15
Negative	10.85	28.62	39.47

Table 2.2 Mean percentages of different types of feedback given by infant, junior and secondary teachers

Type of feedback	Infant (n = 16)	Junior (n = 16)	Secondary (n = 18)
Positive academic	60.31	61.84	50.81
Positive social	4.09	4.69	2.91
Negative academic	11.44	7.35	12.16
Negative social	22.86	22.91	36.23

Comment/activity

At this point, you might be curious about the amounts of positive and negative feedback you yourself give to academic and social behaviour. You could get a rough idea of the relative amounts if you just note each instance during a couple of short periods in your lessons. Alternatively, if you have a classroom assistant you could arrange to be observed more thoroughly. You will find the necessary definitions given earlier in this chapter.

The advantage of recording what the teachers said was that we were able to scrutinise the teachers' feedback in greater detail than other studies. Careful analysis of each tape allowed a record to be made of whether teachers at all three levels included descriptions of pupils' behaviour in both their positive and negative feedback, as shown in Table 2.3.

These figures show quite a variation. While the results for the infant and junior teachers are broadly similar, the secondary schoolteachers seem to use far less description when they give negative feedback, i.e. when the pupils are doing something wrong. Perhaps they assume the pupils are old enough to know what they are doing wrong.

The tapes were also analysed to ascertain the extent to which teachers used pupils' own names when providing feedback. This feature of feedback has not been extensively researched, but as Hattie and Timperley (2007) point out, any feedback that is directed to a named individual is likely to become more effective because it is specifically aimed at an individual and is therefore less likely to be ignored. In psychology, you often hear the term the 'cocktail party effect'. The reader might have experienced this when talking to someone at a party and then hearing their name

Table 2.3 Mean percentages of positive and negative teacher feedback containing a description of behaviour

Type of school	Percentage of positive feedback with description	Percentage of negative feedback with description
Infant (n = 16)	44.36	69.26
Junior (n = 16)	32.76	52.70
Secondary (n = 18)	48.48	26.86

spoken by someone behind. Immediately, some attention is switched to what is being said.

As Table 2.4 shows, the teachers used pupils' names very little when giving positive feedback to their pupils. It could be that a lot of this type of feedback is given privately, when, for instance, a teacher is checking pupils' work, while negative feedback is often given publically when the teacher spies something amiss on the other side of the classroom. Also of note is the lower proportion of named feedback given by secondary schoolteachers. That may well be explained by secondary schoolteachers having less opportunity to learn the names of all their pupils because of the variety of classes taught.

In the analysis of the extent to which feedback was given to individuals and to groups, the size of groups varied from two, i.e. 'Be quiet you two boys at the back', to the whole class, i.e. 'Well done class for lining up well.' Overall, the majority of feedback (85.89 per cent) was directed to individuals and only around 14 per cent was directed to groups.

As far as feedback to individuals is concerned, both in terms of the rate and proportion, positive individual feedback was double that of negative individual feedback. By the same token, teachers seemed to use group feedback more predominantly to provide their pupils with negative feedback. The actual rates and proportions of the different types of feedback are presented in Table 2.5.

There was a considerable similarity between the proportions and types of feedback given to pupils across all three levels of schooling. This was especially the case when considering proportions of negative feedback directed towards groups, which are all within 0.5 per cent of one another.

The percentage of negative feedback with redirection is shown in Table 2.6.

There was only a small difference in the percentage of redirection used by junior and secondary teachers at around a quarter of all negative feedback containing

Table 2.4 Mean percentages of positive and negative feedback that included the pupils' names

Type of school	Percentage of positive feedback with name	Percentage of negative feedback with name
Infant (n = 16)	9.83	41.03
Junior (n = 16)	10.21	48.30
Secondary (n = 18)	5.93	25.42

Table 2.5 Mean percentages of positive and negative feedback-directed to groups and individual pupils

Type of school	Individual		Group	
	Positive	Negative	Positive	Negative
Infant	58.90	25.70	6.13	9.14
Junior	67.70	18.12	4.96	9.16
Secondary	50.42	36.54	3.39	9.63

Table 2.6 Mean percentages of negative feedback that included a redirection

Type of school	Percentage of feedback including redirection
Infant (*n* = 16)	36.16
Junior (*n* = 16)	24.38
Secondary (*n* = 18)	27.90
Overall (*n* = 50)	28.95

a redirection. Infant teachers, however, used redirection in over one-third of their negative feedback. Moreover, they also gave considerably more description with negative feedback than the other two groups of teachers (Table 2.3). It seems very likely that the teachers were aware that such young children need an extra element of direction.

On-task pupil behaviour

As stated previously, the behaviour of the pupils in this study was assessed by observing the on-task behaviour of the pupils in all classes using the Pupil Behavioural Schedule (Jolly and McNamara, 1992). This schedule gives a good measure of pupil engagement, and also measures the types of off-task behaviour. The on-task behaviour for each set of pupils is shown in Table 2.7 (overleaf).

The results show a remarkable similarity between the classes at the different types of school. It is clear that, in this study, there is no substantial difference between the levels of on-task behaviour shown by pupils of different ages.

Comparison between this study and others is difficult because, as has been pointed out earlier, the method of calculating on-task behaviour has varied between different studies. However, these results show a remarkable similarity with some of the other studies carried out in England with secondary aged pupils (Rutter *et al.* (1979) at 81.5 per cent; Wheldall *et al.* (1989a) at 80.5 per cent).

Comment/activity

If you have a teaching assistant who can do some observing you might like to have the on-task behaviour of your pupils measured. The way to record that behaviour is to have your observer look at each pupil in turn in a predetermined order at 10-second intervals and note whether the pupil was on-task or off-task at the instant in which they are observed. With a little practice, it should also be possible for the observer to record what kind of off-task behaviour is being displayed, using the categories of off-task behaviour defined earlier in this chapter. When each pupil has been observed, the sequence can be repeated and be carried on until the agreed observation period is completed. That done, you can compare the performance of your pupils with those of the teachers we observed (see Table 2.8).

Table 2.7 Percentage of on-task behaviour for infant, junior and secondary school classes

Type of school	Mean	Range
Infant (n = 16)	81.24	66.66–92.50
Junior (n = 16)	78.47	41.00–95.70
Secondary (n = 18)	81.58	59.10–96.90
Total (n = 50)	80.48	41.00–96.90

Types of off-task behaviour

Different types of off-task behaviour recorded are displayed in Table 2.8.

Although there is some variation between the off-task behaviour of pupils from different types of school, these differences are quite small in most cases. The only exceptions are in the cases of 'in-seat behaviour', when we see secondary school pupils appear to have done much less fidgeting, turning the head, etc., than the pupils in infant and junior schools, 'out-of-seat' behaviour, which appears to account for around 5 per cent of off-task behaviour of infant and junior pupils but only 1.5 per cent of that of secondary pupils and 'disturbing other pupils', which in secondary classes appears to occur almost three times more often than in primary classes. In all other respects, there appears to be a relative similarity between the type of behaviour recorded by pupils at all levels. This similarity exists despite the considerable variation in the types of lesson observed, from Year 11 pupils preparing for their GCSEs to five-year-olds just starting school.

Talking and inattention were observed taking place in all classes. Shouting out that disrupted the whole class was observed on only seven occasions. Only one example of arguing with the teacher was recorded.

Although so far as we are aware other research has not been published using this schedule, it is worth emphasising that these results are not dissimilar from those of Rutter *et al.* (1979), who found that it was low-level talking between pupils rather than major disruptive incidents that were typical of the average class. Similarly, surveys of teachers, e.g. Gray and Sime (1988), suggest that it is low-level disruptive behaviour, such as talking out of turn or being inattentive, that are the most frequent types of disruption to lessons.

Table 2.8 Percentage of different types of off-task behaviour for infant, junior and secondary aged pupils

Types of off-task behaviour	Infant (n = 16)	Junior (n = 16)	Secondary (n = 18)
In seat	13.0	10.6	4.7
Out of seat	25.0	25.0	8.4
Shouting	0.5	0.4	1.2
Talking	30.0	27.0	46.0
Disturbing other pupils	1.5	1.3	4.5
Arguing	0.2	0	0
Distracting teacher	2.0	0	3.5
Inattention	34.0	28.0	29.0

Relationship between teacher verbal feedback and pupil behaviour

The relationship between teacher verbal feedback and pupil behaviour was one of the key elements of our research. We were able to look at not only the effect of positive and negative feedback but also the way in which they had a combined effect. We did this by looking at the ratio of positive to negative feedback in all classes. When looking at these results, it must be remembered that the majority of positive feedback was directed towards pupils' work, one must presume in an attempt to encourage such endeavour, and the vast majority of negative feedback was directed to pupils' behaviour, one must presume in an attempt to reduce the behaviour. Very little positive feedback was directed towards pupils' behaviour. The results were on the whole in the expected direction. Positive feedback from teachers tended to be positively related to pupils' on-task behaviour, while negative feedback tended to be negatively related to on-task behaviour. While a consistent picture emerged between the three levels of schooling as far as positive feedback was concerned, for negative feedback such was not the case. For the infant and junior school classes, there was a very small negative relationship between on-task behaviour of pupils and negative feedback, but a much more substantial relationship in secondary school classes. (See appendix for a statistical analysis.)

When the results for individual teachers were examined, the pattern for the infant schools teachers' use of negative feedback suggested that there might be a curvilinear relationship between negative feedback and on-task behaviour. The higher rates of on-task behaviour were associated with mid-range levels of disapproval, while lower rates of on-task behaviour were associated with both low and high levels of disapproval. It should also be remembered that there was a noticeable difference between the teachers of infants in their use of negative feedback and the two other groups of teachers. Infant teachers used far more description when giving negative feedback, almost 70 per cent, compared with junior teachers at just over 50 per cent and secondary teachers at around 25 per cent (see Table 2.3). In addition, infant teachers included a higher proportion of redirection following negative feedback (36 per cent) than the other teachers (juniors 24 per cent, secondary 27 per cent) (Table 2.6). The fact that the inverted 'U' shape, as seen in Figure 2.1, is not apparent for the other two groups of teachers may indicate that different factors were at work. Certainly the fact that the majority of negative feedback to infants included a description must be important, especially when the class is showing comparatively high levels of off-task behaviour.

In contrast, the pattern of secondary teachers is very different indeed. Here there was a strong negative relationship between teachers' rates of disapproval and on-task behaviour. In classes with high rates of on-task behaviour, the rates of negative feedback were very low, as shown in Figure 2.2.

Where on-task rates were high, one would expect rates of negative feedback to be low, after all, the teacher has very little to complain about. Conversely, when on-task rates were low then the teachers have a great deal to complain about and, consequently, the rates of teacher negative feedback were very high indeed, almost double the rate observed in both infant and junior classes. Whatever the reasons behind the tactics the secondary teachers were using with their classes, one thing is clear: their use of high

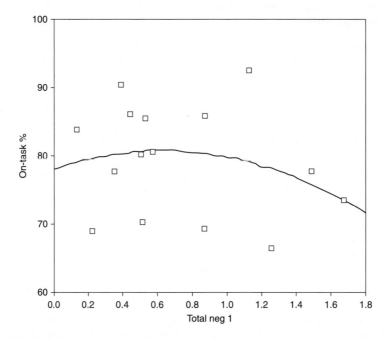

Figure 2.1 Relationship between negative feedback and on-task behaviour in infant classes.

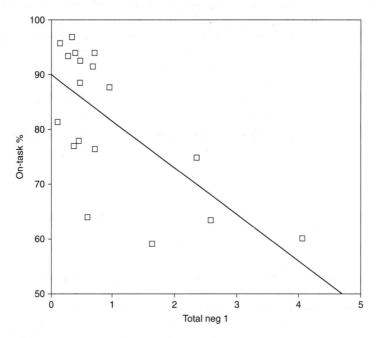

Figure 2.2 Relationship between negative feedback and on-task behaviour in secondary school classes.

rates of negative feedback did not appear to be an effective strategy for getting the students back to work.

The effect of the ratio of positive to negative feedback on pupil behaviour

Wheldall *et al.* (1989b) suggest that one way to assess the overall effect of both positive and negative teacher feedback is to express it in the form of a ratio, i.e. positive feedback divided by negative feedback. They argue that the advantage of treating the data in this way is that it can provide an insight into the overall effect that the balance of both types of verbal feedback, positive and negative, has on pupil behaviour.

The results of analysing the data in terms of the ratio of positive to negative feedback showed that, in all three levels of schooling, there was a strong relationship between the ratio and pupil on-task behaviour. The results were in line with those of Wheldall and his colleagues, the higher the ratio the more pupil on-task behaviour was displayed. (See appendix for a statistical analysis.)

Summary of results

The proportions of verbal feedback directed towards pupils' work and behaviour were similar to those found in other studies in that the majority of positive feedback was directed towards pupils' work while the majority of negative feedback was directed towards pupils' behaviour. Very little positive feedback was directed towards pupils' behaviour. This pattern was found in infant, junior and secondary classes.

More positive than negative feedback was apparent at all three levels of schooling. The ratio was smaller at the secondary level.

The rates at which teachers gave feedback were very similar across all levels of schooling.

When we looked at teachers' feedback that included description, we noted that positive feedback seems very similar across the three levels of schooling. There would appear, however, to be differences when considering negative feedback. The proportion of negative feedback containing a description was approximately 70 per cent for infant schoolteachers, 50 per cent for junior schoolteachers and only 25 per cent for secondary schoolteachers.

Teachers' use of pupils' names when providing feedback also varied: infant and junior schoolteachers used pupils' names in approximately 10 per cent of positive feedback and 45 per cent of negative feedback, but for secondary teachers the figures were 6 per cent and 25 per cent respectively.

Redirections following negative feedback tended to be used more by infant teachers (36 per cent), while in junior and secondary classes the proportion was 24 per cent and 28 per cent respectively.

The majority of verbal feedback was directed to individual pupils (86 per cent) rather than to groups. The rate of positive individual feedback was twice the rate of individual negative feedback. This was the reverse of the rates for group feedback, where the rate of negative feedback was twice that for positive feedback.

High rates of teacher positive feedback tended to be associated with high rates of pupil on-task behaviour and, conversely, high rates of teacher negative feedback tended to be associated with low rates of pupil on-task behaviour.

The second investigation

A further study arose out of interest that was taken in our original research. We were approached by two educational psychologists. Both had seen the value of our work with teachers and they suggested asking educational psychologists from all over the country to take part in a nationwide survey of classroom behaviour. After some discussion, 71 educational psychologists carried out observations in over 140 classes in England, Wales and Scotland. This became the largest and most widespread survey undertaken of British primary teachers and their pupils' behaviour.

The survey used an observational schedule that recorded the following five categories: teacher academic positives (TAP), teacher academic negatives (TAN), teacher social positives (TSP), teacher social negatives (TSN) and academic redirections, explanations, questions (ARD), as well as pupil on-task behaviour from a random sample of pupils. The observations were made in sets of two so that most classes were observed in the morning and afternoon. Note was made of the presence of any teaching assistants present during a lesson, the size of class and the effect that social deprivation, as measured by the percentage of free school meals, might have on the behaviour of the pupils.

Our results in terms of the relationship between positive feedback from the teachers and the behaviour of the pupils were, perhaps not surprisingly, very similar to previous research. We found a positive relationship between 'teacher academic positives' and pupil on-task behaviour. We also found that teachers who were especially positive also tended to use more redirections, explanations and questions. One of the most telling findings is best displayed in the form of a scattergram showing the relationship between teachers' academic positives and pupil on-task behaviour (Figure 2.3).

This shows that there were no classes in our sample where the teacher was being reasonably positive in which the pupils were other than well-behaved. That is a very powerful image of the influence that teacher positive feedback can have on pupil behaviour.

The one finding that did show a slight difference was in terms of the proportion of positive feedback directed to pupils' behaviour. Earlier studies had found comparatively low rates of this type of feedback (Swinson and Harrop, 2005, 4 per cent; Merrett and Wheldall, 1987, 6 per cent), whereas in this survey, it was assessed at almost 15 per cent. The reason for this difference is difficult to interpret and may well be due to differences in methodology.

The widespread nature of the research also allowed us to look at a range of other factors. We found that both pupil and teacher behaviour was very similar in both the morning and afternoon and that class size, the presence of a teaching assistant or the proportion of the pupils having free school meals had little effect on behaviour. We did find that inner-city teachers did more talking within the categories observed than others, especially in terms of giving both positive and negative feedback in response to behaviour. We also found that in very structured parts of the lesson, when the teachers were delivering parts of the national literacy or numeracy sessions, teachers tended to give more feedback to their pupils and the pupils themselves were more attentive. Finally, we

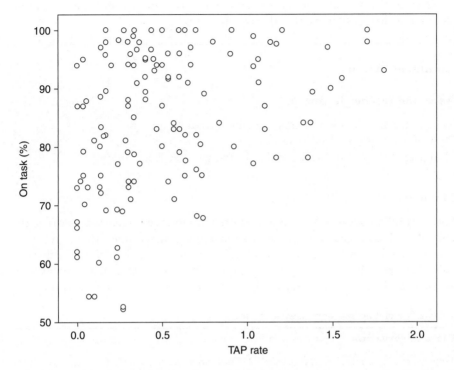

Figure 2.3 Scattergram showing the relationship between positive teacher feedback and on-task behaviour in primary schools (from Apter, Arnold & Swinson, 2010).

found that the most effective teachers, those who gave their pupils the most effective feedback, were those teachers at the end of each key stage, in other words Year 2 and Year 6 teachers. It might not be an accident that such effective teachers taught these groups because, in the UK, that is when pupils take their national SATS assessments.

General comments

The two investigations just recounted are links in a sequence of studies that has extended over at least the past 30 years. Interest in this area of inquiry has continued, presumably because it has been felt that teacher feedback was, is, and will continue to be a very important element of good teaching and our aim has been to bring the reader up to date with recent developments.

What next?

We have demonstrated that there is a very strong link between the positive nature of teachers' feedback to their pupils and the behaviour of the pupils themselves.

It could be, of course, that it is the good behaviour of the pupils that leads the teachers to be more positive. While there may be an element of truth in this supposition, it is perhaps more logical to assume that it is, in fact, the teachers' positive attitude and behaviour that is leading to enhanced pupil behaviour. We shall be explaining in the following chapter how we tested this hypothesis.

Comment/activity

Assessing teacher feedback

Teacher feedback is a key element in all good teaching!
How effective is your feedback?
Two simple ways of recording and assessing your feedback follow.

Method 1

Find a trusted colleague in school and offer to observe one another during the course of a lesson when one of you has some non-contact time. All you need is a simple record sheet to record each occasion when a certain type of feedback is delivered (see Table 2.9). Alternatively, if you have access to a classroom assistant ask them to do it. We know one teacher who asked two of her pupils to record her.

Table 2.9 Example teacher assessment form

Class observation

Time start..   Time finish..

Class..   Number of pupils..

Type of feedback	Positive	Negative
Academic/work		
Behaviour		
Redirections		
Instructions/directions		

Method 2

In our original research, we used a 'Walkman' device (for younger readers, this is a small cassette recorder) to tape our teachers. A number of teachers asked to hear their own tapes and others taped themselves. Technology has moved on so it is now easy to tape yourselves using a mobile phone, iPhone, iPod or Blackberry.

Simply record yourself over half an hour of teaching and analyse your feedback using the record sheet.

(It may be advisable to discuss with your head teacher the fact that you plan to record, and also tell your pupils.)

Most teachers feel they are more positive than they actually are. How positive are you?

Comment/activity

We have written about investigations in which different teachers were observed and the overall relationships found between verbal feedback and on-task behaviour. What hasn't been done, as far as we are aware, is an investigation by a single teacher in her or his own classroom into the relationship between verbal feedback and on-task behaviour with different kinds of lesson (in the primary school) or with different classes (in the secondary school). It shouldn't be too difficult to set up such an investigation, provided you can arrange for observations to be done, and the results would be most interesting.

If it isn't possible to arrange for someone to observe, you can at least monitor your own performance and see if there appear to be any relationships.

Appendix: statistical analyses

Table A2.1 Correlations (Pearson's *r*) between types of teacher verbal feedback and pupil on-task behaviour (*n* = 50)

Types of feedback	Pearson's r	Probability
Total positive	.312	.027*
Academic positive	.339	.016*
Behaviour positive	−.219	.126
Total negative	−.463	.001**
Academic negative	.082	.571
Behaviour negative	−.493	.000**
Total feedback	−.104	.471

* Correlation is significant at the 0.05 level (2-tailed)

** Correlation is significant at the 0.01 level (2-tailed)

Table A2.2 Correlation between the on-task behaviour of pupils in infant, junior and secondary schools and the negative verbal feedback of their teachers

Type of school	Pearson's r correlation	Level of significance
Infant	−0.213	0.429
Junior	−0.325	0.220
Secondary	−0.689**	0.002

** Level of significance at the 0.01 level (2-tailed)

Table A2.3 Correlation between the ratio of teachers' positive and negative feedback and pupils' on-task behaviour

Type of school	Ratio +ve/−ve	Percentage of pupil on-task behaviour	Pearson's r correlation
Infant (*n* = 16)	1.899	81.24	0.560*
Junior (*n* = 16)	1.983	78.47	0.507*
Secondary (*n* = 18)	1.127	81.58	0.545*
Total (*n* = 50)	1.669	80.48	0.422**

* Correlation is significant at the 0.05 level (2-tailed)

** Correlation is significant at the 0.01 level (2-tailed)

This analysis is provided to illustrate the combined effect of both positive and negative feedback on on-task behaviour. However, as has already been outlined, this treatment of the data means that any effect due to the rate of feedback is lost. What is gained, however, appears to be some effect due to combining both forms of feedback. The correlation between the ratio and on-task behaviour is greater than that between rates of positive feedback alone and on-task behaviour for infant, junior and secondary samples. The correlation between ratio and on-task behaviour is greater than correlations between negative feedback rates and on-task behaviour for infant and junior samples, but not for the secondary sample. The reason for this phenomenon is not clear, but may be related to the fact that in secondary classrooms the actual rate of negative feedback is higher than for the infant and junior sample.

Chapter 3

Positive strategies
Four essential steps

In the previous chapter, we outlined the relationship between teachers' use of positive and negative feedback and the behaviour of their pupils. The research presented and discussed was generally concerned with investigating relationships, a method normally referred to as *correlational research*. In interpreting the results, however, we pointed out that it was difficult to know precisely whether it was the pupils' good behaviour that prompted the teachers to become more positive or the positive teachers' feedback that encouraged the pupils' good behaviour. To answer that question, we must turn to experimental research that we used in evaluating a training programme for teachers.

There have been a number of studies, including some by the authors of this book, that have looked at the effect of encouraging teachers to become more specific in their use of feedback and to become more positive in their responses to pupils' behaviour that have been incorporated into a number of training packages aimed at helping teachers become better classroom managers. An early example of such training can be found in a report by Harrop (1974). Working together with an educational psychologist, he developed a six-week series of 'behavioural workshops' in which teachers were encouraged to develop class rules, ignore inappropriate behaviour and whenever possible praise appropriate behaviour. Evaluations of the workshops by the teachers involved were very positive in terms of improved pupil behaviour.

Later, Wheldall and Merrett (1988) developed a programme called the behavioural approaches to teaching package (BATPACK), which consisted of six one-hour training sessions, delivered either in school or in a university setting. It also included homework, which comprised classroom observations of other teachers and of the participants, in addition to reading assignments.

Another training programme that received considerable publicity when it was launched in the United Kingdom in the 1990s (see Makins, 1991; Cohen, 1993), was an American programme known as 'Assertive Discipline', devised by Canter and Canter (1992). Like the others, the programme was based on behavioural principles. It consisted of six hours of training, which included many examples of good practice shown to the teachers on video. Teachers were given advice on many aspects of good discipline including the use of sanctions, but the central message of the programme was to emphasise to teachers the need to recognise and praise those pupils who were doing as they had been asked. Advice was also given on how to deal with off-task pupils by redirecting their behaviour and praising them once they had re-engaged in the lesson.

The 'Assertive Discipline' programme was extremely popular in some areas of the country. In Liverpool, staff from over 70 schools were trained in the technique (see government White Paper, 'Excellence in Education', 1997). It has been estimated by its British distributors that some 400,000 teachers across the United Kingdom have received training in the programme, but the extent to which the principles and practices of the approach have been applied is unknown.

An interesting point is that although 'Assertive Discipline' training includes some very specific advice on dealing with disruptive behaviour in a very systematic fashion using a hierarchy of sanctions, in reality, teachers tend to choose not to use them. When we asked the teachers why this was, they pointed out that their increased use of positive feedback appeared to lead to more pupil engagement, less disruption and therefore less need to use sanctions.

It is important to note that the changes in teacher and pupil behaviour shown in both of the last two training packages discussed include not only advice on teachers' use of praise and acknowledgement, but also advice on other strategies. BATPACK includes advice on seating plans and assertive discipline provides detailed instruction on the use of sanctions. Therefore, although teachers following both training programmes show an increase in their positive feedback to pupils, it cannot be said that changes in pupil behaviour are solely the product of that increase.

The investigation

That being the case, it was the aim of the investigation described here to use a methodology that was as rigorous as possible in addressing the effects of teacher feedback alone, both quantitative and qualitative, on pupil on-task behaviour. Consequently, we embarked on a major investigation with which a group of six schools, one secondary and five primary, agreed to take part (see Swinson and Harrop, 2005). The schools had been nominated by their head teachers for whole school training in classroom management. In the investigation, we were intent on examining the extent to which changes in teachers' verbal feedback altered the behaviour of their pupils.

The methods for both the recording of the teachers' verbal behaviour and the recording of the pupil behaviour were exactly the same as those used in the previous study, outlined in detail in the preceding chapter.

A group of teachers from each school volunteered to allow observations to be made in their classroom. The total sample included six teachers from infant schools, six from junior schools and seven from secondary schools. The initial set of observations took place in school during the week prior to the training. The second set of observations of each teacher and their pupils took place between four and six weeks after the training at the same time and day of the week as for the first set. The lesson content, of course, varied but all lessons were of a similar type in terms of organisation and structure.

The training

The training consisted of two elements:

1   *Element 1*. A presentation and discussion of the results of a series of detailed observations carried out in a number of classes in each school was shown to the teachers in each school.

2 **Element 2**. A PowerPoint presentation, 'Managing behaviour – four essential steps', was presented to all the staff.

In most schools, the presentation took only a couple of hours, although in the secondary school more time was allowed for discussion at departmental level.

Element 1

The feedback on the teachers' current use of verbal feedback was based on an analysis of the original sets of pre-training recordings similar to the ones we used in our original study (Harrop and Swinson, 2000) using a 'Walkman'. The identity of individual teachers was kept confidential, the results were reported only on the basis of the whole school results and were reported back only in terms of percentages of feedback given. Thus each school was informed of the following details as average values for their school:

- percentage of positive feedback
- percentage of negative feedback
- percentage of positive feedback for work (academic)
- percentage of positive feedback for behaviour (social)
- percentage of negative feedback for work (academic)
- percentage of negative feedback for behaviour (social).

Staff of the schools were told that, on the whole, most feedback was delivered to individuals not groups and that only a minority of feedback contained a description. It was not possible to provide any more detailed analysis at this point in terms of teachers' use of pupils' names or their use of redirection.

The teachers were informed that, without exception, the results showed a consistent pattern that reflected the results of research outlined in the previous chapter. In other words, most positive feedback was reserved for pupils' work, while most negative feedback was directed towards pupils' behaviour. Some negative feedback was given for pupils' work, but very little, if any, positive feedback appeared to be directed towards pupil behaviour.

The proportion of negative feedback that was followed by a redirection was discussed, as was the use made by the teachers of descriptions of both unwanted and desired behaviour.

Comparisons were made with previous research in this area and, not surprisingly, the results from each school proved to be very similar to those of previous research in both Great Britain and also across the world.

It was pointed out to the teachers that their current teaching style was essentially a reactive one in that much of their feedback, especially their negative feedback to social behaviour, was in response to pupils or groups of pupils who basically were not doing as they were told. It was explained that telling off pupils was essentially a very limited strategy, which yielded only short-lived changes in behaviour. It was argued that a much more proactive strategy, one that involved providing a great deal more in terms of positive feedback, especially positive feedback aimed towards the pupils' behaviour, might prove a much more effective way of leading to improved pupil behaviour and learning. Generally at this point, a discussion of these issues took place. In all the schools, no teachers presented any major objection to the central argument that being proactive and making a deliberate effort to be more positive towards pupils would result in better behaved pupils and in more time spent by the pupils on their work.

Element 2: Four Essential Steps

This element was the training course. The programme was devised by the first named author and two colleagues: Richard Melling, an educational psychologist, and Mike Cording, a head teacher and behavioural consultant. It developed from a consideration of the research by the first author and Richard Melling into the effectiveness of the 'Assertive Discipline' training (Swinson and Melling, 1995). It had been noticed in this research, as mentioned before, that despite the fact that the programme included considerable advice on the use of sanctions, in practice, teachers did not use these. The reason for this was, we assumed, that the advice in the training on the use of positive feedback was so effective in modifying the pupils' behaviour that any use of sanctions became superfluous. We were also conscious in previous training we had given that teachers found it very hard indeed to ignore disruptive or other off-task behaviour by pupils, a tactic suggested by many earlier practitioners (e.g. Madsen *et al.*, 1968; Harrop, 1974) and, indeed, in BATPACK (Wheldall and Merrett, 1988). Hence we included a section in the training on positive responses to disruptive and off-task behaviour.

The four essential steps can be summarised as follows:

1 Always make your instructions and directions to the class absolutely clear.
2 Follow any instruction or direction by looking for those pupils who are doing as they have been asked and acknowledging them.
3 Frequently acknowledge the pupils when they are doing whatever they have been requested to do.
4 Always know exactly what to do to deal with inappropriate behaviour.

A detailed description of the 'four essential steps' presentation is included in the appendix.

Comment/activity

Read 'four essential steps'. Concentrate on two of the most important pieces of advice.
Always look for the behaviour that you want rather than the behaviour that you don't want.
And
Every time you give an instruction or direction, look for two pupils who have followed the instruction and praise them.
Try this out in your lesson.

Ask a colleague to observe the lesson and measure your rate of positive and negative feedback (as in the advice at the end of the last chapter). If you are a secondary school teacher, start with one of your less demanding classes before trying it with the most difficult.

The presentation was received well by most teachers. A number of them asked a series of questions but none raised any practical or philosophical objection to the approach.

The head teacher of each school was asked to be present during the training and at the end of the training session was asked to make a comment. All head teachers were complimentary about the content and encouraged their teachers to adopt the approaches outlined in the training.

Between a month and six weeks after we had given the training to the teachers we went back and carried out a second series of observations. This was not only to evaluate our training in terms of changes in teacher behaviour but also to provide us with an opportunity to look at the effect that any changes in teachers' use of feedback might have had on the behaviour and engagement of their pupils.

Since the emphasis of the training was to increase both the nature and quantity of feedback provided by teachers to their pupils, we expected to find an increase in the amount of feedback given by the teachers and, in particular, an increase in the proportion of positive feedback given. That is broadly what we found.

Teacher verbal feedback

The mean rates of feedback of all types were recorded and are presented in Table 3.1.

As can be seen in Table 3.1, the rate of feedback did, in fact, increase for both the teachers of infant and of juniors, but not for the secondary school teachers. We did see, however, substantial changes in the types of feedback given, as demonstrated in Table 3.2.

Table 3.1 Mean rate of instances of feedback per minute given by teachers pre- and post-training

Type of school	Pre-training	Post-training	Difference
Infant (n = 6)	1.592	2.200	+0.608
Junior (n = 6)	2.301	2.618	+0.317
Secondary (n = 7)	2.342	2.109	−0.331
Total (n = 19)	2.091	2.298	+0.207

Table 3.2 Changes in mean rates of different types of feedback pre- and post-training (n = 19)

Type of feedback	Pre-training rate	Post-training rate
Positive for work	0.955	1.556
Positive for behaviour	0.138	0.350
Total positive	1.093	1.906
Negative for work	0.231	0.117
Negative for behaviour	0.768	0.275
Total negative	0.999	0.392
Ratio positive/negative	3.036	10.646

The changes in the rates for the various types of feedback were all in the direction anticipated by the training, i.e. to increase the proportion of positive feedback and to decrease the proportion of negative, especially that directed towards pupil behaviour. In fact, the rate of positive feedback almost doubled while the rate of negative feedback was reduced by two-thirds. (See appendix for a statistical analysis.)

The pattern can be seen more clearly when the changes in the proportion of each type of feedback are presented.

Table 3.3 shows a major shift in the teaching strategies of the teachers we trained. The smallest change in absolute terms was the change in the percentage of negative feedback directed towards work, which fell in percentage terms by some 6 per cent. That figure does, however, show more than a halving of the rate. Other changes are considerable, i.e. the proportion of total positive feedback shows an increase of over 50 per cent, the increase in positive feedback towards behaviour being threefold. Bearing in mind that the overall rate of feedback changed very little after training (see Table 3.1), these changes in all types of positive feedback have been largely responsible for a threefold reduction in the negative feedback directed towards behaviour. Teachers therefore appear to have adopted a more positively based strategy than before training for encouraging both good work and for encouraging good behaviour.

Perhaps the best way of demonstrating the changes in the pattern of feedback is to look at the ratio of positive to negative feedback given by the teachers in the three types of class. A ratio greater than 1 indicates teachers are being more positive than negative.

(See appendix for a statistical analysis.)

The data presented in Table 3.4 show that the teachers in infant and junior schools increased the positive to negative feedback ratio by a factor of over seven. The increase in ratio for secondary teachers was less dramatic, but even so they more than doubled their ratio. The reasons for these differences are not obvious. Perhaps secondary teachers feel less at ease giving praise to older pupils or worry about possible effects on their pupils of too much approval.

Table 3.3 Changes in the percentage of different types of feedback post-training (n = 19)

Feedback	Positive Pre- − Post-	Negative Pre- − Post-
Work	48.0 − 67.9	11.7 − 5.28
Behaviour	5.6 − 17.1	34.6 − 9.6
Total	53.6 − 85.0	46.3 − 14.8

Table 3.4 Mean ratios of positive to negative feedback given by teachers pre- and post-training

Type of school	Pre-training Positive/Negative	Post-training Positive/Negative
Infant	2.07	14.92
Junior	1.88	14.08
Secondary	1.15	3.32

What is clear from our research is that the classes we observed after training were very positive places to be in and much more positive than before. The pupils were receiving a great deal of positive encouragement for both their work and their behaviour. The essential step of catching children being good and acknowledging them appears to have been implemented well.

Group versus individual feedback

We felt that the use of positive feedback to the whole class or groups within any class was underused. Therefore the training contained advice that one simple way of ensuring that every pupil in the class felt valued and their behaviour or work approved by the teacher was to use forms of positive feedback directed to the group, rather than to rely solely on individual feedback. For many teachers, the rates of group feedback, especially before training, was very low.

The changes in the pattern of feedback from pre- to post-training are outlined in Table 3.5.

In all cases, as a result of the training, there appeared to be a shift in the nature of the type of feedback given by teachers in that a higher proportion of all types of feedback appears to be directed towards groups. This is, of course, against a backdrop of increases in the use of all types of positive feedback and a drop in the rate of all forms of negative feedback.

The teachers from the different stages of schooling responded to the training in a very similar fashion and it is interesting to note that the most frequently used form of group feedback was negative feedback about behaviour. We guess all teachers would recognise themselves admonishing a class along the lines of: '3B you are making too much noise. I've already told you to work quietly.'

That statement is a form of class instruction, but phrased in a very negative way. A far better way of achieving the same effect would have been to remind the class of the instruction and note and approve of one or two class members who were working quietly.

Table 3.5 Changes in percentages of group and individual feedback pre- and post-training (*n* = 19)

Feedback	Individual		Group	
	Pre-training	Post-training	Pre-training	Post-training
Positive	92.3	85.0	7.7	15.0
Negative	84.3	75.6	15.7	24.4

Use of pupils' names

There is some evidence that use of a personal name increases the value or power of any feedback (Andrews and Kozma, 1990) and can raise the status of the praised child (Flanders and Havumaki, 1960). Therefore, in the training, teachers were encouraged to increase their use of pupils' names both with positive and negative feedback. The results are reported in terms of percentage of feedback including a name (see Table 3.6).

Table 3.6 Percentage of positive and negative feedback pre- and post-training including pupils' names

Type of school	Type of feedback	Pre-training	Post-training	Percentage change
Infant	Positive	19	15	−21
	Negative	34	22	−35
Junior	Positive	10	21.2	+89
	Negative	33.7	23.7	−30
Secondary	Positive	15.5	12.3	−21
	Negative	26	28.8	+11
Total	Positive	14.8	16.2	−10
	Negative	31.2	24.8	−21

These results are very mixed and, as a consequence, we feel that this aspect of the training was not felt to be important by the teachers and may not have, as we will see later, a great influence on pupil behaviour.

Teachers' use of description as part of feedback

The training contained a section encouraging teachers, both in their use of positive and negative feedback, to describe the behaviour or work that was the subject of their approval or disapproval. The results of changes in their use of descriptions are shown in Table 3.7.

We were very encouraged with the effects of this aspect of the training as we felt the use of descriptions following feedback increases its power, especially in spelling out to pupils exactly what it is about their behaviour or work that the teacher feels is important. These results are largely in the direction expected as a result of the training. Generally, the teachers increased their use of descriptions for both positive and negative feedback. The exception to this appeared to be junior teachers in their use of positive feedback. It is difficult to explain this phenomenon. It is noticeable that the largest change occurred in teachers' use of a description when providing negative feedback. This was especially apparent for junior school teachers. Their use of descriptions

Table 3.7 Teachers' mean verbal feedback that contained a description pre- and post-training, expressed as a percentage (*n* = 19)

Type of school	Type of feedback	Pre-training percentage	Post-training percentage	Percentage change
Infant	Positive	41	49.5	+21
	Negative	53	70	+32
Junior	Positive	17.6	9	−51
	Negative	25.5	53	+108
Secondary	Positive	37	49	+32
	Negative	17.9	22.5	+26
Total	Positive	31.9	35.8	+13
	Negative	35.8	48.5	+35

when giving negative feedback more than doubled. For some reason, the junior school teachers, unlike the other two groups, seemed to have focused on giving description with negative feedback.

Teachers' use of redirection following negative feedback, before and after training

In the training, teachers were encouraged to include a redirection following the use of negative feedback, e.g. 'Tommy please do not turn around and talk, I need to see you finishing off those sums.' The results are reported in Table 3.8.

The results in all three types of school were in the direction expected as a result of the training. However, the results showed only a small increase in the use of redirection for infant and secondary teachers but a large increase in junior teachers' behaviour. It is difficult to account for these differences. What is clear is that the training did result in an overall increase in the proportion of teachers' use of redirections, of over 50 per cent. It should also be borne in mind that this was against a background of an overall decrease in the rate at which teachers were giving all forms of negative feedback by a factor of three (see Table 3.2). This change represents another major shift in the way the teachers dealt with their pupils.

Table 3.8 Percentage of negative feedback that included use of redirection pre- and post-training ($n = 19$)

Type of school	Pre-training including redirection	Post-training including redirection	Percentage change
Infant	37.4	40.7	+9.2
Junior	30.6	76.8	+153
Secondary	34.9	39.6	+13
Total	34.3	52.4	+53

Pupil behaviour

The teachers who took part in the training were observed teaching both before and after they took part in the training. During these observations, the behaviour of the pupils in their classes was also observed in order to ascertain if the application of the teachers' new-found skills had any influence on the behaviour of their pupils. The changes in pupil behaviour are presented in Table 3.9. (See appendix for a statistical analysis.)

The changes in pupil on-task behaviour were not only in the direction expected as a result of the training but were very impressive changes that were strikingly similar at all three levels. This is very strong evidence of a shift in pupil behaviour as a result of changes in teachers' verbal feedback. Moreover, it shows that the training was equally effective in the infant, junior and secondary schools.

Looking at the data, a reader could form the impression that the lessons we observed were ones in which rows of silent automata toiled away in total obedience. That was manifestly not the case. Most lessons were as lively and as entertaining as they had been before the training. The single most important change was essentially that of pupil

Table 3.9 Changes in mean percentages of on-task behaviour of pupils pre- and post-training

Type of school	Pre-training on-task	Post-training on-task	Difference in on-task
Infant (n = 6)	78.68	93.76	+15.08
Junior (n = 6)	77.72	95.93	+18.21
Secondary (n = 7)	76.23	92.68	+16.45
Total (n = 19)	77.48	94.05	+16.57

engagement. After the training, the pupils were doing more of what the teacher had planned for them to be doing, be that reading quietly, playing badminton, making a CD disc holder or discussing the life of Henry VIII.

Types of off-task behaviour

In addition, a record was made of the nature of the different types of off-task behaviour observed in all the classes both before and after the teachers' training. The results of these observations are given in Table 3.10.

The results show that the changes in the teachers' verbal feedback resulted in a decline in virtually all types of off-task behaviour. The strategies appeared to be particularly effective in reducing rates of in-seat misbehaviour, i.e. rocking on chair and turning around, and especially out-of-seat behaviour, which showed a dramatic reduction, especially in the junior sample. There were also reductions by almost two-thirds in pupils' most indulged-in forms of off-task behaviour, namely talking and inattention. Anyone scrutinising the data carefully will have noticed that, in the secondary classes, the in-seat misbehaviour increased after training. That should be taken in conjunction with the reduction in all other forms of misbehaviour, particularly 'out-of-seat,' since reducing time 'out-of-seat' inevitably means more time 'in-seat'.

Table 3.10 Mean percentage of different types of off-task behaviour in infant, junior and secondary pupils pre- and post-training

Types of off-task behaviour	Infant (n = 6)	Junior (n = 6)	Secondary (n = 7)	Total (n = 19)
In seat	0 (2.47)	0 (2.40)	1.23 (0.73)	0.41 (1.86)
Out of seat	2.13 (5.40)	0.30 (10.40)	0.30 (2.80)	0.91 (6.20)
Shouting	0.25 (0)	0 (0.10)	0 (0.34)	0.08 (0.15)
Talking	1.33 (4.51)	1.96 (5.82)	3.16 (9.15)	2.15 (6.48)
Disturbing other pupils	0 (0.20)	0.25 (0.10)	0 (2.50)	0.08 (0.80)
Arguing	0 (0)	0 (0)	0 (0)	0 (0)
Distracting teacher	0 (0.10)	0 (0)	0 (2.10)	0 (0.49)
Inattention	2.72 (6.95)	1.72 (6.70)	3.17 (6.38)	2.54 (6.68)

Note: Pre-training percentages in parentheses

Relationship between changes in teachers' verbal feedback and pupil behaviour

Our evaluation of the four essential steps training showed that, with the exception of attempting to use pupils' names more, the teachers we trained were able to successfully incorporate our advice into their teaching. This was illustrated in Table 3.3, in which we saw the mean proportion of positive feedback increase by over 50 per cent and negative decrease to less than one-third of its level after training. If we look at the changes in the ratios of positive to negative feedback in the three different levels of school (as shown in Table 3.4) and compare them with the changes in percentages of on-task behaviour (as shown in Table 3.9), we can get a visual illustration of the relationships involved in Table 3.11.

We can see, for example, that although the teachers of secondary age pupils showed the smallest change in the ratio, their pupils still increased their on-task behaviour substantially. The change in ratio from 1.15 to 3.32 looks small in comparison to the changes for the teachers in the infant and junior school, yet it represents a more than doubling of the ratio. It is evident that doubling the ratio was quite sufficient to increase their pupils' on-task behaviour. That is interesting and will probably lead to all kinds of speculation in the readers' mind, focused around the differences in the pupils, the school organisations, etc. We, however, are not going to indulge in speculation at this point, remaining content to note that secondary school teachers made a smaller adjustment in their ratio of positive to negative feedback and obtained more or less the same results as the teachers of younger pupils.

It is worth noting that the mean rates of on-task behaviour that were recorded in the classes after the teachers had had the training were all at a higher level than has been observed in other classes in separate studies in the United Kingdom, USA, Hong Kong, Australia or New Zealand.

Discussion of the results of the investigation

The investigation was aimed at examining the effects of changing teacher feedback on pupil behaviour and this was done through a training programme designed to provide teachers with strategies that would help improve the behaviour of pupils in their classrooms, by increasing their rates of approval and decreasing their rates of disapproval and by improving the quality of approval and disapproval. The results show that the programme successfully fulfilled that aim. The changes in teacher feedback were accompanied by marked increases in the on-task behaviour of the pupils in the teachers' classes.

Table 3.11 Changes in ratios of positive to negative feedback at the three levels together with increases of pupil on-task behaviour

Type of school	Pre-training positive to negative ratio	Post-training positive to negative ratio	Increase in pupil percentage on-task rate
Infant	2.07	14.92	15.08
Junior	1.88	14.08	18.21
Secondary	1.15	3.32	16.87

The changes in teacher behaviour and consequent changes in pupil behaviour achieved in this study bear comparison with those achieved by others in the field, e.g. those of Harrop (1974) and Wheldall and Merrett (1988). It is important to emphasise, however, that the training packages discussed previously vary in some aspects of their content and also in their style of presentation. Harrop's behavioural workshops and Merrett and Wheldall's BATPACK were based on a series of workshops for teachers, while the Canters' assertive discipline programme was a very professional series of video presentations with a textbook and workbook. All these training packages involved at least six hours' training presented either over a number of sessions or during a whole day. In contrast, the training in this study took just over two hours to deliver. Consequently, it is worth considering the elements of the training used in this study that proved to make it so powerful.

Three aspects of the training given to the teachers were essential to its success. The first aspect occurred in other programmes, but the others did not.

The first aspect, advice given to teachers, was based very firmly on sound research in educational psychology. In this respect, the training was no different from the others quoted earlier. It did allow the presenters to tell the teachers that 'we recommend you treat pupils in this way because we have sound evidence that if you do, it will work', rather than giving them a series of rather bland suggestions that they might like to try. In some ways, this was the tone of the presentation. The teachers were given an opportunity to discuss how they might implement the strategies they learned about, but there was little opportunity to debate whether or not it might or might not work.

Second, unlike other training packages, at the beginning of the presentation teachers at each school were given a brief outline of their current use of verbal feedback, using group mean scores as recorded at the pre-training observation. Individual teachers were not identified. The results for each school were invariably similar, allowing the presenter to highlight the underuse of positive feedback for behaviour and the overuse of negative feedback. Teachers were then given an opportunity to reflect on their current performance. Teachers' underuse of positive feedback led to a discussion of alternative strategies and an acceptance by most teachers that an alternative praise-based approach was at least worth attempting.

Third, every attempt was made to keep the content of the presentation as simple as possible. This was exemplified by the use of the 'four essential steps of classroom management', which formed the core of the presentation. Teachers appeared to understand its simple message and, as the results of the post-training observations showed, they employed these strategies in their classrooms. Although the course did contain other levels of advice, e.g. redirection following disapproval, close listening to the recordings of the teachers revealed that these techniques did not appear to have been incorporated into teachers' practice to the same extent as other more basic advice had. In other words, it was the simplest aspect of the training, i.e. to catch children doing the 'right thing' and positively acknowledging this behaviour, that was most obviously implemented.

As a result of the evidence we have highlighted, we can say that our research clearly demonstrates that the use of positive approaches in the classroom can be very successful in reducing unwanted behaviour and improving pupil engagement and hence pupil learning. Having said that, a fundamental question is whether teachers can sustain these techniques. The answer to this question is *yes*, especially if they are supported by the school management, school systems and policies. We were able to follow up the schools in our study in the subsequent years. All the teachers we trained continued to use the approach for several years. The schools that were most successful, however, were those that asked for 'top-up' training and especially asked for training for new members of staff.

Other questions are concerned with whether the approach works with all pupils, even the most difficult ones, and whether the approach can be incorporated across an entire school. Both of these questions will be dealt with in subsequent chapters.

Comment/activity

Now that you have read details of the short course 'Managing behaviour – four essential steps,' it would be a valuable exercise if you could investigate to find out whether reading about the course and its results has had any effect on *your* teaching, whether or not you consciously try to apply the advice contained in the course. You may have previously investigated the feedback you give to the pupils and/or their level of on-task behaviour. If so, repeating that investigation now will give you some interesting information.

Appendix

Four Essential Steps

Table A3.1 Changes in rates of different types of verbal feedback, pre- and post-training ($n = 19$)

Type of feedback	Pre-training rate	Post-training rate	T	Statistical significance
Positive for work	0.955	1.556	−4.592	0.000**
Positive for behaviour	0.138	0.350	−3.886	0.001**
Total positive	1.093	1.906	−5.624	0.000**
Negative for work	0.231	0.117	2.280	0.035*
Negative for behaviour	0.768	0.275	3.018	0.007**
Total negative	0.999	0.392	3.793	0.001**
Ratio +ve/−ve	3.036	10.646	−3.031	0.007**

** Significant at $p < 0.01$ level   * Significant at $p < 0.05$ level

Table A3.2 Mean ratios of positive to negative feedback given by teachers pre- and post-training

Type of school	Pre-training	Post-training
Infant	2.07	14.92**
Junior	1.88	14.08**
Secondary	1.15	3.32*

** Significant at $p < 0.01$ level   * Significant at p < 0.05 level

Table A3.3 Changes in mean percentages of on-task behaviour of pupils post-training

Type of school	Pre-training on-task	Post-training on-task	Difference in on-task	T	Level of statistical significance
Infant (n = 6)	78.68	93.76	+15.08	−4.14	0.009**
Junior (n = 6)	77.72	95.93	+18.21	−7.058	0.001**
Secondary (n = 7)	76.23	92.68	+16.45	−3.284	0.017*
Total (n = 19)	77.48	94.05	+16.57	−7.474	0.000**

** Significant at $p < 0.01$ * Significant at $p < 0.05$

General preamble

Teaching a class of 30 young people of whatever age is difficult. In their training, teachers are given a considerable amount of advice on how best to achieve a smooth-running classroom. A great deal of that advice is very sound and we do not wish to suggest that we have a monopoly on all that is good in the field. Generally, the advice given to teachers centres around three areas:

- content of the lesson
- management of pupils and resources
- relationships with the children.

We are not experts on the curriculum, but, as psychologists, we do know something about the behaviour of children and teachers and therefore will limit our advice to these areas. What we do know is that if the behaviour of the pupils is cooperative, if they are polite to one another and to their teacher and they follow the requests of their teacher, then the prospects of a good lesson are set fair. In short, the teacher can teach and the pupils can learn. If the pupils are not cooperative with the teacher and are unable to get along with each other, then the prospect of their learning anything from the lesson is bleak. This course is all about how teachers can achieve that peaceful cooperative learning environment through their use of feedback.

There is a great deal of evidence that methods based on what are called behavioural approaches, in which, in broad terms, good behaviour by the child is followed by a pleasing consequence for the child, can be an effective way of achieving a well-behaved child. The application of this approach to whole class settings has been exemplified by a number of teacher training schemes, namely BATPACK (Wheldall and Merrett, 1988) and more recently an American programme, assertive discipline (Canter and Canter, 1992). Both these programmes contain a great deal of behaviourally based advice that has influenced our approach, as have the writings of Bill Rodgers (Rodgers, 1998). It was as a result of reading these sources and having a series of extensive discussions with two former colleagues from Liverpool, Mike Cording, the former head teacher of a specialist school for children with emotional and behaviour difficulties (EBD) and an educational psychologist, Richard Melling, that we developed a training approach, which we called 'four essential steps to classroom management'. Over the years it has been modified and different emphases made but its essential core has remained intact.

Step I

Always make your instructions and directions to the class absolutely clear

Right at the start of any lesson, and before you give any directions, it is important that as many of the children as possible are quiet and are listening to you. You therefore need a short instruction to get attention. Something like, 'OK, class 3, I need all eyes and ears on me.' As soon as this instruction is given, you need to look for pupils or groups of pupils who are doing as you have asked and acknowledge them: 'Well done boys at the front, you're ready to listen; well done Kevin, nice to see you're listening.'

You then need to give the class the instructions they need to start the lesson. This will, of course, vary with the type of lesson and age of the pupil, but some simple examples would be:

- **Infant:** 'OK class, I need you all to be sitting on the mat, so walking slowly and quietly, could you all find a place.' **Or** 'Green table, you all need to find a green crayon and help yourself to a piece of white paper from this pile and then listen to my next instruction.'
- **Junior:** 'OK class, I need all of you to sit quietly in your place, facing the whiteboard with your rough notebooks open in front of you.'
- **Secondary:** '3B, I need all of you to be sitting quietly at your desks with your maths textbook open on page 64, ready to go through example one on the whiteboard.'

Although these initial instructions to a class vary, they all contain a number of essential elements.

1   They are simple, clear and unambiguous. They are not open to misinterpretation and they are observable.
2   The instructions are limited in number. Don't expect any pupil to remember more than three elements of any instruction.
3   They all indicate an instruction relating to behaviour, especially the level of noise you as the teacher expect.
4   They all include mention of the materials the pupil will need to participate in the lesson.

A good way of remembering this phase of the lesson is MINC:

M = Materials needed by each pupil.
I = In- or out-of-seat.
N = Noise level.
C = Communication: how each child is expected to communicate with the teacher (hands up?).

Once the pupils are ready and in position the teacher can then start the next phase of the lesson. The same principles apply of simple, clear unambiguous instructions:

- **Infant:** 'Well done, table 1, you all have green crayons and some white paper. Today we are thinking about triangles. With your green crayon, I want you to very carefully draw a triangle shape just like the one on the whiteboard.'
- **Junior:** 'Well done, class. Today we are going to do some writing about ghosts. To begin with I want you to listen to this short taped story. I need everyone to be very quiet and really listen as when it is over I will be asking questions. Is everybody quiet? Is everybody ready? Good, then here we go. Everybody listening carefully.'
- **Secondary:** 'Well done, class, everybody has their book open at the right page, page 64. Remember last lesson we did some long division; today we are going to do some more but involving decimal points. Everybody needs to listen and look this way before I show them how it is done. OK here goes.'

The opening three or four minutes are very important to set the tone of the lesson. It is vital that every single class member understands what is expected of them in terms of what they have to do in order to take part in the lesson. Obviously, all classes are different. Classes new to the teacher will require extra time to learn new procedures and ways of working and, of course, very young children will require to be taught how to behave. A number of techniques can be very useful here.

First, the teacher can question for understanding. Taking the secondary example from earlier the teacher can question members of the class whom she/he feels may not have listened that well or may not have a history of always doing as they are asked. For example, 'Right, what book do you need in front of you? Charles? Yes, that's right, your textbook. Good and what page should it be open at? Christine? Page 64? Good. Have all of you got that? Page 64! Have all of you got it open at page 64?'

The purpose of the questioning is not only to put some pupils on the spot, but, of course, to repeat the instructions for the rest of the class. In short, the crucial information about the appropriate page is, in effect, repeated three times.

The second technique that can be used, especially with younger children, is to use role play to demonstrate an instruction. A simple example could occur when in a PE lesson the class is given an instruction to divide into groups. If the pupils do not do it well at first, then call the class back together and say:

Sorry that was shambolic. My instructions were for the groups to quietly form up at the four corners of the pitch. Only green group did it well. They did it without talking and lined up as I asked. Could you show us green group? See how they are walking not running and doing it quietly. Well done greens. Now let's see how reds do.

This technique of keeping instructions very clear, simple and therefore easy to follow is an essential element of all classroom management. It is vital at the beginning of the lesson and in the course of a lesson when the teacher requires transition from one activity to the next. All instructions must contain an element of the behaviour required by each pupil. In most of the cases previously given, this concerned noise level but behavioural instructions could also include what pupils should do if they get stuck or don't understand.

However, probably the most important step is what the teacher needs to do immediately the instruction or direction is given. This is step 2.

Step 2

Follow any instruction or direction by looking for those pupils who are doing as they have been asked and acknowledging them

This step is the most powerful piece of advice to any teacher. We believe if teachers only follow one piece of our advice in this book that this would be the one to choose as it can by itself change the behaviour of even the most difficult class. It also is the exact opposite of what we most often observe in lessons.

Typically a teacher will say, 'OK, class, could you please line up at the door?' They then look for pupils who have failed to respond and say something like, 'Billy, did you hear me? I told you to line up with the rest of them . . . Julie could you please join us lining up? Kevin, are you a member of this class? Please line up!'

This is not a particularly effective way of dealing with the problem, it draws attention to the miscreants and, most importantly, it ignores those pupils who have done what they have been told.

Therefore our advice is very clear. As soon as the teacher has given an instruction, they need to look for pupils who have followed that instruction and acknowledge them. To use the previous example, our suggestion would be: 'Listen, class, I now want you to line up quietly at the door . . . Well done, Julie, I see you're ahead of the rest, you've already lined up . . . Good to see all of table 5 on their way . . . We're almost all there, and we're all quiet . . . Well done everyone.'

You will notice that during the course of that acknowledgement, the original instruction, to line up quietly, is repeated. This is important as it gives the opportunity for any pupils who did not hear the instructions to have them repeated.

This technique of the teacher paying attention to those pupils who are following instructions can be used not only for instructions that concern behaviour such as lining up, but also can be used to emphasise teaching points, such as:

> Listen in class, I want to read you something that Julie has just written . . . see how she has used adjectives, 'mean' and 'ugly' to describe the monster; that's just what I'm looking for . . . well done, Julie!
>
> I know this business of tens and units is difficult . . . But it is so important to write both the tens and the units in separate columns . . . look here at Tom's. See, he has the tens here in one column and the units to the right in another column. Let's see if I can find other people who have done the same.

The effect of this technique is threefold. It acknowledges those children who have done as they have been asked, they feel good about themselves as a result of the attention they have been given, and they will therefore, at least in theory, be more likely to do the same thing again. Second, it allows the instructions or teaching point to be repeated to the whole class, which, in turn, allows all children to be made aware of the expectations of the teacher and, third, it informs all the class what they need to do in order for them to receive praise for their work or behaviour.

Catching children doing as they have been asked is the most significant tool in any teacher's armoury for building up good behaviour in their class, for improving the pupils' skills and abilities and developing positive images of themselves. It is also the key to the next step in good classroom behavioural management.

Step 3

Frequently acknowledge the pupils when they are doing whatever they have been requested to do

Any individual's attention span is limited and that of children tends to be less than that of adults. Classrooms are full of people and can be distracting environments. Therefore it is essential that once children have been set a task or an activity, they are encouraged to stick at that task. If the task is difficult, they may need encouragement in order to stick at it and the teacher may need to check on progress from time to time to ensure it is being completed successfully. In order to keep the pupils on task, the teacher needs to acknowledge those pupils by providing positive verbal feedback.

In order to be effective, this feedback needs to incorporate a number of important features. First, feedback should be individualised. By this we mean it should, as far as possible, include the name of the pupil or pupils. Thus: 'Well done, Jimmy, that's very neat writing' is better than, 'That's good work.'

The practice of naming can, of course, also apply to a group of pupils, e.g. 'Well done, blue team, your display was excellent. I liked the way everyone in the team took part' or 'Good back row, you're all sitting up quietly ready to work.' Psychological investigations have shown that the use of a name increases the likelihood of an instruction being carried out by up to 30 per cent.

Second, any feedback needs to be sincere. Young people are acutely aware when teachers and others mean what they say. It is therefore vital that any feedback is sincerely given.

Third, feedback needs to be age appropriate: 'Let's give a class clap to Julie for this lovely painting' works well in an infant class, but would be counterproductive delivered to a group of teenagers. Generally speaking, older pupils tend to appreciate feedback delivered personally and privately. This can be done during a lesson by talking quietly and individually to the pupil, or in some cases asking to speak to the pupil briefly at the end of the lesson, e.g. 'James, I really appreciate how well you have behaved this lesson, keep it up.'

Finally, it is important that any feedback we give to pupils is descriptive. All pupils need to know why they are being praised thus: 'I like the way you have kept the tens and units in separate columns' confirms to the young person what it is about what they have done that the teacher approves of. It reinforces that particular aspect of the young person's behaviour and, most importantly, it reiterates to other pupils within hearing distance what it is that you the teachers are hoping all the pupils in the class will achieve.

It is this constant repetition to the class, in a positive form, of what it is that the teacher is expecting of them that is a fundamental key to good classroom management. If all pupils in a class are fully aware of the expectations of the teacher, both in terms of what they have to do in the learning task but also what is expected of them in terms of their behaviour, then the chances of a well-behaved class learning well are substantially increased.

The style of teaching in which pupils are being constantly, but positively, informed of what they need to do and how they are expected to behave cannot occur if the teacher remains seated at a desk or standing at the front of the class. At several points in the lesson, teachers need to be scanning the class to ensure pupils are on-task, and circulating around the room to deliver encouragement and appropriate praise.

Obviously, once pupils are settled to a task the amount of feedback teachers give to the pupils can be reduced. However, the amount of feedback needs to be increased when pupils are expected to move from one activity to the next and, of course, if the teacher notices the class is becoming restless. This last advice is probably the opposite of what happens in most classes, which is that when the class becomes unsettled, the majority of teachers start telling the pupils off!

Step 4

Always know exactly what to do to deal with inappropriate behaviour

There are essentially three types of inappropriate behaviour that most teachers would recognise. It is important for teachers to note the difference as the three types of behaviour all require a different strategy. These three types of behaviour are:

1   non-disruptive off-task behaviour
2   disruptive off-task behaviour, such as talking
3   severe disruptive behaviour that stops the class from functioning.

The difference between the three and the way to handle each type of incident will be explained.

Non-disruptive off-task

This is the type of behaviour that is typical of pupils who have lost concentration. The teacher should be able to notice these pupils when scanning the class. The behaviour such as staring out of the window, doodling, playing with their pencil or rocking on the chair does not interfere with other children, but it is important that it is dealt with quickly because it is the type of behaviour that can lead to potentially more disruptive behaviour. When dealing with this type of behaviour, it is important not to draw attention to the behaviour that you don't want, e.g. 'Paul, stop fiddling with your pen.'

It is far better to deal with the behaviour by using strategies such as 'the look', simply making eye contact with the pupil and frowning, by standing next to the pupil or by simply mentioning his name, e.g. 'As you all know, especially Paul, the square root of 49 is 7; isn't that right, Paul?'

Another powerful technique is called 'proximity praise'. In this technique, praise is given to two pupils seated near the 'off-task' student, e.g. 'Well done, Julie, well done. Peter, I can see you're both concentrating well and finishing your writing.'

The likelihood is that Paul will have heard the feedback, heard the repetition of the teacher's instruction and returned to work.

The basic principle of this advice is not to draw attention from the rest of the class to the off-task pupil but to ensure that the pupil is gently reminded what behaviour is expected of him or her.

Low-level disruptive behaviour

Disruptive behaviour is essentially any behaviour by one pupil that stops other pupils from learning. It includes such behaviours as talking, shouting out, making inappropriate comments, pushing, leaving seat, walking around the room and many more. There are a number of basic principles involved in successfully dealing with this type of behaviour that are essential if the behaviour of the pupil is to be turned around.

First, it is important never to ignore such behaviour. It will not go away by itself and will probably get worse in time. Second, it is important for the teacher to stay calm. Disruptive behaviour is to be expected in all classes, so all teachers should have a series of techniques to deal with it in a reasonably effective fashion. Third, and most important, disruptive behaviour is best dealt with by the minimal amount of fuss and without drawing the attention of the rest of the class to the teacher's intervention. Many pupils thrive on attention, so if the teacher inadvertently draws the attention of the rest of the class to the incident, then they may be providing the disruptive student with exactly what they want: publicity! For this reason, reprimands or redirections are best given personally and privately. The teacher therefore needs to get close to the pupil, make eye contact if possible and quietly state what they, the teacher, wants the pupil to do. In other words, the teacher needs to focus on the desired behaviour rather than the undesired behaviour. An example of this would be if a teacher spotted a pupil wandering around the class. The teacher would need to approach the pupil and focus on the desired behaviour thus:

> Jimmy, I need you to return to your seat please, you know the class rule.
> But, sir, I just need a rubber.
> Jimmy, I need you to return to your seat, there should be a rubber on your table, if not you should have put your hand up . . . please return to your seat and then we can sort out the rubber.

You will notice the teacher here repeats the instruction to return to the seat three times. The child is, therefore, in no doubt what he is required to do. Last, of course, assuming the child does respond appropriately and does begin to return to his seat, the teacher then needs to acknowledge this by saying something like: 'Good choice, Jimmy, I'll sort out the rubber.'

Not all intervention will go this smoothly but the basic principles of focusing on the behaviour the teacher wants rather than the behaviour that is not wanted remains. With some pupils, it may be necessary to use the 'broken record' technique in which the instructions need to be repeated several times. Here is an example:

> Debbie, I need you to work quietly, you know the rule about not talking.
> But, sir, Lucy started talking first.
> Debbie, I'll deal with Lucy next . . . I need to see you working quietly.
> But she started talking to me.

Debbie, I need you to finish your work off in silence.

Sir, you're always picking on me.

Debbie, I've told you what I want . . . I need you to finish off the work on the board in silence . . . make the right choice . . . well done.

Some pupils like Debbie do not respond first time and may need telling more than once. Debbie, as we can see, is also good at trying to distract the teacher from their task of getting them to work quietly. They use the well-worn tactic of deflecting attention to another pupil, Lucy, and then by accusing the teacher of bias. It is important that these attempts are ignored. What Debbie wants is attention and an argument. It is important that the teacher is not drawn into any argument that will, in the end, disturb the whole class. Therefore the teacher needs to avoid arguments and other distractions and focus on the desired behaviour. This technique if often called the 'broken record' because the instructions are repeated again and again. Some teachers, if accused of bias in this way, may wish to address the issue with the pupil, but the middle of a lesson is the wrong time to address this. To deal with the accusation when you are trying to teach would distract you from teaching, which may be what the pupil wants. This is best done at the end of the lesson in the absence of the rest of the class.

One of the most common sources of disruption is the pupil who doesn't follow instructions and appears to ignore the teacher. Usually such behaviour is calculated. In short, the pupil wants to do what he wants to do and not what the teacher wants him to do. It is important that at this time the teacher concentrates on the behaviour that they want rather than the behaviour they don't want. For instance, if the teacher has entered a class and asked them all to sit down quietly and notices a group at the back which has ignored the request, the teacher must immediately go to the back of the room and deal with the issue. We have found that 'I need' statements work better than 'you need' statements. Therefore the teacher needs to say something like: 'Come on, boys, I need you to sit down quietly so I can start the lesson.'

If some respond but one remains standing and appears not to respond, the statement needs to be repeated but directed to the individual: 'Jason, I've asked you once; please take your seat so we can start.'

If he still refuses to conform, then the instruction needs to be repeated yet again but this time with a warning of potential consequences: 'Jason could you please sit down so we can start? If you don't, you will have to stay behind at the end of the lesson or report to me at the end of school.'

It is good practice at this point to move away and give Jason a few seconds to conform. Most pupils will respond positively at this point but Jason appears to want a confrontation, in which case it's important not to give him one! So, very coolly, the teacher needs to remind him again of the consequences in this way: 'Jason, you are making some bad choices here. I'm asking you once again to sit down. If you don't, you will have to go to the referral room and your parents will be invited into school.'

If Jason does do as he has been asked, all well and good. If not, then the teacher will have no option but to enforce school procedures for this type of behaviour, which, in this case, would be going to the referral room.

Through all these processes, the emphasis has been on the pupil, in this case Jason, taking responsibility and ownership of his own behaviour. It is not a case of 'Jason do as I say or I will send you to the referral room', it is more a case of 'Jason, you are making some bad decisions here. Unless you conform, I the teacher have no option but to ask you to go to the referral room.' Therefore the confrontation is less about who is in charge, but more about allowing the child to take a reasoned decision. In this case, therefore, the teacher is, in fact, helping the pupil to make the right choice.

Whatever the outcome of this altercation, the teacher will need to have a quiet word with Jason at the end of the lesson to discuss his behaviour. This discussion needs to be on the basis of the teacher explaining their decisions and the expectation that his behaviour will be better next lesson.

This careful, staged approach works well enough for most disruptive behaviour but is inappropriate for more severe behaviour that hopefully may not occur that often but which we classify as severely disruptive.

Dealing with severely disruptive behaviour

We classify severely disruptive behaviour as any behaviour when a student:

- wilfully hurts another child
- deliberately damages property
- overtly refuses to do as they are told
- engages in behaviour that stops others from learning
- engages in racist language or behaviour.

In most schools, this type of behaviour does not happen too often. It is, however, behaviour that all teachers should be aware might occur in even one of their well-prepared lessons. All teachers must, therefore, have a plan to deal with such incidents and all teachers should expect their school to have a policy to support that. This plan usually involves the pupil leaving the classroom in secondary and junior schools. In secondary schools, this may mean being sent to a referral room, in junior schools it may mean 'time out' outside the classroom in the corridor under the supervision of a classroom assistant or in infant schools 'time out' in the classroom away from the other pupils.

In view of the seriousness, it is inappropriate to use the staged approach used for less serious behaviour as outlined in the previous section. Instead, the teacher needs to intervene as soon as possible, not offer the pupil any choices but state very clearly: 'Matt, that is unacceptable behaviour. I need you to go to the referral room at once.'

With younger children, we need to be equally direct and make very plain to them what behaviour we don't allow: 'Cheryl, we do not hit each other in this class. Please cool off in the corridor with Ms Cole.'

Two points need to be made about the use of time out. Time out should be time limited. Generally, we feel that the time spent in 'time out' should be related to the age of the child. Five year olds should never do more than five minutes, while 10 year olds should be able to cope with 10 minutes. Usually, in secondary schools, pupils are sent to the referral room for the rest of the lesson.

It is important to realise two things about punishments. First, any form of time out is only of limited value in changing pupils' behaviour. There is no evidence that punishments of any form have any measured effect on changing pupils' behaviour. What changes pupils' behaviour is the second element of the intervention, the restorative element. It is important to separate punishment from this restorative element. When pupils have lost their temper or been really confrontational, it is not the time to explain to them the error of their ways. This is far better achieved when tempers have cooled and the pupils have had time to reflect. For primary school children who are generally the responsibility of one teacher, this restorative procedure needs to be carried out before the child returns to class. The teacher needs to stress not only the unacceptability of the child's behaviour but, more importantly, place an emphasis on the type of behaviour they expect in the future.

> Graham, I was very disappointed with your pushing and shoving of the smaller children at playtime. This is totally unacceptable. You need to learn to be friendly and play sensibly with the younger children in the yard. I know you can behave well because you were very good last week. I will be keeping a special eye on you next playtime.

The teacher needs to be true to their word and will need to keep a close eye on Graham and, of course, praise him for behaving better next playtime, if, in fact, that is the case. For older children, naturally, a different style is needed:

> Colin, I hope you realise why I asked you to leave the class. You know we cannot tolerate racist comments in class. We need to respect each other at all times. You realise I will have to log this and discuss this matter further with your head of year. In my view, this is out of character. I know you usually get on well with the rest of the class and don't make such remarks. You need to make sure this doesn't happen again. I will want to see you at the end of the week to discuss this further and I'll check up on your behaviour up till then.

There are some basic principles that all teachers need to be aware of. 'Telling off' or disapproving of behaviour does not fundamentally change pupil behaviour. Pupils who engage in disruptive behaviour must be encouraged to adopt new and more appropriate behaviour and this can only be achieved by adopting positive strategies such as those that have been outlined in this chapter. This is a very important principle and a difficult one for teachers to learn. It is further complicated by the fact that telling pupils off or administrating punishments appears, at least at face value, to be effective. The explanation is simple: Jimmy is out of his seat; the teacher notices and says: 'Jimmy, stop wandering around. Sit down in your place.' Jimmy sits down. The teacher is annoyed with him but feels that the 'telling off' has worked because, after all, he did return to his seat. The teacher gets an immediate reward. Later in the lesson, however, Jimmy may start wandering around again and the process is repeated. Each time the scenario is repeated the teacher feels that the 'telling off' has worked, because the child does return to his seat. In the long term, however, the strategy does not work.

Chapter 4

Working with particular groups of pupils

We saw in Chapter 2 the pattern of feedback that teachers generally use. Most commonly in normal teaching, they use positive feedback directed towards pupils' work and negative feedback in response to pupils' behaviour. In this chapter, we delve a little more deeply and examine ways in which teachers respond to different groups of pupils. There have been a number of such studies and we are going to look at some concerned with pupil ability, race, pupil behaviour and gender.

Pupil ability

Heller and White (1975), in the USA, compared styles of teachers' verbal behaviour directed towards groups of pupils of high and low ability. Ten teachers were observed as they taught different sets during maths or social studies lessons.

Heller and White found that when teachers taught the pupils of low ability they tended to use more disapproval, especially of a 'managerial' type, than when they were teaching the abler pupils. Unfortunately, Heller and White did not simultaneously record the behaviour of the pupils in the different classes during their observations so that we don't know the extent to which each group of pupils was behaving appropriately during the lessons. It could have been that the low-ability classes behaved less appropriately than those in the higher ability classes and consequently received more disapproval.

These factors were addressed in a more recent study by Myhill (2002) in Britain. The pupils she looked at were described by her as 'underachieving' and 'overachieving.' With younger middle school pupils (around eight years old), she found the underachievers were more off-task and received more teacher attention than the over-achievers. The majority of the attention was negative feedback about their behaviour. She also found that some of the high-achieving boys were more off-task than the equivalent group of girls and that they received higher proportions of admonishments. At the age of 14, the low achievers were still significantly more off-task and were still being 'told off' more often than their high-achieving classmates who were, in turn, the subject of more positive feedback than their less engaged low-achieving classmates.

It seems, then, that from the research of Heller and White and that of Myhill, we can conclude that while the more able/overachieving pupils show more appropriate behaviour than the less able/underachieving pupils, the pattern of teacher attention is determined by the pupils' behaviour.

Race

The issue of race in education is invariably contentious. According to government statistics (Ofsted, 1996), while some ethnic groups do very well in their exam performance, e.g. ethnic Chinese and Indian, other groups, such as those pupils from Bangladesh and, especially, Afro-Caribbean boys, tend to do less well. It has also been extensively reported that Afro-Caribbean pupils are over-represented in those excluded from school, presumably because of their behaviour (Gillborn and Gibbs, 1996; Osler, 1997).

Little attention, certainly in the UK, has been paid to how teachers treat pupils from different ethnic groups. There is some evidence from studies in American schools. The work of Byers and Byers (1972), Hillman and Davenport (1978) and Aaron and Powell (1982) suggest that teacher attention was generally spread reasonably equitably among pupils of different ethnicities, with the exception that black pupils tended to receive more negative feedback for both their work and behaviour. Irvine (1985) also reported that black pupils received more 'positive–negative statements, e.g. 'That's a good answer but next time raise your hand.'

Not all studies were in agreement. Meyer and Lindstrom (1969), in a nursery, found no difference in teacher attention, neither did Corabieth and Korth (1980) or Barnes (1978) in other school settings. Most of these studies are, however, more than 30 years old and were not based in the UK. We could only find two relevant British reports. Ofsted (1996) reported that black pupils were criticised and disciplined more often and for more minor offences than were white pupils, and Connolly (1995), in a study of infant classes, found that African-Caribbean pupils were reprimanded publicly more than other groups.

We were also involved in a study with an educational psychologist colleague, Hema Ward. A series of observations was conducted in a junior school in the Midlands (Hathiwala-Ward and Swinson, 1999). In the classes we observed, 75 per cent of the pupils were white, 17 per cent Afro-Caribbean and 8 per cent of Asian descent. We found that teachers tended to give comparatively more feedback to the Afro-Caribbean pupils than to the others, but this was not positive feedback, which was equally shared between the different racial groups, but negative feedback directed towards behaviour.

The reasons for this disproportionate negative attention are difficult to explain. Unfortunately, in this study, we did not have the opportunity to measure the actual behaviour of the pupils. Consequently, it could be that the Afro-Caribbean pupils were more disruptive than the rest, although that did not seem to be the case to us when we were observing. An alternative explanation could be one of teacher attitude. Teachers are no different from the rest of society and may adopt negative attitudes towards black students including negative attitudes concerning deviant behaviour (see Gottlieb, 1964; Eaves, 1975; Beady and Hansell, 1981). We also know from a study by Russell and Lin (1977), to be discussed later, that teachers tend to adopt a negative strategy when dealing with those students they perceive as being potential trouble. The former explanation suggests that it was the pupils' behaviour that produced the negative teacher feedback, while the latter suggests that it was the teachers' negative feedback that produced the pupils' behaviour. Moreover, it could be a combination of pupils' inappropriate behaviour and teachers' attitudes that caused the effect. The teachers' negative feedback may also, of course, be at least part of the basis of the perception of many black students that they are 'picked on' by teachers (Verma, 1986).

Pupil behaviour

A number of studies have looked at the way teachers responded to different types of pupil in terms of their perceived behaviour. Russell and Lin (1977) conducted a study in an Australian secondary school that examined the way that one teacher responded to two groups of children classified by other teachers who taught them as the 'worst behaved' and as the 'best behaved'. Observers recorded not only the teacher's praise and criticism but also contact, facial attention and ignoring. They found that the teacher gave far more attention to the 'worst behaved' group both as attention for inappropriate behaviour (admonishment, frowning, etc.) and also for appropriate behaviour (praise). Russell and Lin argued that the appropriate behaviour of the 'best behaved' group was not being maintained by the teacher's attention.

A larger study by Fry (1983) observed teacher–pupil interactions over a four-month period in a junior school. In this study, teacher approvals and disapprovals were not recorded directly, but a method involving an observational schedule that measured 15 teacher–pupil variables covering eight teacher behaviours and seven pupil behaviours was used. The results showed, contrary to Russell and Lin's findings, that 'problem pupils' received more negative attention and less positive attention than other pupils. In Fry's study, the problem children had fewer social contacts with teachers and were asked fewer questions than other pupils. Interestingly, Fry (1983) found that the differences in teacher attention became more pronounced over the four-month period of the study, in that towards the end, the 'problem pupils', as they were described, received less and less teacher attention. This reduction in teacher attention was accompanied by a decline in behaviour.

Strain, et al. (1983) investigated the behaviour of 19 teachers and their pupils in the USA. These were young children, from kindergarten to Grade 3 (eight year olds). Children were rated by their teachers on the basis of their adjustment to school, from poor to high. Strain et al. (1983) recorded teachers' gestures as well as verbal responses, finding that the teachers only responded to the children's compliance to any request at a ratio of once every 10 episodes. The vast majority (82 per cent) of the children rated as poorly adjusted to school never received any positive social consequences as a result of their behaviour compared with 27 per cent of the highly rated group.

The three studies reported here, which looked at teacher response, were carried out between 30 and 15 years ago; none was conducted in Britain. We could find no similar study that had been carried out in a British context, which prompted us to carry out our own investigation (Swinson and Knight, 2007).

The investigation was carried out in a large secondary school in Liverpool and its aim was to investigate the pattern of teacher feedback in a sample of British secondary school teachers to see if there were any variation between the quality and quantity of feedback directed towards those pupils designated as having behaviour problems and those pupils in the rest of the class. We asked the teachers to nominate who they regarded as the worst three or four pupils in each class. We observed the classes over a period of two weeks, collecting data not only on the behaviour of the pupils in the class, but also on the pattern of feedback given by the teachers and to whom that feedback was directed.

Twenty-four pupils were selected from one year group by their form tutors as being particularly difficult to teach because of their behaviour. These pupils came from six different classes, 18 were boys and six were girls. Twenty different teachers were observed teaching a total of 303 pupils, an average of 15 pupils per class.

Observations of pupil engagement were made using the Pupil Behaviour Schedule (Jolly and McNamara, 1992) which we had used in much of our earlier research. As detailed in Chapter 2, the schedule assesses on-task behaviour and various types of off-task behaviour. Simultaneously, a record was kept of teacher feedback recorded in terms of positive and negative comments, whether directed towards individuals or groups and whether directed towards academic or social behaviour. A note was also made if the feedback was directed at one of the designated 'worst' pupils. Since the schedule allows the on-task behaviour of each individual pupil to be measured separately, the on-task behaviour of the whole class and of those designated as 'worst' pupils was calculated.

The results showed those pupils designated as 'worst', i.e. those having challenging behaviour, were more off task than the pupils in the rest of the class, as Table 4.1 shows. (See appendix for a statistical analysis.)

We found little difference in the types of off-task behaviour we observed with the exception of the 'shouting out', which was three times higher for the designated pupils (see Table 4.2).

To take the analysis a stage further we decided to examine the behaviour of the designated pupils in a range of classes in which pupils were found to have higher than average on-task rates, average classes and classes where average on-task rates were low. We suspected that in well-run classes all the pupils, including those designated as displaying challenging behaviour, would tend to conform to the expectations of their teacher and conversely that they would be more likely to be non-compliant in classes

Table 4.1 Percentage on-task/off-task behaviour of two groups of pupils

	On-task	Off-task
Whole class	76.3	23.7
Designated pupils	65.7	34.3

Table 4.2 Percentages of types of off-task behaviour by class and designated pupils

Behaviour	Whole class	Designated pupils
In seat	28.3	24.5
Out of seat	10.5	13.6
Shouting	2.9	9.5
Talking	32.8	28.5
Distracting other pupils	1.9	1.2
Arguing	0.1	0.1
Distracting teacher	2.3	3.2
Inattention	20.1	18.9

where the on-task rates for the whole class were comparatively low. Therefore, we made an analysis of the behaviour of the designated pupils in classes where the on-task behaviour of the rest of the class was assessed as either high (91 per cent and above), average (below 91 per cent and above 61 per cent) and low (61 per cent and below), using the time-honoured convention of defining high as one standard deviation above the average (mean) and low as one standard deviation below the mean. The behaviour of the designated pupils in those classes was classified in the same way, i.e. as high, average and low. This analysis is presented in Table 4.3. (See appendix for a statistical analysis.)

As Table 4.3 shows there is a big difference between the way in which the pupils designated as 'worst' behaved in the below average and the above average classes. These frequencies are presented graphically in Figure 4.1.

It would appear that in well-run lessons where the average on-task rate of all the pupils was high, it was also high for the designated pupils. In classes where the on-task rates of the whole class were in the average range, similar rates are found for the designated pupils. Finally, in classes where on-task rates for the whole class were found to be low, the behaviour of the designated pupils was almost inevitably also very poor in terms of low on-task behaviour. The behaviour of the designated pupils was invariably either satisfactory or good in well-run classes and the disruptive behaviour of the designated pupils seemed to be reserved for the less well-run lessons.

Table 4.3 Frequency of on-task behaviour of designated pupils, classified as above average, average or below average, in classes of above average, average and below average on-task behaviour (*n* = 49)

		Designated pupil behaviour		
		Below average	*Average*	*Above average*
Behaviour of whole class	Below average	8	1	0
	Average	10	14	4
	Above average	1	3	8

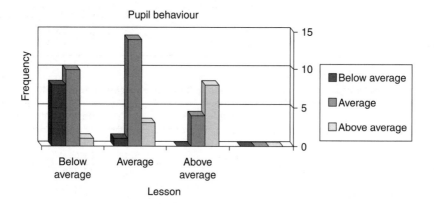

Figure 4.1 Bar chart of the frequency of above average, average or below average on-task behaviour of designated pupils in classes of below average, average and above average on-task rates.

We also looked at the teachers' use of positive and negative feedback as recorded in the Pupil Behaviour Schedule (Jolly and McNamara, 1992) and whether this feedback was directed to pupils' social behaviour or academic work. The results are presented in Table 4.4.

These proportions were very different from our previous studies (Harrop and Swinson, 2000) in that the teachers in this study were far more negative and less positive in their feedback than has been apparent in almost all previous studies. The feedback that was directed to the designated pupils and the rest of the class was also recorded and is presented in Table 4.5.

The proportion of designated pupils in classes was 14.6 per cent, i.e. about one-seventh of the pupils were designated, so that if we look at total feedback it is clear that the designated pupils received a higher proportion of teacher attention than the rest of the class. They received a much higher proportion of positive feedback than their classmates and very few critical remarks were made about their work. It is also clear, however, that they received an over-proportionate degree of negative feedback for their behaviour and unlike the rest of the class received almost no positive feedback at all for appropriate behaviour, only one positive remark about their behaviour being recorded.

As in previous research, we also noted that the vast majority of feedback was directed at individuals, 79 per cent, most of which was negative directed to social behaviour, and only 21 per cent was directed to the whole class, again most of which was also negative.

In this study, we did not find a marked relationship between teacher feedback and pupil behaviour for the whole classes, perhaps because the teachers used so much negative feedback. However, when we looked at the feedback that was directed towards the designated pupils, we did find a strong relationship between feedback personally directed towards them and their behaviour. (See appendix for a statistical analysis.)

Table 4.4 Percentage of teachers' feedback directed at pupils' social behaviour and academic work

Behaviour	Positive feedback	Negative feedback
Academic	14.0	5.3
Social	6.9	72.9

Table 4.5 Percentage of different types of teacher verbal feedback directed towards designated and non-designated pupils (*n* = 20)

Types of feedback	Non-designated pupils	Designated pupils
Total feedback	73.9	26.1
Positive feedback for work	10.45	5.65
Negative feedback for work	5.66	0.018
Positive feedback for social behaviour	3.92	0.004
Negative feedback for social behaviour	53.87	20.50
Proportion of designated/non-designated pupils	85.4	14.6

The relationships are as expected, i.e. a positive relationship between teachers' positive feedback and on-task behaviour and a negative relationship between teachers negative feedback and on-task behaviour, suggesting that individual praise and censure may have a stronger influence on the behaviour of our particularly difficult pupils than feedback directed to the class as a whole, or indeed feedback directed to other pupils.

The use of the Pupil Observation Schedule allowed us to separate the feedback directed by teachers towards specific individuals from feedback directed to the whole class and to examine the effects. Some 20 per cent of teacher feedback was directed to the class as a whole, including both sets of pupils, and was predominantly negative. This negative feedback, together with individually directed feedback, did not appear to be related to our measures of classroom behaviour. It was only positive feedback that was predominantly individually directed to the pupils; that appeared to be significantly related to on-task behaviour.

A comparison between this study and other earlier studies shows similarities in overall on-task rates at around 76 per cent, e.g. Merrett and Wheldall (1987) and Swinson and Harrop (2002). However, as mentioned previously, the pattern of teacher feedback was markedly different in that the teachers in this study used a higher proportion of negative feedback, largely directed to pupil behaviour, than had been found in the other studies. This could be a product of the context of the school in which the study was conducted, the non-random selection of classes or a reflection of the fact that the majority of classes observed in this study came from lower-attainment sets in the school. This phenomenon was also described by Heller and White (1975), who found that teachers tend to reserve more negative comments for pupils described as low ability. An alternative explanation could be found within labelling theory (Becker, 1963). The selection of the designated pupils was made entirely on a subjective basis as a result of a group discussion with a group of teachers who knew the pupils. Labelling theory would suggest that, as these pupils had been singled out and labelled as being especially difficult and disruptive, two phenomena would occur. First, from the teachers' perspective as the pupils were labelled and 'known' to be 'troublemakers', the teachers would treat them differently. Second, from the designated pupils' point of view, having been labelled as disruptive troublemakers they might well be expected to 'live up' to their label and behave in a more disruptive fashion.

It was beyond the scope of this study to ascertain the motivation that led to either the teachers' or the pupils' behaviour. Neither was it possible to ascertain whether the designated pupils were admonished more by their teachers because they were observed to be less on-task than the rest of the class or whether their higher levels of off-task behaviour were a consequence of repeatedly being 'told off'.

This study also shows that the teachers were accurate in their selection of the challenging pupils, in that our results showed their chosen sample to be significantly less on-task than the rest of the class. It is interesting to note that when a comparison was made between the designated group and the rest of the class in terms of the types of off-task behaviour they exhibited, it was only the 'shouting out' behaviour of this group that differentiated them from the rest of the class. The significance of this finding may have a resonance for many teachers, as 'shouting out', unlike some of the other off-task behaviours, is the one behaviour that tends to disrupt the whole of the rest of the class, disturbs concentration, is difficult for a teacher to ignore and therefore requires some form of teacher intervention, which again could disrupt the flow of a lesson. It may well be that the teachers' selection of designated pupils was strongly influenced by whether the pupils shouted out or not.

Overall, the behaviour of the designated pupils was not universally a cause for concern. As was demonstrated in Table 4.3 and Figure 4.1, in well-ordered classes, i.e. those with high on-task rates, all the pupils, including the designated ones, were doing what their teacher had directed them to do. This finding is very similar to that of Swinson, Woolf and Melling (2001), who looked at the behaviour of SEBD pupils placed in a mainstream school.

As regards teachers' feedback, we found these teachers to be more negative than those in other studies. We also found that they gave the designated pupils overall more attention than other pupils in the class. They gave those pupils a higher proportion of positive feedback for their work than the rest of the class and very rarely criticised their work. Compared with the rest of the class, they gave the designated pupils a much higher proportion of negative feedback directed towards their social behaviour and almost never praised them individually about their appropriate behaviour.

In the school, there did not appear to be a concerted whole school approach to classroom management or for the treatment of those pupils who the teachers themselves singled out as being potentially difficult to teach. Some teachers gave very little feedback at all to their pupils and appeared to ignore the designated pupils even when the pupils themselves behaved well and were observed to be following instructions. Other teachers appeared to over-rely on a 'telling-off' strategy. One teacher was recorded as telling off the class no fewer than 55 times during the course of the lesson, to little effect. In contrast, others not only gave a great deal of positive feedback to the whole class, they also singled out the designated pupils for special attention. It was those teachers who incorporated high levels of pupil approval into their teaching style who appeared to be the most successful in engaging all pupils, including those who were designated as potentially disruptive, in the lesson and keeping them involved throughout the teaching period.

In short, while the teachers in this study appear to have used a proactive, positive, praise-based strategy for encouraging all pupils' work, they adopted a very negative reactive response to pupil behaviour. This appears to be especially the case with the pupils who the teachers themselves designated as being poorly behaved.

The significance of this style of management should not be lost when considering the results of the relationships found in this investigation. Although the relationship between positive and negative feedback and pupil behaviour was not strong when considering the results on a whole class basis, the results did show, as far as the designated pupils were concerned, a strong positive relationship between positive feedback and on-task behaviour and, conversely, a strong negative relationship between negative feedback and on-task behaviour.

It seems, therefore, that it would be wise for teachers to adopt positive based strategies if they wish to improve the on-task behaviour of those pupils who are a cause for concern rather than to over-rely on admonishments.

It is impossible, within the confines of this study, to ascertain whether the designated pupils we observed received a disproportionate amount of teacher attention, and especially negative attention, from their teachers as a result of their behaviour, or conversely, as a result of being labelled as disruptive (Becker, 1963). What is clear, however, is that the teachers in this study adopted a significantly different style of management towards the designated pupils. Whatever the reason, the teachers in this study were not adopting a style of pupil management that was likely to improve the behaviour of the most difficult to teach pupils in their class.

No one would doubt that teaching pupils who display challenging behaviours can be extremely demanding in terms both of the professional skills needed to deliver successful lessons and of the emotional energy needed to deal with disruptive behaviour. However, it is apparent from this study and our work, as outlined in the previous chapter, that a positively based strategy is more likely to yield an increase in appropriate behaviour, not only for the class as a whole, but especially for challenging pupils. It would also appear to be good advice to all teachers that such strategies include a number that are aimed specifically at reducing the highly disruptive 'shouting-out' behaviour that appears to be the one behaviour that differentiates most clearly between those pupils who are designated as real problems and the rest of the class. These strategies could include individual behavioural contracts or perhaps the use of whole class rewards for all pupils putting their hand up appropriately, a technique recommended by Canter and Canter (1992).

Gender

The attention that teachers pay to pupils of different genders has long been of interest to educational researchers. It has been assumed by almost all teachers as a given fact that boys receive more attention than girls. Indeed, French and French (1984) (p.127) put it very simply, saying: 'It is now well established that in mixed sex classrooms male pupils receive more attention than do females.' However, as we shall explain, this situation is not as simple as the Frenches would have us believe.

There are numerous well-respected studies that support the notion that boys get more attention. Clarricoates (1980) and Spender (1982) both reported boys dominating class discussion. Also two large-scale analyses, by Kelly (1988) of over 80 studies and more lately by Jones and Dinda (2004) of over 32 studies, seem to confirm this view. Additionally, a large-scale study of over 200 pupils in 50 schools in the UK by Mortimore et al. (1988) noted that teachers tended to communicate more with boys but noted that this was often in the form of negative interactions. More recently Davies (2008), in a small-scale study of four male and four female primary teachers, reported that the teachers gave more negative feedback to boys but also more positive feedback.

A contrary view is that of Galton et al. (1999) in a large-scale study of primary school classes. This study was a follow-up to previous research carried out in the 1970s. Galton noted that there was little difference between boys and girls in terms of teacher attention between the 1970s and 1990s, except that there had been a slight shift towards girls receiving greater proportions of the teachers' attention, as a result of whole class-based interactions; but with this exception the data showed that just as boys and girls received almost identical proportions of the teachers' time in the ORACLE 1976 classroom, so too did they in the ORACLE 1996 study (p.97). One other study worthy of mention is that by Croll (1985). Croll had been part of the original ORACLE study team. His work showed that on average boys did, in fact, receive slightly more attention from teachers than did girls. However, when he looked more closely at his data, he discovered that it appeared that this uneven attention was because teachers were spending a disproportionate amount of time with a very few boys in each class. It appeared that the attention given to this small number of boys had skewed the results. That, of course, raises the question: 'What was it about this small number of boys that resulted in all the teacher attention?' We suspect it may have something to do with behaviour. To look at this, we carried out a series of investigations in both primary and secondary schools.

In designing our investigation, we were aware that Hammersley (1990) had raised concerns about a number of previous investigations into teachers' attention and gender. He criticised the small scale of a number of studies and the key fact that very few studies took into account the behaviour of the pupils. We were aware of only two studies that took into account pupil behaviour.

In one such investigation, Merrett and Wheldall (1992) conducted a study in 38 secondary classrooms. They found that the on-task behaviour of boys and girls was broadly similar, but that teachers talked significantly more to the boys than to the girls. The second study was one we mentioned earlier, that of Apter et al. (2010). They found that girls and boys in primary schools all over the UK were similarly behaved and were treated reasonably equally in terms of the attention they received from teachers.

We conducted two studies, one in primary schools and one in secondary schools. Our primary school study involved observations in 18 junior classrooms (Swinson and Harrop, 2009; Harrop and Swinson, 2011). We recorded pupil behaviour and the teachers' attention to both girls and boys. In the junior classrooms we observed, we found the girls to be much more on-task (93 per cent) than the boys (85.5 per cent). Our method of observation allowed us to look at the off-task behaviour of individual pupils and the results may be seen in Table 4.6.

From Table 4.6, it appears that in these classes, boys were more likely to be spotted by their teacher as being off-task, being more persistent in their behaviour. However, the off-task behaviour of the boys was not confined to a small group of boys. It was more generalised, with over 60 per cent of the boys being off-task at least once. As far as the teachers' verbal behaviour was concerned, we found significant differences. Boys received two–thirds more instructions and redirections, they received 50 per cent more disapproval for their social behaviour and more approval for their school work. It was only in their use of questions that our teachers allocated equal attention to the two groups.

The following year we carried out a similar investigation but this time with classes in two secondary schools. The results of our observations were very different from those of the primary schools. We found that secondary school teachers seemed to treat their boys and girls in a very similar fashion. Although boys received slightly more questions

Table 4.6 Number of junior pupils of each gender who were never off-task (0), were off-task once (1), twice (2) or thrice (3)

Off-task	0	1	2	3	N
Girls	121	44	12	1	178
Boys	77	56	26	7	166

and slightly more disapproval, these differences were not significant. Interestingly, when we looked at the behaviour of the two genders, we found them to be very similar indeed; the on–task rates of the boys was 84.7 per cent and of the girls 86.8 per cent. Also, unlike the primary school pupils, the pattern of persistent off–task behaviour was very similar for the two groups as is demonstrated in Table 4.7.

It is tempting to conclude that the differences we observed in teacher behaviour were simply a function of the different types of school in which we carried out our observations. However, a more plausible explanation lies in the relationship between pupil behaviour and teacher behaviour. In all our studies (Swinson and Harrop, 2009; Apter *et al.*, 2010; Harrop and Swinson, 2011), when the behaviour of the boys and girls has been similar, then teachers treat both sexes similarly, but when, in the case of our primary study, the boys are less engaged in the lesson, they receive more attention.

Table 4.7 Number of secondary pupils of each gender who were never off-task (0), were off-task once (1), twice (2) or thrice (3)

Off-task	0	1	2	3	N
Girls	100	43	23	19	185
Boys	94	77	32	25	288

Summary

Looking across the range of studies, it would seem to be the case that, *on the whole*, teachers do not respond differently to pupils on the grounds of their ability, gender, previous history, or even their reputation, but, rather, it is the pupils' behaviour in the class that appears to be the greatest determinant of teacher behaviour. The only possible exception to this case would appear to be the issue of race, but it is worthwhile stressing that while a number of authors, notably Blyth and Milner (1996), have suggested that there is a tendency for teachers to perceive black students, especially Afro-Caribbean, as potential troublemakers and therefore to adopt a negative strategy in dealing with those pupils, we have found no study that has looked into this issue with sufficient rigour to substantiate the case, as all studies to date, including one of our own, have failed to include a measure of pupil behaviour in their analysis.

The overwhelming evidence we have is that it is the behaviour of the pupils in front of the teacher that determines both the quantity and indeed quality of the teachers' interactions with the class. Almost without exception, it is especially the pupils' lack of engagement in their work and other types of low level off-task behaviour that results in more teacher attention, and especially negative feedback, directed towards their social behaviour. As we have seen, in particular, in our study of pupils singled out by their teachers as being especially disruptive (Swinson and Knight, 2007), the adoption of such a negative strategy does not appear to be especially successful in that high rates of negative feedback do not result in well-behaved pupils. On the contrary it is high rates of positive feedback that appear to be associated with well-behaved and hard-working students.

How do especially difficult students respond to positive approaches?

As we have demonstrated, on the whole, teachers in the studies we have looked at tend to respond to difficult students by adopting quite negative strategies, ones that involve a lot of 'telling off'. As we have also shown, this is not an especially effective strategy, so one might ask whether especially difficult pupils respond to positive approaches as well as do other pupils. There are those who have suggested that they might not. Hanko (1993), for example, has stated that many very discouraged and disaffected pupils were 'immune to praise'. Interestingly, she did not supply any evidence to support her assertion and, in our opinion, she would have found that very difficult. It is true some pupils can be reluctant to become engaged in lessons but in our experience there is usually an approach or strategy based on positive psychology that will remedy the situation. We will mention some of these at the end of this chapter, but before that we are going to consider the way that some of the more difficult pupils respond to positive strategies.

In Chapter 3, we looked in some detail at the results of a training study in which we encouraged teachers in a variety of schools to adopt our 'four essential steps' programme. The results were very encouraging indeed (Swinson and Harrop, 2005). We were also able to use the data we collected at that time to examine the way the more difficult children in the classes responded to the approach. To do this, we looked at the engagement or 'on-task' behaviour of the least attentive 5 per cent in each class, that is, the worse behaved, and compared their rate of improvement with the improvements we had observed in the rest of the class. The results, as presented in Table 4.8, make very interesting reading.

There are two important points to note from these data. One is that all pupils, even those who may be particularly inattentive and unengaged and therefore more prone to be potentially disruptive, appear to have responded to the positive strategies of the teachers. Second, it would appear that the rate of improvement of the least well-behaved is actually better than that of the rest of the class. This seems to refute Hanko's (1993) assertion of unresponsive pupils immune to praise and confirm our assertion that all students respond to positively based strategies and, most importantly, that in well-ordered, well-run classes, which these were, all pupils tend to behave well and become engaged in the lesson.

The fact that all pupils, even those who find behaving difficult, respond to positive feedback came as no surprise to us. Some years ago one of us was engaged in an evaluation of the 'Assertive Discipline' training programme (Canter and Canter, 1992).

Table 4.8 Percentage on-task rates of the whole class and least well-behaved (bottom 5%) before and after 'four essential steps' training

Group	Before training		After training	
	Whole class	Bottom 5%	Whole class	Bottom 5%
Infant	79	53	94	73
Junior	78	61	96	80
Secondary	76	66	93	79

'Assertive Discipline', which we discussed in Chapter 2, is an American teacher training programme in which teachers are encouraged to use classroom rules, to have firm and clear consequences for misbehaviour and, above all, to praise children more, especially for behaviour. Our evaluation (Swinson and Cording, 2002) was carried out in an SEBD special school (a school for pupils with social, emotional and behavioural difficulties). All the pupils in this type of school have been seen by an educational psychologist who has judged that they need to be taught in small classes by specialist teachers because their behaviour has been such that it was felt they couldn't cope in a mainstream school and would benefit from being in a special school.

Our evaluation showed that as a result of the programme, on average, the number of praise statements made by the teachers increased from 2.1 per lesson to 9.3 per lesson while the number of negative statements fell by a similar proportion. As a consequence, the behaviour of the pupils in terms of their 'on-task' behaviour improved from 65 per cent to 86 per cent while the number of disruptive incidents fell from 8.6 per lesson to 3.8. This result further confirms our contention that all children, including those with major behavioural problems, do respond to praise-based strategies. One interesting further point about our training with this particular group of teachers was the extent to which we encouraged them to use a system of awarding class points. This system is easy to operate. The class teacher simply awards points whenever he or she catches pupils being good. In one system with young pupils, the class teacher drops marbles in a jar, while at secondary level points may be marked on a board. When a set number has been achieved the whole class gets a reward. The reward can be very simple, such as five minutes' free time at the end of each lesson or a class quiz. One teacher in the school in which we carried out our study asked his class what they would like and they told him it was to have the radio on in class. The teacher, who taught craft, then allowed the radio to be played once 25 points had been earned. He allowed the pupil who gained the 25th point to choose the radio station. An important feature of this technique is that the teachers remain in control of the system. They decide what points are awarded for. For instance, if the class is noisy, points can be awarded for 'working quietly' or if the pupils are prone to 'shouting out', points are awarded for raising hands. A teacher can also decide when the reward is finally earned. A teacher we worked with invariably awarded the 25th point about five minutes before the end of the lesson, thereby maximising its effectiveness.

We hope we have established that all pupils, including those who can be very challenging in terms of their behaviour, can and do respond to positive strategies. We cannot over-emphasise our view that it is vital for teachers to ensure, among other aspects of their classroom organisation, that they carefully consider the positive feedback they give to all pupils, both individually and collectively, before they embark on an individual intervention aimed at a particularly difficult pupil. The evidence we have collected over the years indicates that in well-run classes, all children tend to be engaged in the lesson and are reasonably well-behaved.

That being said, there are a number of techniques that we will outline in the remaining section of the chapter, which will focus on approaches that can be used to turn around some of the particularly difficult-to-manage young people. We will start with interventions that are more suitable for younger pupils and end with those more suitable for older pupils.

Individual behaviour plans

If any pupil in a class appears to be responding less well to the class-wide strategies than the other pupils, it may be necessary to devise an individual approach to help that pupil achieve the level of engagement and behaviour of all the rest of the class. Some of these approaches have already been described in some detail in Chapter 1, but it is worthwhile repeating some of the basic principles.

Individual behaviour plans can be used by any teacher for children of any age. First, it is important that the teacher identifies exactly what behaviours they feel are interfering with or getting in the way of the pupils' learning and then, most importantly, decides what behaviour they are looking for from the child to maximise their learning. If, for example, the behaviour that is causing problems is walking around the room interfering with others, then the behaviour that is needed is staying in the seat and working. If the behaviour causing concern is shouting out in class then the behaviour that is required is raising a hand to ask questions. Next, the teacher needs to decide on any reward other than praise that they feel may add to the positive outcome for the pupil. A very simple individual plan may look something like that shown in Figure 4.2.

Once the teacher has worked out the plan it needs to be explained to the pupil. This is the most important moment of any intervention. It is vital that any plan is introduced in a positive manner as an exercise in problem solving rather than as a punitive exercise. We suggest that the teacher creates an opportunity for a one-to-one session with the child concerned and outlines the plan to the child thus:

> Gemma, I have been very concerned about you wandering around the class in literacy and maths sessions when you should be finishing off your work. I want you to make a special effort to stay in your seat and complete the work you have been set. Remember to put your hand up if you want any help. I will do my best to support you. I will be awarding class points to you and others who do well. If you are out of your seat I will simply remind you of the 'stay in your seat rule'. Do you think you can try to do that?

This example is a very simple and low key attempt to improve a pupil's behaviour and learning. If the behaviour is more serious or if the type of intervention outlined does not work, it may be necessary to tighten up any programme. This can be achieved in terms of the specificity of the behaviour but also in terms of the positive outcomes on offer and any consequences. Figure 4.3 is a plan for a pupil for whom a simple intervention has not worked.

Individual behaviour plan for …		
Pupil	**Gemma**	**Age 6**
Problem behaviour	Walking around class during maths and literacy sessions	
Desired behaviour	Staying in seat and completing maths and literacy assignments	
Positive strategy	Catch Gemma on-task in maths and literacy sessions, positive feedback, 'well done for working well', award of class points	
	Individual feedback at end of each session	
Negative strategy	Remind Gemma of 'stay in seat' rule, ask to return to seat	

Figure 4.2 Example individual behaviour plan.

Individual behaviour plan for ...		
Pupil	**Andrew**	**Age 11**
Problem behaviour	Shouting out in class, in both asking and answering questions	
Desired behaviour	Putting hand up to ask and answer questions	
Positive strategy	Praise when put hand up. Star at the end of each successful lesson	
	Letter or phone call home when 10 stars awarded	
Negative strategy	Remind Andrew of 'hand up' rule, reminder at end of lesson	

Figure 4.3 When simple intervention does not work

Again, this plan would need to be discussed with Andrew in a one-to-one discussion and, of course, with his parents who need to be aware of any intervention. This can be done either at a brief meeting after school or perhaps in a telephone conversation. It is vital that any discussion with parents is couched in positive terms as a problem-solving exercise rather than in any punitive terms. So a conversation might go something like this:

> Mrs Jones, I'm worried about one aspect of Andrew's behaviour which I feel we need to sort out before he goes to secondary school. I feel he tends to shout out in class both when asking and when answering questions. I have had a word with him and we have a plan, which I will send to you, whereby he will collect stars on a chart for good behaviour. Once he has collected ten stars I will send a brief note home.

The aspect of this plan that is worthy of note is that it incorporates a number of important features. First, the collection of stars on a chart is motivating for the pupil as they can see progress towards an agreed target (10 stars), which is in itself motivating and it employs the most desired reward valued by the pupils themselves (see Harrop and Williams, 1992), that of their parents being informed of good work or behaviour. Second, the contact with Andrew's parents is very positive. The teacher does not take an opportunity to complain about Andrew, even though they may have wanted to, but instead, asks for their support in solving a problem. We have found that virtually all parents value this type of approach and are more than willing to support such an initiative. Parents often ask when contacted in this way if they can reward their child when he achieves his target. The answer we give is that it is not necessary, as just their being informed that the child has achieved the target is often enough. However, if they wish, a small reward such as staying up later on Friday or Saturday night can be appropriate. We point out that a substantial reward is best kept for when the behaviour has been maintained for an extended period.

Research note

The key elements behind the success of this type of intervention are threefold. First, there is a need for teachers to work out precisely the type of behaviour they require from the pupils in order for learning to take place. Second, they need to provide feedback to the pupils, and also reward them when that behaviour has been achieved. The third important element is the consultation with the pupils themselves. Any intervention needs to be discussed with the pupils not only to clarify the terms of the plan but also to establish ownership. If the pupils feel part of the process they are more likely to be willing participants and more likely to want the intervention to succeed.

Fair pairs

One of the reservations that some teachers have about individual plans such as we have described earlier is that they can lead to giving more attention and reward to troublesome pupils. One technique that overcomes this problem is a called 'fair pairs' or 'three-part praise' (Eaton and Hansen, 1978; White and Haring, 1980). It is not dissimilar to a technique called 'proximity praise' that we have mentioned in Chapter 3.

In the fair pairs approach, just like in the individual behaviour plans, the unwanted behaviour of the pupil is defined, as is the behaviour that the teacher feels the pupil needs to achieve so that learning can take place. Once this has been done, in all subsequent lessons whenever the pupil who is the cause for concern exhibits the unwanted behaviour, say, 'pushing into the line,' the teacher draws attention to others in the line who are behaving appropriately and says, 'Well done, Jimmy, for lining up properly. Yes, I can also see Tracy standing still wanting to go out to play.'

The key elements of this approach are that the behaviour is clearly defined and the teacher repeats what is required every time the other children in the class are praised for their behaviour.

Research note

This technique introduces an important element we have not noted before, one of social learning. Bandura (1977) has shown that a great deal of children's social learning is achieved by observing and copying others. He cites four core elements influencing copying: effective models, motivation to copy, ability to copy and ability to remember model behaviour. This fair pairs technique seems to contain these elements, by the teacher drawing attention to the behaviour, drawing attention to good models of behaviour and by praising the 'models' to provide the motivation for the child concerned to change.

One important aspect of this approach is that it can and should be used by all adults in the class not just the teacher. Increasingly, many classes have teaching assistants and helpers in the class. This approach works best if everyone concerned uses it. Williams (2012) gives an account of teaching assistants in Birmingham being trained how to use these techniques with great success. One last point is that, although the example we have given is of a primary aged pupil, this technique has been used equally with older pupils. We have seen it used successfully with pupils up to the age of 16. In fact, one astute young man said to one of us: 'I know what you're doing, you praise the others whenever I misbehave.' We told him he was right, but, interestingly, he continued to respond to the programme.

On report

The on-report system has been around for several decades, usually in secondary schools, but as McNamara (1999) has stressed, placing a pupil 'on report' has generally been seen as a punishment aimed at reducing inappropriate behaviour. In fact, one author can remember being 'on report,' himself, in the 1960s. Invariably, being 'on report' means that the pupil has to carry a report card and at the end of each lesson the teacher rates behaviour, usually as 'unsatisfactory' or 'satisfactory'. The report has to be signed off by either the head of year or deputy head teacher at the end of the day. Bad reports inevitably lead to further punishment.

On report can, however, also be constructed on a positive basis, where points can be awarded for good behaviour and targets set that can lead to commendations or even rewards. An example of such use with a particularly clever but apparently unmotivated secondary school pupil is described here. Until our intervention, he would sit at the back of the class in each lesson, barely completing the minimum amount of work with no real effort. After discussion with him and his parents, it was decided to put him on a positive report system, which we outline in Figure 4.4.

On-report card

Name ....   **Form** ....   **Date** ....

Please rate behaviour in each lesson for:

　　Arriving at lesson with correct equipment

　　Completing work assigned

　　Active participation in lesson (asking and answering questions etc.)

Please award 1 point for each target behaviour (maximum 3 points per lesson)

	Period					Total	Signed
Day	1	2	3	4	5		
Monday							
Tuesday							
Wednesday							
Thursday							
Friday							

Weekly total ....

Signed by parents ....

Figure 4.4 Example on-report card.

In our discussion with the young man, we asked him what reward he would like. He said would like to visit the Natural History Museum in London. This is more expensive than the usual reward we suggest, but after consultation with his parents we found they were willing to foot the bill. In this case, we agreed a target of 450, which, at a maximum rate of 75 points a week, would take the minimum of six weeks to achieve. In the end, he reached his target in eight weeks and earned his trip. This proved a turning point in his school career from which he never looked back. Normally, we don't suggest using large rewards such as this because, in our view, small rewards given often are more appropriate rewards for most children. Very young pupils can wait for up to two or three days for a reward but tend to lose motivation if they have to wait longer. Older pupils are capable of waiting longer, but weekly rewards tend to work for most of them.

It is important to emphasise here that it is not the rewards themselves that are the most important element of this type of system, but the feedback that the pupils receive at the end of each lesson and at the end of each day when they meet up with the head of year and report to their parents on progress. Very often, as we have mentioned previously, some pupils have had little positive feedback for their school work and receiving positive feedback with the rewards can lead to them valuing the positive feedback on its own later.

Self-report

A variation of the principle of having reports done on performance at every lesson is to get the pupils themselves to rate their own behaviour. This is generally known as pupil self-monitoring or student self-report. In this technique, the onus is on the pupils themselves to provide judgements of their behaviour or work during each lesson. It is a technique that works best with older pupils who are sufficiently motivated to change or improve their performance in school. It places all the responsibility on the pupils themselves to take control of their own behaviour (see Figure 4.5).

An example of self-report follows. The pupil concerned was 15 years old and was referred because although he was known to be bright, he was putting very little effort

Self-report card					
Please report effort in lessons and completion of any homework					
2 = Good 1 = Satisfactory 0 = Unsatisfactory					
Target	**Lesson 1**	**Lesson 2**	**Lesson 3**	**Lesson 4**	**Lesson 5**
Work in lesson					
Homework					
Date					
Parent					

Figure 4.5 Example self-report card.

into course work for his GCSE exams. Kevin was heading for failure unless he changed his ways. A meeting was organised between him, his parents, teachers and the educational psychologist. His teachers voiced their concerns, as did his parents. He reported that eventually he wanted to go to college and acknowledged that he was not doing enough work. He said that he did not want to go on report as he viewed it as a punishment, but he accepted that the psychologist's suggestion of self-monitoring was worth a try. He agreed to carry the cards, which were stapled together to form a booklet, to all lessons and to show it to his parents at the end of each day. A further meeting was scheduled in three weeks' time to assess progress.

After three weeks both teachers and parents reported a vast improvement. Kevin agreed to continue monitoring his progress but after only a further week he announced it was too much trouble and he was allowed to discontinue. He did, however, continue to put effort into his work and he did sufficiently well in his GCSE exams eventually to make it to college.

The key elements in this intervention that led to its success were present at the initial meeting between, his teachers and parents. At this meeting, Kevin acknowledged that what was being said about him was true and he was sufficiently motivated by the prospect of going to college to accept responsibility to change his behaviour. He did not want his teachers to monitor his behaviour but was happy to accept responsibility for himself. Kanfer and Spates (1977) have shown that such self-evaluations and self-monitoring techniques can be very effective indeed in changing young people's behaviour and increasing and maintaining motivation. However, not all pupils are sufficiently motivated for this technique, but there are other techniques that are available to support them. These are behavioural contracts and motivational interviewing.

Behavioural contracts

Behavioural contracts are essentially written agreements drawn up between teachers, parents and pupils concerning the behaviour or learning of the pupils. The rationale on which they are based stems from the work of Levy (1977), who found that the people he worked with were more likely to follow a course of treatment if they made a verbal commitment to do so and even more likely if the agreement was written down and signed. Behavioural contracts were first reported by Stuart (1971) in his work with delinquent families but were subsequently used in schools (see DfE, 1994).

Behavioural contracts are especially effective over issues such as school attendance but can also be used for other behaviours in school. They can often involve the suspension of a pupil's pocket money or of other privileges which the pupil can then earn back consequent on certain conditions.

Behavioural contracts have to be drawn up at a meeting between all parties in which everyone has a chance to put their side of the argument. Even though, in any contract, some privileges may be withdrawn, it is important that the young person has an opportunity to earn them back and perhaps also receive a bonus for continued good behaviour. Clearly, the young persons must be able to see some benefit to themselves by taking part. (You can read about one such contract in Chapter 9, in which the reward was playing badminton at lunchtime.)

The following case (Figure 4.6) involved a Year 11 pupil, Brian, who, although he was reasonably able, found it easier to stay in bed and miss school than to attend. His

---

Behavioural contract

Brian	1	I wish to improve my attendance at school
	2	I agree to attend every day and have a report signed by Mr Mitchell
Mrs Jones	1	Agree to withdraw Brian's allowance
	2	Agree to reinstate 90p for each day attended
	3	Agree to pay a bonus of £1.50 for every full week
	4	Agree to wake Brian every morning before 8.00 am
Mr Mitchell	1	Agree to ensure Brian has an attendance report card
	2	Agree to sign report each day
	3	Agree to telephone Mrs Jones if Brian is not in school
Signed		Brian ....
		Mrs Jones ....
		Mr Mitchell ....

It is agreed to meet again in three weeks' time to review progress

Date ....

Figure 4.6 Behavioural contract for case study.

mother worked and had to leave the house early and was not in the house when he was due to leave for school. Following a meeting at school a contract was drawn up.

It is important to note that Brian's allowance was £5.00 a week and by agreeing to the contract, he had the opportunity to earn more (£4.50 + £1.50 bonus). This monetary reward in itself would probably not be a sufficient incentive to change his behaviour but, of course, failure to attend on any one day would be costly as both the bonus of £1.50 and the daily earnings of 90p would be lost.

Another case we were involved with concerned a boy of 16 in his last year of schooling. His teachers were concerned that although the rest of the class were working diligently towards their exams, Chris continued to muck about in class, making jokes and distracting the others. When we talked to Chris, he said he wasn't really worried about exams as he had a job lined up. When we talked to his mother, she told us that getting Chris to work for his pocket money wouldn't be effective because he earned £10 working every weekend for his brother. However, we got around this by persuading his brother to become part of the contract. Thus the contract looked as shown in Figure 4.7.

This contract proved remarkably successful. Chris behaved well without exception for the rest of his time at school. This contract worked because we found the right reward, no punitive sanctions were involved at all, other than the right not to earn extra money via working.

The most important feature of any contract is the statement of intent in which the young person agrees to change. In Brian's case it was: 'I agree to attend school every day.' Behavioural contracts will only work with a level of commitment. If, for any reason, the young person is not willing to agree to change or not willing to sign such an

---

Behavioural contract

Between Chris W., Wixsted High School, Mrs W (mother) and Mr Y (his brother)

Chris *agrees* to try to behave well in all lessons and ensure his report card is signed

The school *agrees* to monitor Chris's behaviour via a report card

Mrs W *agrees* to sign the report card and inform Mr Y if Chris can work at weekends

Mr Y *agrees* to allow Chris to work if he scores at least 20 good lessons per week (max = 25)

Signed   Chris ....
               School ....
               Mrs W ....
               Mrs Y ....

Date ....

Figure 4.7 Behavioural contract for second case study.

agreement then an approach involving motivational interviewing may be needed. Another important feature of any successful contract is that it has to be written so that there is some benefit to the young person. There is a tendency in some contracts for them to become over-punitive towards the pupil or to expect 100 per cent compliance before any benefit accrues to the pupil. This is why, for example, the contract with Chris only asks for 20 out of 25 good lessons a week. If 100 per cent compliance is required and the pupil misses his target for one lesson, then the value of the contract will be lost for the rest of the week as the target becomes unachievable. In general, a contract will work if the target is achievable and the outcome is beneficial for the young person, both in terms of any reward on offer and for their participation in any lesson.

Motivational interviewing

Implicit in any of the techniques we have discussed so far in this chapter is the assumption that the young person concerned acknowledges that there is an issue in terms of learning, motivation or behaviour and that they are at least willing to cooperate with adults, either teachers and or parents, to try and change. However, not all pupils we meet in school have such motivation and some may not even admit there is a problem. English comedienne, Catherine Tate, created a schoolgirl character who, whenever her behaviour was criticised merely replied: 'Bovvered? –I ain't bovvered.' In other words, she did not acknowledge she had any problem and was certainly disinclined to do anything about it. Such attitudes, from a very small minority of pupils, make it very hard for teachers to implement an intervention that is likely to be effective.

However, a friend and colleague, Dr Eddie McNamara, has pioneered the use of an approach called 'motivational interviewing' in schools to help in these situations. Motivational interviewing was originally described by Van Bilsen (1991) and has been used in the treatment of drug addicts, among other things, in an attempt to persuade them to join treatment programmes (Miller and Rollnick, 1991). McNamara has adapted the approach for use with young people in schools (McNamara, 1999, 2009).

There is not sufficient space in this book to give a full account of the technique, but essentially it is a six-stage model to help the young person and the teachers or parents understand the stage at which the young person may be, why they are resistant to any change and, most importantly, how they may be helped to accept the need for change.

The six stages are:

Stage 1. Precontemplation (pupil sees no problem but others disapprove).
Stage 2. Contemplation (weighing up the pros and contras of changing).
Stage 3. Determinism (do I carry on as before or do I change?).
Stage 4. Active change (putting the decision to change into practice).
Stage 5. Maintenance (actively maintaining change).
Stage 6. Relapse (return to old behaviours).

The motivational interview includes a great many techniques that give the adults concerned, be they parents, teachers, social workers or psychologists, a means of understanding why a young person may be resistant to change or unwilling to cooperate. Most importantly, it contains a number of techniques that the adult can use to help the young person understand their own behaviour more clearly and move towards a position where they become willing to work with the adult to accept the need for change. In his book, McNamara (2009) cites examples from both within and outside education where the techniques have been very successful in changing the behaviour of some very difficult and hard-to-reach young people.

In order to use some of the techniques included in motivational interviewing, teachers would need to be trained in the techniques involved. This is also true of some of the other possible interventions such as cognitive behavioural therapy (see Squires, 2001). Such an intervention, without appropriate training, may be out of the reach of most teachers and therefore beyond the scope of this book. It is, however, worth noting that all the approaches we have outlined in this chapter, and indeed in this whole book, have two common features.

First, whatever the technique, the child or young person who is the subject of the intervention has continual feedback about their current performance and, second, the outcome is most likely to be beneficial both in terms of rewards and in terms of them fitting in better with the rest of the class and learning more effectively. In short, they stand to benefit.

A number of interventions that we have seen practised, especially with very difficult children, seem to be structured in a way to benefit the teachers and not the young people, e.g.: 'Unless you can behave until the end of term, you're out of this school!' Although the prospect of a class free from a particularly troublesome young person is often very tempting to contemplate, it is not a solution that is often in that child's best interests and, as we have outlined, there are many positive approaches that can and do work with this very difficult and challenging group of young people.

Appendix

Table A4.1 Percentage on-task/off-task behaviour of the two groups of pupils

	On-task	Off-task
Whole class	76.3	23.7
Designated pupils	65.7	34.3

$t = 4.605$, $df = 347$, $p < 0.001$

Table A4.2 Frequency of on-task behaviour of designated pupils, classified as above average, average or below average, in classes of above average, average, and below average on-task behaviour ($n = 49$)

		Designated pupil behaviour		
		Below average	Average	Above average
Behaviour of whole class	Below average	8	1	0
	Average	10	14	4
	Above average	1	3	8

Analysis of these figures using a chi square test shows the differences to be statistically significant; $\chi^2 = 24.26$, $df = 4$, $p < 0.001$

Table A4.3 Correlations using Pearson's r between positive and negative feedback directed at designated pupils and individual on-task behaviour ($n = 20$)

Correlation	Pearson's r	Statistical significance
Individual positive feedback and individual on-task behaviour	0.4971	0.05
Individual negative feedback and individual on-task behaviour	−0.4325	0.10

Chapter 5

The whole school

Introduction

In the preceding chapters, we looked at the use of positive based strategies with both individual pupils and with classes. We have pointed out that, on the whole, even potentially difficult pupils tend to be reasonably well-behaved in well-run classes. In this chapter, we will extend our coverage beyond the level of the individual and the class. Much of our experience in this area stems from a period when the first author worked as part of a specialist behaviour team in the city of Liverpool. The team had the remit to work with schools to help develop behaviour policy and practice at a whole school level. This work also included giving advice to teachers with very difficult classes or year groups.

Working with a challenging class

During the course of their teaching career most teachers will come across a 'difficult-to-teach class', one whose pupils do not seem to respond to the routines and techniques that appear to have worked with other groups. There may be many reasons for this, e.g. a chance collection of difficult characters or perhaps the class contains a higher than usual group of pupils with learning problems. In secondary schools, most teachers complain about Year 9 (pupils aged between 13 and 14), which may be a reflection of the emotional maturity of pupils of that age or the fact that they haven't got major exams coming up to provide them with a focus.

Whatever the reason, blaming the pupils is not a strategy that is likely to work. What is needed is a plan to help pupils to become more engaged in lessons and to help them improve their social relationships between one another.

An early involvement by one of us in consulting with both teachers and their pupils to help find a solution to what was regarded as a problem class taught us a great deal about this process (Swinson, 1990). Teachers in a small comprehensive school were extremely concerned about the pupils in a Year 9 class who were the source of concern for almost all their teachers because of their poor behaviour in class, poor motivation and general lack of progress in their work. A series of meetings with both the pupils and their teachers were set up and information about the pupils' attitudes was collected by questionnaire. The questionnaire we used was developed by Raymond (1987) and consisted of two sets of a dozen statements that the pupils had to rate. One set was called 'Things that encourage me in school' and the second set 'Things that discourage me in school'. The results of the questionnaires were fascinating. The pupils said that they liked teachers who took control of lessons and stopped disruption, they did not feel they were praised enough when they tried hard and they did not like the use of their surname when being told off. The meeting of the pupils with the author and one teacher got off to a bad start when some class members tended to blame one or two boys for starting off all the 'messing' as they called it. However, things turned in a much more positive direction when the pupils were asked what they thought they might do to improve their behaviour and learning. Several pupils thought that if the potential troublemakers could sit next to some well-motivated pupils then there would be fewer problems. Several students volunteered to act as 'good behaviour buddies'.

The meeting with those teachers who taught the class found them all agreed about how difficult the pupils were to teach. Most teachers complained about low-level disruption, such as talking in class, distracting others, failure to complete work etc., and the fact that the group failed to respond to the usual telling off and occasional punishment. Things became more positive when the teachers learned about the pupils' responses to the questionnaire. When we focused on solutions to the challenges the class posed, one teacher in particular, who agreed they could be very difficult, told the group that his solution was to introduce the set routines he used, especially at the beginning of each lesson. He said that he ensured they lined up quietly outside the classroom and that at the beginning of each lesson they sat in their prescribed seats and that initially this was in a boy–girl–boy–girl arrangement. He said that the pupils didn't like that at first, but he devised a plan that if, towards the end of the lesson, they had completed the work and behaved well they could move to sit next to their friends. That use of a seating plan has been proved to be a very effective way of improving behaviour and increasing pupil engagement (Wheldall and Lam, 1987).

It was decided to implement these seating plan arrangements in all lessons. Together with that the teachers agreed to be more positive and to allow pupils to use the buddy system to remind one another if anyone started 'messing'.

The school had a monitoring system whereby the classes were awarded points at the end of each lesson, so that it was easy to follow the progress of the class in the following weeks. The results were startling. The class in question moved from getting least points each week to getting most and their attendance became the best of their year group. The teachers were delighted with the improved behaviour, motivation and learning of the group but, more importantly, the pupils themselves told us how much they now enjoyed school, especially the way their teachers were now so encouraging and positive.

This intervention had a number of elements that are worth exploring in more detail. First, the intervention was very solution focused. Not too much time was spent analysing the problem, the focus was all geared to finding a solution. What is more, the 'solution' came not from an 'expert', but, essentially, from the teachers themselves. All the 'expert' did was to allow them the opportunity to discuss what strategies they found successful. The second important element was the involvement of the pupils themselves. Pupils of all ages like to be consulted, especially at secondary age. The pupils in this case were genuinely flattered to be asked their opinion. Their remarks about what they expected from their teachers, especially in terms of the need for teachers to be more positive, were very important in changing the attitudes of some of their teachers. They also came up with some very perceptive solutions to help improve the functioning of the class. Thus the functioning of their class became an issue not solely for their teachers. It became one of shared responsibility in which the pupils had a stake and hence they became more motivated to change.

(The role that pupils can play in changing the school *system* will be discussed later in the chapter.)

There have been a number of more recent reports of projects aimed at improving the behaviour of difficult classes, e.g. that of Berg and Shilts (2004, 2005), 'working with what works' (WWW). These initiatives tend to be very teacher based and any evaluations tend to be based on teachers' and pupils' perceptions of change rather than using any direct observations of improvement.

Whole school interventions

There is no shortage of advice to schools on how they can improve the learning and behaviour of their pupils. *Building a Better Behaved School* (Galvin et al., 1990) is a good example and there are many others. While the guidance given in such publications is invariably very sound and, in the best examples, is based on a solid research base, there tends to be a dearth of evidence where the advice given is put into practice and scientifically evaluated.

Changing policy and practice in a large organisation such as a secondary school can be difficult. To be successful, it is important to involve all sections of a school community. Guidance was issued to schools (DfES, 2003) to encourage schools to take account of pupils' views on behaviour through discussions with school councils (Macbeath et al., 2003). Osler (2000), Pearce and Hallgarten (2000), Read (2005) and Rowe (2006) all argue that whole school policies in which pupils are involved in their development are the most likely to be successful. Davie and Galloway (1996), Breen and Littlejohn (2000) and Lewis and Lindsay (2000) all emphasise that pupil involvement leads to a great sense of ownership of the policy by the pupils, who are consequently more likely to understand its underlying philosophy and purpose.

However, while there is evidence of pupil involvement in the development of anti-bullying policies (see Sharp and Thompson, 1994), accounts of pupil involvement in the development of whole school behaviour policies would appear to be rare.

The first author was a member of a multidisciplinary team that included an advisory teacher and an educational consultant and was managed by a member of the education authority's advisory team. We were invited by the senior management team of a school that had come to a decision that it needed to revise its behaviour management policy. The initiative was aimed at developing school policy and improving behaviour in the classroom. It was hoped that by focusing specifically on pupil behaviour and involving both pupils and teaching staff in policy development that improvements in other areas, such as pupil attainments and attendance, might also be apparent.

The school was an 11 to 18 comprehensive school with a roll of approximately 1200. A high proportion of the pupils were on free school meals. At an initial meeting with the senior management of the school, we were told they were concerned about the standard of behaviour in their school, especially that of the Year 9s (13–14 year olds) and the impact that this had on the pupils' learning.

The advisory team explained to the management that they did not wish to appear as 'hero innovators' and impose a new system, but, rather as Georgiades and Phillimore

(1975) suggested, they would be seeking solutions from those who worked day to day with the problems. As a result, the team embarked on a series of consultations with the three key elements of the school: the parents, the teachers, and especially the pupils. The aims were to learn about the current discipline system in the school, to find out how each group felt it was working and to work with all three partners to develop and improve the school's behaviour policy and practice.

The project took place in three phases spread over one school year. Initial consultations between the school staff and the team began in the autumn term:

- *Phase 1* consisted of consultations with teachers, parents and pupils and a series of classroom observations whose aim was to see how the current behaviour policy was working in practice. This took place in the first half of the spring term.
- *Phase 2* was the planning and introduction of the new, revised system and occurred in the second half of the spring term. It was during this time that the staff training took place. The revised system was introduced to the pupils at the beginning of the summer term.
- *Phase 3* was an evaluation of the initiative. This involved a number of classroom observations, pupil, teacher and parent interviews and took place at the end of the summer term. Further evaluation was through the school records.

Phase I. Assessment of current practice

The teachers were consulted through a series of staff meetings and the completion of simple questionnaires. At the initial meeting, it was made clear that the team was working with the school to find a solution to its concerns and not to impose answers. The team made it clear that unless the eventual proposals had the support of the staff they would not work. A small working group was formed to work with the team. This working group deliberately included only one member of the senior management team and consisted of a cross-section of staff in age and experience.

The staff completed two questionnaires. One was that used by Gray and Sime (1988) as part of a national survey of teachers' experience of classroom behaviour, in which teachers were asked to report their experience of various disruptive behaviours that had occurred in their class over the past week or past month. The other was a questionnaire used by Harrop and Holmes (1993), which asked secondary school teachers to rate the effectiveness of various rewards and punishments.

All parents of Year 9 pupils were sent a brief questionnaire asking for their experience of the school's behaviour policy together with an invitation to attend a consultation meeting. Only a small number of questionnaires were returned (12 per cent) and only a handful of parents attended the meeting. The parents who did turn up at the meeting told us they were happy to be consulted but felt that it was up to the teachers to sort out the behaviour, not them. These attitudes are quite common (see Miller, 2003).

The pupils' views were collected via two pairs of rating scales used in earlier research. One was a device used by both Raymond (1987) and Swinson (1990), which asked pupils to rate what it was that most encouraged and discouraged them at school, and the other was a version of the scales used with the teachers by Harrop and Holmes (1993) in which the pupils rated their perceptions of the value of various rewards and punishments.

These rating scales were completed by the pupils as part of a PSHE lesson. During the rest of the lesson they were invited to give their views on the current school behaviour/discipline policy and asked how they felt it could be improved.

A series of observations of Year 9 classes was carried out over a period of three days by the team, using an observation schedule devised to record the pupil behaviours identified by Gray and Sime (1988). It recorded incidents of disruptive behaviour and the number of positive and negative statements directed to the pupils made by the teachers. It also allowed us to estimate the on-task rates of a random group of six pupils from each class.

Phase 2. Planning and implementation

The results of Phase 1 of the project were fed back to the teachers at a staff meeting and to the pupils during a PSHE lesson.

The results of the survey of pupil behaviour were almost identical to the national survey of Gray and Sime (1988). This showed that what concerned teachers most was not major disruptive incidents such as fighting or pupil insolence, which, in this school, happened only rarely, but with low-level disruption such as talking in class, distracting other pupils or pupil inattention. In the Harrop and Holmes (1993) questionnaire, the teachers tended to regard the formal sanctions of being sent to the head of year as effective punishments and thought that praise in front of the class was an effective reward. The teachers told us that they did not think the current merit system of filling in 'merit slips' at the end of lessons was useful, as they took too long to give out and that as a result they rarely used it.

In discussions, most teachers felt the current system of referring disruptive pupils to the heads of year was not effective. The heads of year agreed and told us that they were often faced with dealing with pupils who were disruptive in only a handful of lessons but were otherwise reasonably well-behaved.

The few parents who responded to the survey told us they did not feel they knew enough about the behaviour of their children in school and only heard from the school when their child was in trouble.

The results of the 'encourage/discourage questionnaire' (Raymond, 1987) showed a high degree of consistency and were very similar to the results we received when working with the very difficult class (Swinson, 1990). The vast majority of pupils told us they wanted:

- more praise
- to be spoken to in a pleasant tone of voice
- for teachers to have control of lessons and to let them get on with the work
- for teachers to be consistent, especially when it came to being told off
- to be told off privately and for teachers not to use their surname during admonishment.

As far as the pupil ratings of punishments and rewards were concerned, on the Harrop and Holmes (1993) questionnaire, these were substantially different from those of the teachers, as indeed Harrop and Holmes had found in their original study in classrooms. As far as rewards were concerned the top five pupil ratings were:

1   parents informed about good work or behaviour
2   good marks
3   positive comments written on work
4   merit/house points
5   whole class praise.

As far as sanctions were concerned, their ratings in order of perceived effectiveness were:

1   parents informed about behaviour
2   being sent to the head or deputy
3   being sent to tutor or head of year
4   being on report
5   detention.

Discussion with the pupils also yielded valuable information. They told us that teachers were very inconsistent in their use of the current 'merit' system: 'You can get 10 merits for helping move the piano, but Mr. P. never gives you any.' They were also very clear over whose responsibility it was to establish good order in class: 'It's up to the teachers to get us quiet,' and 'We all work hard if the lesson is interesting and the teacher is in charge.'

When these results were fed back to the teachers and to the pupils, there was a genuine interest in each others' responses. The teachers acknowledged that they had not given enough thought to how pupils valued rewards and punishments. They also agreed with the parents that at present there was little opportunity to make contact, especially in response to favourable reports on their children. They were pleasantly surprised at the pupils' responses on what they felt encouraged them in school. The pupils, by way of contrast, seemed pleased that the teachers were taking their views seriously and remained resolute in their view that it was the teachers' job to establish good order in the lessons and to make lessons informative and interesting.

Planning policy

The small working party that was charged with planning the new policy did so based on the evidence gathered, especially that the pupils most valued any rewards or positive encouragement offered, that parents needed to be more involved, particularly in terms of positive feedback, that low-level disruption was best dealt with by using positive strategies, that merits needed to be given more regularly and consistently and that there needed to be greater consistency in the use of referrals to heads of year and, most fundamentally, that the behaviour in the school would not improve unless there were significant changes in classroom practice.

The group met a number of times over a period of half a term during which time a new policy was formulated and presented to the staff and governors. It was accepted with only one significant change (involving the use of merit stickers for Years 10 and 11, which the teachers felt would not be effective with older pupils). A launch date was set for the beginning of the summer term, prior to which a full day of Inset training was delivered to all the staff in order to ensure that the principles of the policy as well as the practicalities were understood by all. Much of the training concentrated on good classroom practice but, more specifically, on teachers' use of verbal feedback. It was argued that positive verbal feedback was possibly the most powerful and effective tool available to teachers and certainly one that was valued by the pupils. Evidence was presented to the teachers that showed that increasing positive feedback was the key element to effective behavioural interventions (Elwell and Tiberio, 1994; Webster-Stratton and Hammond, 1997; Webster-Stratton and Reid, 2004; Swinson and Harrop, 2005). In fact, the training was based on the 'four essential steps of classroom management' outlined in Chapter 3, which argued that teachers needed to 'catch' pupils working and behaving well and that giving acknowledgment or praise to them helped increase appropriate behaviour and decrease disruptive behaviour. The point was made to the teachers that the low-level disruptive behaviour that they reported as being of concern was much more effectively dealt with by using positive strategies than by sanctions.

The key features of the policy that marked a change from the previous practice were the use of merit stickers, the increased involvement of parents and the referral of 'difficult-to-teach pupils'. The team felt that the former merit system lacked credibility with both pupils and teachers and that it was underused. In the new policy, merit stickers were introduced. These were awarded at the end of lessons for good work, effort and good behaviour. Teachers agreed to award these at the rate of at least two every lesson and the pupils were advised that this was the expected rate and, if teachers forgot to give them out, they were (politely!) to remind their teacher. The stickers were to be placed in a special section of each pupil's homework diary that would then be seen and signed every day by their parents. In this way, both pupils and their parents would receive regular, tangible feedback of the pupils' work effort and behaviour. The stickers would also be used to record merits gained by each form group and would provide a record for each pupil of the total number of merits they had gained. When pupils had collected 25, 50 or 75 merit stickers, they were to be presented with an appropriate certificate.

As far as referrals made by teachers to the heads of year concerning especially disruptive pupils was concerned, the planning group felt that these were made in a rather *ad hoc* manner and without any definite criteria. The new policy placed a greater emphasis on the responsibility of each academic department for the behaviour of difficult pupils. It was agreed that, in future, if a pupil was a cause for concern because of his or her behaviour that the issue should be discussed at a departmental meeting and a strategy devised to deal with this specific problem. Often this would take the form of a change of teaching group for a set period or support from a departmental teaching assistant or head of department. Heads of year would be informed of such arrangements but would only become involved if a pupil was referred by more than one department.

The new policy was introduced to the school at the beginning of the summer term and presented to the pupils at year assemblies. It was agreed that the policy should be applied through all the school with the exception of Year 10 and 11, because the staff felt that those pupils would not be motivated by stickers. For these students, it was decided to use a form of praise letter instead.

Phase 3. Evaluation

The working of the new system was evaluated at the end of the summer term and a longer term perspective was also made possible by an examination of the school's published examination results, exclusions and attendance records.

At the end of the summer term one member of the team returned to the school and carried out a series of classroom observations with the same Year 9 teachers and teaching groups that had formed part of the original observations in the previous term. The same observational schedule was used in a sample of 17 classes, thus a comparison of on-task behaviour, disruptive incidents, use of merits and the use of praise and censure by teachers was made. The results are presented in Table 5.1.

The pupil on-task behaviour, the increase in positive feedback and the decrease in negative feedback were all analysed statistically and found to be significant changes (see appendix for details).

All the changes in both pupil and teacher behaviour were in the direction anticipated as a result of the new policy. The new policy together with the training given to all staff appeared to have resulted in positive changes in both the teachers' and the pupils' behaviour. This was seen especially in the case of positive feedback to pupils, which increased by nearly 50 per cent, and the number of merits given out, which increased from the negligible figure of 0.20, or one every five lessons, to a mean of 2.30 per lesson.

In addition to these quantitative data, a series of meeting were arranged to gather the opinions of teachers and pupils. Additionally, parents were invited to write comments about the new system in the homework diaries.

The teachers felt the new policy was more effective than the old one. As far as they were concerned, it was easier to administer since pupils were given the responsibility for keeping their own record of merits. It gave form tutors a way of monitoring an individual's performance over a week or month. The teachers also felt that the new system, whereby disruptive pupils were dealt with in the first instance at departmental level, appeared to be working. Fewer pupils were being referred to heads of year, who now felt able to deal better with the fewer children being referred to them.

The pupils' response was even more enthusiastic. They especially liked the way they were allowed to remind teachers if they failed to remember to give merit stickers out. They reported that all the teachers were keeping to the system and as a result they felt that behaviour in classes had improved. They were appreciative of the way they had been consulted over the new system and glad that their voice had been heard and acknowledged. Two weeks into the new term the head teacher received a delegation from the Year 10 pupils demanding the school gave them stickers again. Two weeks later he was approached by a group of Year 11 pupils asking whether they, too, could

Table 5.1 Mean changes in Year 9 pupil and teacher behaviour before and after introducing a new behaviour policy

Indicator	Old policy	New policy	Change
Percentage on-task behaviour	78.3	85.9	+7.60
Rate of positive feedback per minute	0.85	1.25	+0.40
Rate of negative feedback per minute	0.96	0.36	−0.60
Disruptive incidents* per lesson	18.4	9.50	−8.90
Merits per lesson	0.20	2.30	+2.10
Year 9 detentions per week	20.5	8.30	−12.20

* Disruptive incidents were categorised as those that stopped the teacher from teaching or pupils from working, i.e. shouting, talking loudly, calling out, out of seat, arguing or distracting the teacher

become part of the system. The parents were equally positive. Those who wrote in were universal in their positive responses. Several commented that it was so nice to realise that their children were being praised on such a regular basis. One parent commented that it was the first time anyone in his family had every received a certificate from school.

Both the pupils and the teachers felt that relationships between staff and pupils had changed immeasurably. One teacher reported that he had not told a pupil off in weeks and that he now had a very positive relationship with some of the groups he had previously found most difficult to teach. Other teachers felt that the whole atmosphere in the school had changed; the staff had become less punitive and the pupils better behaved. Several commented that issues of classroom discipline were now more freely discussed in school and colleagues were more supportive when advice was sought.

Pupils pointed out that not only had behaviour improved in class but they felt that there was a higher degree of mutual respect between pupils that had resulted in calmer playtimes and lunchtimes. They also commented that they felt there was a better atmosphere in school and that relationships between teachers and pupils had changed for the better.

In the longer term, the improved behaviour policy and practice was part of a number of changes at the school that led to improved attendance, a reduction in exclusions and ultimately to vastly improved GCSE exam results.

This initiative was judged a success by all those taking part. The members of the school senior management team were pleased with their new system, and the teachers, parents and pupils were all conscious that the new system worked and that there was a greater sense of communal well-being and endeavour in the school than had hitherto been the case. All parties acknowledged that relationships between teachers and pupils and between teachers and parents had improved.

More general comments

The advising team was drawn from a wide range of different backgrounds combining a broad range of experience in different schools in a number of authorities. Team members were therefore able to draw on a large number of resources in their work. The team was guided by a number of key principles throughout the project. One key principle was taken from the world of business, especially Tom Peters' work *In Search of Excellence* (Peters and Waterman, 2004). Peters makes the point that any successful organisation needs to engage with all those in the organisation to be 'partners in change'. In this project, the team made great efforts throughout the development of the project to seek the participation of all the key players in the school, teachers, parents and, above all, pupils in all aspects of the formation of the new policy. The pupils were consulted about the original school discipline policy, how it could be made better, how teachers could encourage them better, what rewards they thought would be effective and what they thought about sanctions. The pupils appeared to value this level of consultation and therefore felt more part of the process. They were conscious of their contribution to the eventual policy. This was, in essence, a consultation with the 'customer', finding out what they wanted (Peters and Waterman, 2004).

The teachers were also consulted at all stages of the development, formulation and implementation of the new system. They liked the fact that they had been asked about the failings of the former system and asked for their opinion on what type of behaviour, i.e. low- level disruption, they thought the new system ought to address. The fact that the working party, which devised the new system, included a wide range of teachers in terms of experience and also personnel from outside the school was also seen as a positive feature. The teachers never felt the new initiative was a management directive, and because they were so involved in all aspects of the development of the new system they had a sense of ownership of the policy and therefore a commitment to make it work.

The team members were also aware that a mere change in policy would not lead to any change in outcome for the school unless it was accompanied by a change in practice and especially a change in practice at classroom level. It is clear from the results of our observations (see Table 5.1) that there were measurable changes in both teacher and pupil behaviour. One reason for this was that the policy included regular and systematic use of positive feedback to the pupils in the form of the 'merit stickers'. The regularity with which these were awarded was part of the agreed system. The key role that the stickers played within the system was borne out by feedback we received from parents, who told us they took particular notice as their children accumulated them in their homework diaries, and by the pupils themselves when after only one term of operation, the pupils in Years 10 and 11 asked to become part of the system. In this way, the pupils were receiving a double dose of positive feedback for their effort and work, from first, their teachers and then their parents.

The powerful influence that feedback has on behaviour has been fully explored by Hattie and Timperley (2007) and it was this increase in feedback rather than any intrinsic reward value of the stickers these authors argue accounts for changes in pupil behaviour and motivation. It cannot be assumed that the changes in pupil behaviour were solely because the pupils were responding to rewards and punishments, because the stickers themselves did not lead to any material advantage and there was a marked reduction in both admonishments and formal punishments under the new system. The fundamental change lay in the feedback that the pupils and parents received under the new system.

These changes in the use of positive based strategies in the classroom were, we hope, a result of the training that the teachers had been given as part of the introduction of the new system. This training, which took place over the course of one day, placed an emphasis on the teachers acknowledging good behaviour and work effort and not resorting to punitive strategies. Part of the training included mention of the work of Bandura (see Bandura, 1977), in which it was explained to the teachers that they themselves were models of good behaviour to their pupils. Thus if they were kind, rational, well-spoken and positive to the pupils, the pupils themselves were more likely to be kind, rational and well-spoken in return.

The other major and significant change in the new system concerned the approach that was adopted towards disruptive behaviour. Although the teachers continued to use a series of warnings and mild but irksome punishments, like reporting to the teacher at the end of the day as a sanction, these were now used in a more systematic fashion. The evidence suggests such punishments were used less than in the past, probably as a result of an increase in positive feedback and merit stickers. There was also a marked change in the teachers' response to persistently disruptive pupils. These pupils were now discussed at fortnightly departmental meetings and were perceived to be a problem not only for the individual teacher, but for the whole department. The focus of the departmental discussions therefore became one of problem solving and the locus of the concern moved away from the individual pupil to one in which the teachers as a group had to find a solution to problem behaviour. Thus the tendency to scapegoat the pupil became less easy.

The success of the initiative was due in the most part to the commitment of the teachers and the support they received from the pupils and parents. Peterson (2008) lists the features of a good school. These include:

- an articulated and shared vision of the school's purpose
- students' perception that they have control over what happens to them at school
- students' perception of school discipline policies as firm, fair, clear and consistently enforced, with a focus on correction and skills-building rather than punishment
- students' perception of the school reward system as being rational; the school recognises students for their achievements and rewards their positive behaviour.

Pupils in the school with which we worked would, we hope, recognise these statements as being a reasonable description of their own school.

School improvement has been a key issue for governments of all political colours over the past 20 years. All governments have acknowledged the work of Rutter and his colleagues (Rutter *et al.*, 1979), which showed that it is schools as institutions that make a major difference to pupil outcomes. Academic success for schools is strongly linked with both attendance and school behaviour. In fact, in a recent major review of the effectiveness of various interventions covering over 800 analyses across the English-speaking world, Hattie (2009) reported that improving classroom behaviour ranked as the 6th (out of 138) most effective way of improving achievement. Interestingly, improving teacher clarity was ranked 8th and improving teacher feedback was ranked 10th. The training that was given to the teachers included elements of all three of these variables.

We have worked with a number of schools in the way we have described here. Every school is different and therefore any attempt to work with a school to change and improve their systems requires a 'tailor-made' rather than 'off–the-peg' solution. We would, therefore, argue against any school attempting to copy the example we have outlined earlier. There are, however, general principles that we would like to emphasise. These are:

- *Consultation.* Listen and talk to all those involved with the school, teachers, support staff, parents but, above all, the pupils themselves. Ask everyone what they feel the key issues are that affect both learning and behaviour in the school. The more participation in the consultation exercise the more all parties will have a sense of ownership of any new system.
- *Planning.* It is essential that in any planning of a new system there is participation from a wide selection of staff, but any planning team needs to be led by a senior manager who will ultimately have responsibility for carrying out the new policy.
- *Impact at classroom level.* If any change in a school's policy and procedures is to be effective in improving the school's functioning, it *must* include change at a

classroom level. In the example we described earlier that included changes in feedback to pupils in class and increased feedback to parents.

- *Monitoring and review.* In all the schools we have worked with, we have argued that all systems need a designated member of staff who takes responsibility for monitoring the running of any new initiative. Too often staff will agree to certain changes and then fail to follow through by changing their own practice. Part of that review process is to inform staff of the impact that any change is having on the school. Remember, members of staff need positive feedback, too.

Comment/activity

You could make a short list of rewards and a short list of punishments you use in your classroom ranked in order of effectiveness. Randomise the order, present the lists to your pupils and ask them to rank them in order of effectiveness, i.e. in terms of what would help them work and behave better in class. That is essentially what Harrop and Holmes (1993) did. They found some vey interesting differences between the pupils' ranking and that of their teachers. You might find this a very instructive exercise.

Appendix

Table A5.1 Analysis of changes in pupil and teacher behaviour before and after implementation of a new behaviour policy

Indicator	Old policy	New policy	T	Level of statistical significance
Pupil on-task rate	78.3	85.9	3.284	0.017
Rate positive feedback	0.86	1.41	3.043	0.023
Rate negative feedback	1.48	0.70	2.007	0.092

Chapter 6

Pupil learning

As we have seen in previous chapters, the positive approach works very well for changing pupils' behaviour, and while it is very important to focus on ensuring that pupils behave appropriately in class in order that learning can take place, it is equally important, where possible, to focus on improving classroom learning itself. There haven't, however, been many such studies in classrooms using positive psychology, probably because it can be more difficult to measure changes in learning than to measure changes in behaviour. As a consequence, those investigations that have been undertaken tend to be more complex than those with behaviour as their focus. The examples included in this chapter, particularly the first, illustrate that complexity. The first two investigations, which are concerned with writing, were conducted by teachers in their own classes.

Improving creative writing in a comprehensive school

A comprehensive school teacher who was concerned about the level of creative writing that she was able to produce from her third-year middle-band pupils discussed her problem with one of the authors. She felt that the nature of what was required in creative writing made it very difficult for her to give the pupils appropriate feedback. We had considerable discussion about the nature of creative writing, trying to decide what was required of the pupils. Finally, we decided to use three basic components of creative writing, i.e. fluency, elaboration and flexibility, as the initial measuring tools. Fluency was the number of ideas produced, elaboration was the way in which ideas were spelled out within each sentence and was defined in terms of uses of adjectives, adverbs, clauses, phrases, etc., and flexibility referred to changes in perspective from one idea to the next.

As an example, for the essay title 'Just suppose the Martians landed,' one pupil began: *People would be shocked. The police would come to the space ship and surround it. People would be moved away from the area. The Martians might be friendly.* The first sentence would score for fluency but not for flexibility because it was not preceded by an idea. The second would score two points for fluency because it contained two ideas, but would also score one point for flexibility because the first idea was a change in perspective. Sentences 3 and 4 would both score for fluency and for flexibility. Scoring for elaboration is too technical to describe here but can be found in the original article.

Feedback, we decided, would be given to the pupils on these three components. Further, we decided not to introduce feedback on all three at once since that might overburden the pupils with complexity.

To find the pupils' initial level of creative writing, each pupil wrote six essays. These were done during the normal class time for creative writing, over a period of weeks. The essays were scored for fluency, elaboration and flexibility but the scores were not given to the pupils. These first six essays were used as a baseline against which any changes produced by the positive approach could be measured.

Following that baseline, the pupils were told that the teacher was concerned about raising their ability to write creatively and that for the next essays in creative writing they were not to worry about grammar or spelling. She told them that she wanted to see improved work and that she would be writing to the parents of those whose work improved, telling the parents how well they had worked. She explained what fluency, elaboration and flexibility mean and gave them examples of how they could increase their scores on each. She then returned their essays, each marked for fluency, elaboration and flexibility, and answered any of their questions.

For the next six essays, the teacher asked the pupils to try to increase their fluency scores. Points up to a maximum of five were awarded for each essay (up to two for exceeding the class average and up to three to pupils for exceeding their own previous scores). These points were accompanied by appropriate teacher comments, ranging from 'That was really first class' for a five to 'That was OK' for a three and no comment for lower than three. After six essays had been marked for 'fluency', the teacher moved on to 'elaboration' and followed the same procedure. Finally, six essays were completed for 'flexibility'.

The essay titles were drawn at random from a pool of titles that had been compiled before the investigation began. One month was allowed to elapse after the final stage during which no creative writing was done. At the end of that time the pupils were required to write a further six essays without any points being awarded.

The results showed that, after the baseline, with the exception of the final stage, the pupils' average scores increased considerably throughout each stage, i.e. for fluency, followed by elaboration and, finally, flexibility. In the final stage, when the points were not awarded, the pupils' average scores stayed at the level of the penultimate stage, but showed no increases. Naturally enough, the teacher was very pleased with the results.

As an additional check, in case the increases obtained didn't reflect real increases in creativity, but merely represented bizarre writing to obtain points, pairs of essays of similar length were selected from 12 of the pupils, one for each pupil being taken from the baseline and the other from the final set. Six secondary school teachers of English from other schools read each pair of essays without knowing the details of the investigation or when the essays had been written. They were asked to pick which essay of each pair was the more 'creative'. These teachers almost always selected the later essay. As a consequence, the teacher, who had had to put a good deal of work into the marking, was very satisfied with the results, which demonstrated that she had indeed improved her pupils' level of creative writing. She was also pleased to note that the pupils had shown considerable interest in gaining points during the investigation.

Research notes

The use of the three components of creativity, i.e. flexibility, elaboration and fluency, and the requirement that pupils try to increase their scores on each in turn, enabled the teacher to give the pupils simple targets to aim for. The positive feedback of gaining points was very precise. Previously, the teacher had found it very difficult to convey to them what writing creatively involved and she had felt that her feedback was sometimes too complicated for the pupils to understand. In awarding points for each of the three components in turn, she was simplifying the task for them. The feedback was given as each essay was returned and was effective in enabling the pupils to raise their scores.

In the final stage, when points were not awarded, the fact that the scores obtained remained at the level of the previous stage demonstrated two features: first, that the awarding of points had had a strong effect in raising the scores and, second, that the pupils' ability to write creatively was maintained when the points system was withdrawn.

That the three categories used for feedback were important components of 'creative writing' was borne out by the results obtained when the six secondary teachers rated the essays.

It was decided to use a 'favourable letter home' as the reinforcement since previous research had shown that to be the reward that pupils wanted the most.

A 10 per cent sample of the pupils' essays was photocopied before the teacher scored them. The essays were then given for independent scoring. Very high levels of agreement, around 90 percent, were obtained on each of the three components between the teacher's scoring and that of the independent scorer. That was done to check on the objectivity of the teacher's scoring.

For further details on the investigation, you might like to look at Harrop and McCann (1984).

Comment/activity

One important feature of this investigation is that the use of the three categories enabled the teacher to give feedback to the pupils as each piece of work was returned.

Teachers who find creative writing difficult to mark in a way that gives pupils the necessary feedback to improve might like to try out this technique.

Improving writing skills in a primary school

Primary school pupils aged nine to ten wrote stories in their lessons for 30 minutes, twice a week for three weeks, and the number of words per essay produced by each pupil was counted. Following that, the teacher directed the pupils' attention to the brevity of their stories and said that she was going to show them how to increase the length of their stories and that the stories would as a consequence become better and more exciting.

The teacher introduced a self-management game explaining that the aim was to increase the quantity of the pupils' writing little by little and that increases should not be at the expense of quality. The pupils were each given a booklet that contained such features as:

1   a self-recording page on which the pupils were to enter their target scores, plus the scores actually achieved

2   a coloured card with the pupil's own average baseline score and teacher advice, e.g. to try not to repeat the same words and phrases, to avoid disturbing other pupils, to use different adjectives
3   a self-recording chart on which the pupils entered their target number of words, which the teacher advised should be 10 or 20 words longer than the previous average, together with the actual number written in each session
4   an individual histogram for the pupils to complete progressively.

When pupils reached their target score they could select a reward, e.g. sitting in a special 'author's chair', having their essay put on the classroom wall, having three minutes' 'free time', which they could save up and use for a favourite school activity, and so on.

At the end of each writing session, the pupils had to count their words and fill in their records. The game took place over three weeks.

This procedure produced a marked increase in the average number of words produced by the pupils. To check that it was the self-management game that had produced the increase the teacher stopped the game for a further three weeks and the average number of words written decreased. When the game was re-established the average number increased again. To check for the 'quality' of the writing, an evaluator with primary school experience followed a procedure similar to that used in the previous 'creative writing' investigation to see whether quality improved. The conclusion was that there had been an increase in the quality of the essays as well as in the quantity of words produced by the pupils as a consequence of playing the self-management game. To check that the pupils were accurately recording the number of words written, their scores were compared with those of an independent observer and very high levels of percentage agreement were obtained.

Research notes

The feedback obtained by the pupils was very precise, i.e. number of words written. The reinforcement used could be selected by the pupils. The self-management game, apart from helping the pupils to be able to monitor and manage their own learning, also provided a vehicle for the teacher to insert some of her teaching requirements (avoiding repeating words, trying not to disturb other pupils, etc.). As in the previous example, the pupils had feedback following each piece of work.

The fact that when the game was discontinued the number of words decreased and then increased when the game continued, demonstrated that the game was controlling the number of words produced. A discerning reader might wonder why that didn't happen in the 'creative writing' investigation where the score level remained constant when the points system was removed. The explanation lies in the nature of the two investigations. In the 'writing skills' investigation, the pupils' task did not involve the learning of as complex a task as did the 'creative writing' investigation. From this we can deduce that the more complex the learning involved, the more likely it is that pupils' performance will be maintained after any 'artificial' treatment is withdrawn.

The independent observer was necessary both to check that accurate recording was being made and to evaluate the quality of the essays.

For further details of the investigation you might like to consult Panagopoulou-Stamatelatou and Merrett (2000).

Comment/activity

It would be relatively easy for teachers to try out this approach, certainly to help pupils increase the length of their essays, but they need to be aware that if they withdraw the game suddenly, any increases obtained are likely to vanish. Ways around that would include withdrawing the game gradually by reducing the elements in a systematic manner and making sure that increases obtained by the pupils throughout the investigation are accompanied by teacher approval.

The teacher could easily arrange to check that accurate recording had taken place but would have to enlist the aid of a colleague to evaluate changes in quality.

Improving reading attainment in a comprehensive school

A comprehensive school teacher, impatient with the reading progress of some of her pupils, wanted to see whether the promise of a favourable letter to their parents would result in increased reading attainment.

Two mixed-ability classes of pupils aged 11 to 12 years whom she taught were selected for the investigation. The pupils in both the classes were given a test to establish their reading ages. One class had a slightly higher average score than the other and that class was chosen for 'special treatment'. The reason for selecting the class with the higher score was that it had previously been shown that it was easier to improve lower scores than higher scores using the SRA Reading Laboratories, and the teacher wanted to find out unequivocally whether the promise of a favourable letter home would help pupils increase their reading scores.

The pupils in the intervention class were told by the teacher that she was very interested in their reading development using a well-respected reading scheme and that they would be retested after five months to see what progress had been made. She added that she would be writing to the parents of any pupils who had made 'good' progress, to tell the parents how well those pupils had progressed. It was also stressed that no letter would be sent to the parents of those pupils who did not improve. The teacher reminded the pupils at fortnightly intervals of this arrangement. No such comments were made to the pupils of the other (control) class.

At the end of the five months both classes were retested and the average increase in reading scores of the treatment class was more than eight times that of the average increase of the untreated class. The teacher, who was very satisfied with the results, wrote to the parents of most of the pupils in the class telling them how well their children had done.

Research notes

The investigation differs from the previous two most notably in the use of two classes of pupils. Using another class as a 'control' is a useful technique, provided one is available, when trying out the positive approach with a class. Ideally, the two classes should be matched for ability levels, but if they are not some care needs to be taken to ensure that a 'fair test' is being made. In the last example, taking the class less likely to show improvement as the one to have the special treatment ensured that at the end of the investigation it would not be possible to say that that class would have improved more than the other without having had any special treatment.

It is also worth noting that this investigation did not have the advantage possessed by the previous two examples, of being able to provide feedback to the pupils on a regular basis throughout the course of the investigation, although moving from one book to another did give a measure of immediate feedback to the pupils.

Further details of the investigation can be found in Harrop and McCann (1983).

Comment/activity

The investigation relied on the strength of the 'favourable letter home', which appeared to have a powerful effect on the pupils. That being the case, the same reinforcer could be used to achieve other classroom aims although it should be borne in mind that overuse of that particular reinforcer might well weaken its power. In the school in which it was used in this investigation, there was no history of 'favourable letters' home. Indeed, when the idea was first suggested to the head teacher, the response was surprise, followed by the comment that 'letters normally only went home when pupils were causing or having problems in school'.

Teachers who have the opportunity of using two equal ability classes that they themselves teach could use this technique of employing a control class in order to undertake investigations on other topics that concern them.

The teaching of mathematics

The three investigations that have just been summarised were all concerned with literacy in one way or another and in each case it was possible to measure the outcome so that pupil improvement was demonstrated. That raises the question of whether the same can be said for the teaching of mathematics. From a superficial standpoint, improving mathematics performance can seem to be a relatively simple task, and a number of such investigations have taken place in the USA. The basic design has been to measure mathematical output, usually by counting the number of problems or sums completed as a baseline, then introducing some form of intervention, e.g. the awarding of points for completing a set number of problems or sums, the points later being 'cashed in' for time spent on a preferred activity. The increase in output has been taken to demonstrate the effectiveness of the intervention.

It can sound impressive to know that the number of problems solved in an investigation has increased by 50 per cent, but a serious flaw in that kind of investigation becomes evident with the realisation that good mathematics teaching does not require the pupil to keep doing the same kind of work. In good mathematics teaching, the pupil continually moves on to different or more complex work. That makes designing an investigation based on mathematical output with one class of pupils impossible, since comparing baseline output with later output would not be comparing like with like. In good mathematics teaching, learning would be involved in coping with more complex material, e.g. problems which may take longer to solve, so that the number of problems or sums completed would be irrelevant. That is why there are no examples in this chapter of investigations conducted by teachers with their own classes aimed at raising mathematical performance.

As an illustration of what else has been done on mathematics teaching, aside from increasing mathematical performance, we have included here brief summaries of two investigations conducted in the USA. The first was concerned with 'increasing pupils' desire to do mathematics' and the second was concerned with 'pupil preferences for reinforcement based on accuracy' versus 'pupil preference for reinforcement based on time on-task'. Both investigations are somewhat contrived since neither involves pupils progressing to more difficult work, but they do serve as indicators of aspects of lessons that might be investigated in more detail. These two investigations are followed by some details taken from an investigation undertaken in a British primary school aimed at increasing numeracy enjoyment, together with increasing both pupil on-task behaviour and pupils' academic self-concepts.

Increasing pupils' liking for mathematics

Two average ability pupils aged 9 and 11 years in a residential care home had three to five 15-minute sessions per week in which they could choose to undertake any one of three activities based on work sheets, i.e. maths problems, word unscrambling and letter coding. Each maths work sheet had five problems, tailored to the individual concerned. Both pupils were asked to rate how much they liked doing maths on a scale of 1 to 7 (1 = not at all, 7 = very much). After a few sessions in which the pupils selected activities freely, the pupils were told that they could earn stars for completing maths sheets only. These stars could be accumulated and later exchanged for desired items, e.g. a sticker for one star, a yoyo for nine stars. The initial low frequency of choosing maths changed to 100 per cent when the stars were introduced. Later, when the stars were no longer used, the pupils continued to choose maths sheets at a higher rate than previously for a week. Two weeks later, two final sessions were conducted without stars and one of the pupils continued to select maths sheets at a high rate, the other did not. Both boys, however, rated their liking of maths at the end as '7' compared with low initial scores.

Research notes

There were two outcome measures in the investigation, i.e. the rate of selection of maths work sheets and the expressed liking for mathematics. With only two pupils being involved, however, the results can at best be indicative of a possible line of enquiry. The investigation showed quite predictably that the pupils did more maths when they were reinforced by stars exchangeable for other goods, but what is interesting is that both pupils stated by their ratings that they liked maths at the end of the investigation much more than they had at the beginning, even though one pupil stopped selecting maths at a high rate. The finding that the pupils rated maths higher at the end than at the start does point to the possibility that liking for maths can be increased by the use of reinforcers other than teacher's approval. One likely explanation for that occurrence is that increasing the amount of maths done (by doing more work sheets) increases the ability to do maths and that this in turn increases the likelihood of obtaining natural reinforcers in the form of approval or praise from a teacher.

Comment/activity

Given the results, it might be well worth investigating whether increasing the reinforcement given to maths performance can increase pupils' liking for the subject when the increased reinforcement is removed.

The second investigation examined the relationship of reward to the difficulty of the material with which pupils worked.

Pupil preferences for reward for 'accuracy' versus time 'on-task'

An investigation in the USA conducted with 9-year-old pupils examined the preferences of the pupils for rewards based on accuracy compared to rewards based on behaviour during 5-minute maths sessions. The pupils were given easy sums, single digit addition, and more difficult sums, double-digit addition. Points were awarded either for getting sums correct (accuracy) or for the number of times the pupils were seen to be on-task when observed (observations were taken at 30-second intervals).

From observations taken before the awarding of points began, it was arranged that the pupils would receive approximately the same number of points under each condition. The points could be traded in for a choice of items, e.g. a favourably written note to their parents, reward certificate, pencil. The pupils were allowed to select which of the two methods of rewards they wanted.

The results of the investigation showed that the pupils tended to select rewards for accuracy for the easy sums and rewards for time on-task for the more difficult sums.

Comment/activity

This was a relatively simple investigation although the design can be criticised for keeping pupils on easy sums when they had progressed to more difficult ones. The result does, however, point to the possibility that material of different levels of difficulty might well benefit from different means of reinforcement. After reading this, teachers might want to consider their own rewarding priorities when the material pupils are working with changes in difficulty. For example, when pupils first start tackling algebra and are finding it difficult, it might be better to focus approval on time spent working rather than just on approving problems solved.

Numeracy enjoyment and specificity of praise in the primary school

In a complex investigation in two British primary schools with Year 4 classes, Chalk and Bizo (2004) examined the effects of giving pupils approval for their appropriate behaviour versus giving them approval together with detail. The detail included a comment from the teacher telling the pupils why they were being given approval or disapproval and, in the latter case, telling them what they should be doing, e.g. 'Pat. Stop playing with your pen. Open your exercise book and get on with your writing like the rest of the class.' Readers may recognise that detail as the same as 'feedback with description' and 'redirection', used by Swinson and Harrop (2005) and discussed in Chapter 3.

The investigators focused their attention on the numeracy hour. They measured changes in numeracy enjoyment, as well as in pupils' self-concepts and pupils' on-task behaviour. Pupil self-concepts were measured by the Myself-As-Learner-Scale (MALS), which is available for teachers' use. Enjoyment of numeracy lessons was measured by asking the pupils to rate their enjoyment on a 10-point scale, ranging from (1) 'I don't like them,' to (5) 'They are OK,' to (10) 'I really like them.'

All the pupils were given the rating task at the start of the investigation. Following that the teachers of two of the classes gave the pupils approval for their appropriate behaviour and teachers of two classes gave the pupils approval together with detail. The teachers each taught their pupils for four to six lessons before enjoyment of numeracy lessons was measured again. The results showed no change in pupils' expressed enjoyment under either of the two conditions, yet observations taken of the teachers did show that they had been giving their approval in the agreed manner during the lesson.

The inevitable conclusion was that for these four classes, whether the pupils were given approval for appropriate behaviour either on its own, or with more detail, had no effect on the their enjoyment of numeracy lessons. That came as something of a surprise since the pupils' academic self-concepts (measured before and after the intervention) rose in the approval with detail condition by more than in the approval condition, as did the pupils' on-task behaviour. Just why the pupils' enjoyment of the numeracy hour was apparently impervious to changes in the teachers' approval techniques is consequently an open question.

Research notes

The investigation just recounted made use of four classes of pupils and the basis of the design was that two classes were given one form of intervention and two were given the other form of intervention. The same investigation could, of course, have been done with just two relatively equal ability classes, each class receiving a different form of intervention. Using four classes does, however, double the number of pupils involved and that, in turn, increases the investigators' confidence in the result.

In the investigation just recounted, it is quite possible that the time period was too short and that had the investigation continued for some 10 to 15 lessons a different result might have been obtained.

Comment/activity

As mentioned previously, since an essential aim of mathematics teaching is that pupils should continually progress in their understanding of mathematics and in the kind of material with which they work, it is very difficult to devise simple ways of measuring improvement with pupils in one class. A larger scale investigation could, however, be set up using two equal ability classes of pupil, taught by the same teacher, one class being given some form of intervention, perhaps the promise of a letter home if pupils do well after a set period of teaching, the other class (control) being given no such promise. In order to detect whether the promise of a letter home improves pupils' learning, a numeracy test based on the teaching aims could be devised by the teacher and given to both classes of pupils before and after the intervention. The results of the test should reveal whether or not the intervention has had a positive effect.

Concluding comments

In this chapter, we have recounted in some detail three investigations concerned with various forms of literacy and briefly outlined three that involved pupils doing mathematics. The three investigations on literacy should give the reader a good appreciation of how teachers can improve pupil learning in their classrooms using the positive psychology approach. At the same time it should be evident that the investigations were more complex than those concerned with increasing appropriate behaviour in the classroom mainly because, as was mentioned at the start of the chapter, of the difficulties involved in measuring learning. If, however, teachers have access to two classes of more or less equal ability that they teach themselves, they can use one class as a control and design an investigation along similar lines to that on 'improving reading attainment in a comprehensive school'. Care does, of course, have to be taken that the control class is not disadvantaged by the investigation. That shouldn't occur provided the control class is taught in the teacher's normal way while the other class receives a different treatment.

As regards the investigations concerning mathematics, they have been included to broaden the readers' thinking on what the positive approach can achieve. Although both the first two investigations have evident flaws, they do suggest other avenues of interest, e.g. how the liking of pupils for a school subject might be increased and how teachers might decide to apportion their approval to pupils when they are dealing with material of different levels of difficulty. The final investigation was included to show that some aspects of the learning process (in this case, numeracy enjoyment) are more difficult than others to change and to illustrate the usefulness of including a control class, when available, in the investigation.

While the examples have been taken from literacy and numeracy, there is no reason why the approach could not be adapted to other school subjects. We haven't given any such examples because we could find none in the literature. That leaves a good opportunity for someone to do original research. Finally, following on from that comment, it is hoped that reading this chapter will stimulate teachers to try using the positive approach to see the extent to which it helps them achieve their own learning objectives.

Chapter 7

Pupil well-being

Improving pupils' self-concepts

In the previous chapter, we emphasised the value of the positive approach in increasing pupil learning. In this chapter we go further and show how the approach may be applied to increasing the well-being of pupils in school. The first investigation we discuss, which is concerned with pupils' self-concepts, illustrates that process.

Reflecting on the success of positive psychology in improving the behaviour of pupils, one of the authors reasoned that the effects of teachers applying positive psychology in their classrooms may be more far reaching than just improving the behaviour and learning of their pupils. Being treated more positively might result in the pupils seeing themselves in more positive terms. Since a useful way of measuring the extent to which individuals see themselves positively is to measure their self-concepts, it was decided to design an investigation to test whether it was possible to improve pupils' self-concepts by using positive reinforcement.

Five primary school teachers, who were known to the author, were contacted and asked if they were interested in taking part in an investigation to see if the self-concepts of some of their pupils could be raised. After an explanation of what would be involved and some discussion they readily agreed, and permission was gained from their head teachers to go ahead. Three of the classes were in the 7 to 9 age range and two were in the 9 to 11 age range.

Before any intervention took place in the classrooms, the pupils' self-concepts in all five classes were measured by a self-concept questionnaire. The following items, taken at random from the questionnaire, should give a good idea of what was involved:

1   I have good ideas.
2   When I grow up I will be an important person.
3   I worry a lot.
4   I am unpopular.
5   It is usually my fault when things go wrong.

[The pupils were required to answer yes or no to each question.]

Additionally, the pupils completed a self-ranking measure. For this, each pupil was interviewed separately and was shown the names of all the children in the class, written on cards, arranged randomly. The pupil was asked to sort the cards into three groups, one group 'a bit better than you', one group 'about the same as you' and one group 'not better than you'. The pupil was then given the group 'about the same as you' and asked to sort it into two piles, those 'a tiny bit better than you' and those 'a tiny bit worse than you'. These arrangements yielded scores illustrating how the pupils viewed themselves in comparison with the other pupils.

The teachers were presented with their pupils' scores, together with the booklets containing the pupils' answers from the self-concept questionnaire and were given a week to look at the results and to decide which pupils they felt had unreasonably low self-concept scores. It was stressed that that didn't mean just the pupils with the lowest self-concepts. The author met with each teacher after a week to discuss their pupils' scores with the intention of asking each teacher to select three or four pupils in their classes whom they felt had unrealistically low self-concepts. In practice, the teachers were so concerned by the unrealistically low self-concept scores of a number of their pupils that it was decided to select up to six or seven pupils in each class.

After some discussion, the teachers agreed that, for the chosen pupils they would:

- Seek opportunities to reward achievements. If achievements were few, to try and find tasks that the pupils could do and give praise/approval wherever possible.
- Try to avoid giving the pupils tasks they could not perform. If failures occurred, to try to ignore these or at least be encouraging about the attempts.
- Try to give the pupils some status within the class, and reward pupils who made positive comments about the pupils concerned.

The teachers continued treating the pupils in that way for four months and the writer called into the schools every couple of weeks at lunchtime to discuss progress with the teachers. After the four months all the pupils in the classes in the study were retested.

The results showed that for the younger pupils (aged 7 to 9) who were treated, there was a significant average improvement in self-concept scores, which was considerably larger than the increase in the scores of the other pupils in the same class. For the older pupils, no significant improvements were found in the self-concept scores of the pupils.

The author was puzzled by these results at first until some delving into research on children's self-concepts uncovered previous research identifying age 8 as critical in the development of person perception. At about that age, it seems that children become able to perceive people in a more abstract way than before, i.e. in terms of values, dispositions and beliefs, rather than in terms of more concrete views based on appearance, identity and possessions. It looks likely, therefore, that the younger pupils' person perception allowed them to be more influenced than the older pupils by the teachers' change in behaviour. Alternatively, of course, the teacher may just have been a more rewarding person for the younger pupils or it may be that self-concepts become more difficult to influence with age. Whatever the reason, the positive approach seemed to be beneficial for the younger pupils, and teachers of children below the age of nine, particularly, really ought to be aware of their potential influence on the way children perceive themselves.

Improving pupils' academic self-concepts

Chalk and Bizo (2004), whose work on numeracy enjoyment and specific praise was outlined in the previous chapter, included a measure of self-concepts in their research; more precisely, they were concerned with *academic* self-concepts. They began by giving all the pupils in the four classes of 8- to 9-year-olds a 20-item questionnaire, the Myself-As-Learner Scale (MALS) (Burden, 1998). The MALS is concerned with pupils' perceptions of themselves as learners and as problem solvers.

As outlined previously, Chalk and Bizo were investigating the effects of teachers using approval on its own compared with giving approval together with more detail. After the four to six lessons of intervention, the pupils' academic self-concepts were re-measured. The results showed that approval on its own had had no effect, but that approval with detail (specific praise) had significantly raised the average scores of the pupils thus treated.

Research note

The reader will have noticed that in the first investigation recounted the aim was to increase pupils' self-concept scores, while in the second the aim was to increase pupils' academic self-concept scores. The basic difference is that while individuals' self-concepts are normally considered to be concerned with the way they see themselves based on all their characteristics, academic self-concepts are considered to encompass a narrower range of characteristics, namely, those concerned with academic matters.

A second difference between the investigations lies in the fact that the latter was concerned with whole classes of pupils while the former was focused on just those pupils considered by their teachers to have unrealistically low self-concepts.

A third difference lies in the form of intervention used. The latter relied solely on giving approval to the pupils and giving specific details with the approval, while the former used a more comprehensive intervention. Moreover, in the first investigation, the intervention continued for four *months* as compared with four to six *lessons*.

At the time of writing, these two pieces of research appear to be the only ones concerned with increasing pupils' self-concept scores so some care has to be taken in generalising too much from the results. Nevertheless, there does seem to be evidence that the self-concepts of pupils in school aged nine and younger can be improved when they are treated positively by their teachers.

Some general background on the self-concept

The self-concept develops through experience of life, through the feedback individuals receive from their parents, relatives, friends, teachers and others. Some authorities emphasise that as we develop we see ourselves in a kind of 'looking glass', which reflects how others react to us. Other authorities emphasise the many roles individuals play in daily life, roles at first being acted out and later becoming internalised as part of the person. There are a number of such views, but common to all is the notion that social experience is crucial in the development of the self-concept. Teachers are major figures in children's lives from when they are still very young and, as such, we would expect these teachers to have strong influences on the development of pupils' self-concepts.

Comment/activity

It is relatively easy to gain an appreciation of how pupils view themselves, using the self-ranking method outlined previously, without having to resort to standard questionnaires such as those used in the investigations. The criterion on which pupils sort the names of the classmates could be changed from 'a bit better than me' etc., to 'better at schoolwork than me' etc., or whatever suits the purpose.

   Another way that is sometimes used for gaining a good idea of how pupils view themselves is to ask the class to 'cast' a play. The class could be given a list of characters in the play, for example, a star footballer, a star dancer, a clever scientist, a good mother, a friendly young doctor, a bossy older sister, a clumsy, silly child, etc. The pupils could be told to try and fit members of the class, themselves included, into the part each could best play. One teacher who did this recently was very surprised to find the pupil who caused her most trouble in the class was generally put in the role by the other pupils of 'a friendly young doctor'. She said she saw him in a new light as a consequence.

   You could, of course, avail yourself of the Myself-As-Learner Scale (MALS), which Chalk and Bizo used, details of which can be found on the internet.

   Gaining some appreciation of how the pupils view themselves is a valuable exercise in itself. It would also be relatively easy to follow that up with an investigation in the class aimed at improving the way pupils see themselves. One or more of the techniques described in the two investigations outlined in this chapter could be used. At the same time it should be appreciated that so far it appears that there has been no evidence that an improvement can be brought about with pupils over the age of nine.

Up to this point in the chapter, we have confined ourselves to considering how the self-concepts of pupils can be improved. For obvious reasons, there are no investigations to quote in which pupils' self-concepts have been lowered by their teachers. Nevertheless, bearing in mind the way in which the self-concept develops, teachers who are unsympathetic, use excessive disapproval, set tasks that are too difficult for some of their pupils, etc., may well at best be retarding the development of their pupils' self-concepts.

Pupils' explanations of success and failure

If we take the notion of the self-concept a stage further, we come to the realisation that the way in which pupils perform in school depends in large measure on the way in which they perceive themselves, particularly in terms of ability. Their performance depends to a large extent on how competent they perceive themselves to be and how they cope with success and failure. Take, for example, a group of pupils who fail a maths test. Some will consider they failed because they are poor at maths, others might say the test was too hard or that they were badly taught, others yet may consider that they weren't at their best that day, that they didn't really try, that they hadn't prepared properly for the test or that they had the bad luck to get the wrong kind of questions.

In other words, there is a whole variety of potential explanations, known in psychology as *attributions*.

According to attribution theory, children and adults who have healthy, self-enhancing attribution systems attribute success to internal factors, such as effort and ability and failure to external factors, such as task difficulty and luck. Those without such self-enhancing systems may well attribute success to luck and failure to lack of ability. Pupils who attribute their failures to lack of ability can come to expect failure on a regular basis. As a consequence, they can develop the habit of not making any effort to master a task because they think any effort will be in vain. Taken to extremes, attributing the inability to carry out the simplest of tasks to lack of ability can lead to a condition known as 'learned helplessness'. Typically, learned helplessness has its origins in the early years of life and develops through the influences of family interactions. On the other hand, pupils who attribute their failures to lack of effort and not to lack of ability are likely to increase their efforts when faced with a similar task. Those who habitually take this stance are often referred to as being 'mastery oriented'.

Teachers play a critical role in which their own attribution systems interact with those of the pupils. So that, for example, if a teacher continually attributes a pupil's failure to lack of ability, that attribution is likely to be transferred to the pupil's attribution system. A teacher who continually accepts poor performances from a pupil serves to confirm the pupil's attribution of lack of ability.

Alternatively, a teacher who attributes failure to lack of effort may transfer that attribution to the pupil. Provided the tasks set are not too difficult for the pupil and the teacher uses predominantly positive measures, particularly approval for efforts made, the teacher's attribution should subsequently become that of the pupil.

The notion of ability itself is very important in this context. There seems to be a widespread belief that ability is a fixed entity that remains constant throughout life. According to that view, some have more ability than others and the amount any one individual has is unchanging. This belief tends to be maintained by the frequent references made to intelligence quotient (IQ) in our culture, usually with the implication that an individual's IQ is immutable. An alternative view is that ability is subject to change depending on life experiences. In that view, the individual is seen as constantly developing skills and knowledge and, by hard work, study and practice, ability can be increased.

It isn't difficult to see the relationship between these two opposing views of ability and the attributions made by pupils, and indeed by teachers, in schools. It is important, for intellectual development, that pupils, see ability as capable of development, rather than fixed, and that teachers embrace this 'incremental view of ability', which they pass on to their pupils.

Teacher expectations

A piece of research reported by Rosenthal and Jacobson (1968) made such a strong impact in its time that the term 'self-fulfilling prophecy' became strongly established in educational thinking. In their original research, after administering tests to pupils, Rosenthal and Jacobson told a number of teachers that several pupils, chosen at random, who were in their classes, would make significant intellectual gains during the year. At the end of the year, the pupils did indeed make larger gains than were normal. What

Rosenthal and Jacobson had done was to give the teachers the *expectation* that those pupils would improve and this expectation had been followed by increased performances from the pupils.

There were some criticisms of the methodology used by Rosenthal and Jacobson but no one has subsequently questioned the importance of teacher expectations on pupils' performance, although later research has demonstrated that the effect of teacher expectation is stronger with younger pupils than with older pupils and that 'naturally occurring' teacher expectations are more effective than those implanted externally (as was done by Rosenthal and Jacobson).

Naturally enough, teachers have expectations about what their pupils can achieve and while many of these expectations are accurate assessments, based on the best available data, other expectations may be overestimates or underestimates. Some research has shown, for example, teachers overestimating the abilities of preschool children rated as independent and interesting and underestimating the abilities of those rated as immature and anxious (Alvidrez and Weinstein, 1999). While most research has been concerned with teachers' different expectations for pupils within their classes, more recent research has noted that some teachers generally have high expectations for all their pupils whereas others generally have low expectations.

In order to help the reader appreciate how teachers with high and low expectations perceive their pupils, we have included here a brief summary of some of the salient features of a recent research report.

Teacher expectations and perception of pupil attributes

Rubie-Davies (2010) began her investigation by having 24 primary school teachers complete a questionnaire in which they rated their expectations of the achievement of each pupil in their classes. From the school records, the teachers expectations were compared with pupil achievements. From this procedure, six of the teachers were deemed to have high expectations for the end-of-year performance of their pupils, their expectations being significantly higher than the pupils' achievements at the start of the year, and three teachers were deemed to have low expectations, their expectations being significantly lower than the pupils' performance.

The nine teachers were then asked to complete rating scales for each pupil based on a scale of one to seven, from well below average (1) to well above average (7) for a series of 15 pupil characteristics, including perseverance, independence, interest in schoolwork, self-esteem, etc.

When the data were analysed, all the mean scores of the ratings of pupil characteristics of the high expectation teachers were well above pupil achievements. Conversely, just over half the means of the low expectation teachers ratings of pupil characteristics were below the pupil achievement. Moreover, for every pupil characteristic on the rating scale, the high expectation teachers had a higher mean score than the lower expectation teachers.

Interestingly, the low expectancy teachers viewed the following characteristics most positively: interest in schoolwork, classroom behaviour, motivation and homework completion. As Rubie-Davies suggests, these characteristics could indicate that the low expectancy teachers viewed their pupils as trying hard in class yet not being capable of achieving well. That perception of hard-working pupils and low achievement levels could be explained by a belief that ability is a fixed entity. In other words, it seems that no matter how hard the pupils tried, the low expectancy teachers considered that their progress was limited by their ability level.

How teacher expectations are communicated to pupils

So far we have discussed the effects of teacher expectations and have given some idea of what these expectations entail in terms of the way in which teachers perceive their pupils, but we haven't considered how these expectations are communicated from teacher to pupil. For this, we can turn again to Rubie-Davies who, in a previous piece of research (Rubie-Davies, 2007), reported that high expectation teachers 'had pupils working in mixed-ability groups, promoted pupil autonomy in learning activities, carefully explained new concepts, provided pupils with clear feedback, managed behaviour positively and asked a large number of open questions'. Low expectation teachers 'maintained within-class ability groups, directed pupil learning experiences, frequently gave procedural questions, reacted negatively to student misbehaviour and asked mostly closed questions' (p.125).

As regards situations in which teachers have different expectations about the pupils in their classes, there are numerous pieces of research that point to pupils for whom teachers have high expectations being given more difficult questions, more praise for correct answers and more smiles and nods, while pupils for whom teachers have low expectations are given easier questions, less praise for correct answers, more sympathetic responses for inadequate answers, but more criticism for incorrect answers. As Woolfolk, Hughes and Walkup (2008) stress, pupils for whom teachers have low expectations often tend to get rather conflicting feedback messages.

If we raise our sights from the individual level to the level of the classroom and the school, we can identify other potential ways in which expectations are conveyed to the pupils. In the secondary school, the practice of streaming classes by pupil performance has largely been abandoned and has been replaced by banding. In the primary school, the classroom may well be organised into reading tables, each table seating pupils of similar reading levels. Given these arrangements, pupils rapidly learn their perceived ability level. The results of SATS tests and GCSE examinations only tend to confirm the pupils' expectations.

General comments

In this chapter, we have moved beyond our previous focus on behaviour into more abstract explanations of some of the effects that teachers can have on their pupils. We began by looking at pupils' self-concepts and presented two investigations that demonstrated the positive effect teachers can have on their pupils. We moved from that to considering the ways in which pupils interpreted their own successes and failures and showed how that may be explained in terms of attributions made by the pupils. Finally, we presented some of the research done on teachers' expectations and how these may influence the pupils' expectations. We appreciate that these notions of self-concept, attributions and expectation are all interrelated, but the precise relationship is unimportant in a text of this nature. What is important is that between them they give information that teachers should consider in order to be able to help their pupils to appropriately develop their self-concept, to make healthy attributions about success and failure and to see themselves as capable of developing their abilities.

We are aware that there has been a number of investigations into the teaching of well-being and even happiness in schools but many of these have taken the form of lessons that are separate from normal classroom teaching. In our view, such 'bolting on' of separate instruction and activity might well give pupils a valuable crash course in a foreign language, but applying such an approach to something as fundamental as pupil well-being is, at best, a misguided project. It is far better that pupil well-being should be an integral part of the normal way in which the curriculum is taught. In our view, teachers using positive psychology achieve not only better behaved pupils, who learn effectively, but also pupils who are likely to develop healthy self-concepts, so that in a very real sense, pupil well-being is a product of good teaching.

As a consequence, what follows is a set of recommendations best incorporated within normal teaching, which make explicit some of the information covered in the chapter and in previous chapters. For simplicity, these recommendations are presented as guidelines that are presented in two groups, one group for pupils in general and the other for pupils who seem to be struggling with the curriculum. This latter group is likely to include those pupils who have low self-concepts, who attribute their lack of success to low ability and who have low expectations.

We appreciate, of course, that many teachers will already be following most if not all of these guidelines. If they are, they will at least have found sound justification for continuing in that way.

Guidelines

General

1 Explain new concepts carefully.
2 Seek to promote pupil autonomy in learning.
3 Provide pupils with clear feedback.
4 Use open questions where possible.
5 Have pupils working in mixed-ability groups when possible.
6 Give praise/approval for appropriate behaviour and explain why that praise/approval is given.
7 When giving disapproval explain why you disapprove and what the pupil should be doing.
8 Give approval for pupil effort, not just for work completed.
9 Expect a lot from your pupils.
10 Appreciate that pupils' abilities can be developed and seek to communicate that view to all the pupils.

For pupils who seem to be struggling

1 Seek opportunities to reward achievements. If achievements are few, try and find tasks that the pupils can do and give praise/approval where possible.
2 Try to avoid giving the pupils tasks they cannot perform. If failures occur, try to ignore these or at least be encouraging about the attempts.

3   Try to give the pupils some status within the class and reward pupils who make positive comments about the pupils concerned.

4   Try not to give approval too frequently for inadequate answers.

5   Try not to give too much criticism for incorrect answers.

6   Do not be overly reliant on directed learning experiences.

7   Keep a careful watch for pupils who are developing 'learned helplessness' and seek to counter that by arranging that they make small achievements that you can reward. If you feel you are unsuccessful with such pupils, pass on your concerns to someone within the school who has responsibility for special needs.

Comment/activity

If you have one or two pupils in your class or in one of your classes who appear to be moving towards 'learned helplessness' in your lessons, you might consider trying to apply the guidelines suggested in order to help them to become more competent learners. You could measure your success by looking at changes in their self-concept before and after you apply the guidelines and by observing changes in the pupils' learning.

Chapter 8

Principles of the positive approach

So far in this book, we have concentrated almost exclusively on the practice of the positive approach and we hope that we have provided the reader with sufficient evidence of the efficacy of the approach to children's learning, well-being and behaviour. We have said very little about the theoretical basis of the approach, neither for that matter have we said much about the role and use of sanctions, punishments and simple 'telling off'. In this chapter, we will put the approach in the context of various other theoretical positions in psychology and education, consider the role of punishments with children and explain the reasons behind the power of feedback.

A number of theoretical models have been used to provide an explanation as the basis for children's behaviour in school (see Davie, 1993; Porter, 2000). Such models are of little value for teaching unless they can fulfil two important requisites. First, they should provide a perspective or angle from which to look at children's behaviour and thereby help provide some insight or rationale to explain the reasons that make children behave in the way they do. Second, and most important as far as teachers are concerned, the theoretical insight or understanding should lead to practical advice that, when implemented, can produce improved pupil behaviour and learning in their classroom or school.

Davie (1993) described six models, detailed in the following paragraphs and presented in order of their historical development.

Theoretical models to explain child behaviour

Psychodynamic

There are a related series of theoretical models that found their origin in the work of Sigmund Freud and were subsequently developed by Adler, Bowlby, Erikson, and Klein among others. These models are characterised by five common features or assumptions that are inherent, i.e. unconscious processes, anxiety and psychic pain, defence mechanisms, motivational drives and developmental phases, all of which can affect behaviour. According to Winnicott (1971) and Brown and Pedder (1979), the fundamental basis for these theories is that the unconscious exerts a powerful influence on both feelings and behaviour.

These theories focus on how the effects of early childhood experience influence current behaviour. Psychodynamic approaches have been used primarily as a basis for practitioners, usually child therapists, in their work with individual children, but as

Marzillier (2004) has recently pointed out, the evidence base for the effectiveness of a great deal of psychotherapeutic interventions is often thin. Therefore, it is difficult to recommend such approaches.

The only exception to this is the work of Dinkmeyer and Dreikurs (1963), who were strongly influenced by the work of Alfred Adler (1870–1937). Their work pointed to the role that self-evaluation, perceived self-worth and self-esteem had on child and adult behaviour. They emphasised the value of encouraging children and helping them to find appropriate rather than inappropriate ways of having their needs met. They argued for more democratic student–teacher relationships in which school and class rules are negotiated rather than imposed and for schools to abandon competition between pupils.

The work of Dinkmeyer and Dreikurs has had some influence on educational thought, especially in the UK in the 1970s. Some of the principles can still be seen in the advice to teachers in *Building a Better Behaved School* (Galvin, Mercer and Costa, 1990), especially in terms of consulting pupils over aspects of school organisation, and has been incorporated in our work in schools (see Chapter 5 on whole school work).

Behavioural

This model was based on the work of a variety of experimental psychologists who were investigating learning. Unlike the psychodynamic model, the behavioural model makes no assumptions about the unconscious or indeed about inner processes, although features of what is known as the cognitive behavioural model do accommodate aspects of a person's attitudes and beliefs. Essentially, the behavioural model is based on learning theory and the quintessential principle that behaviour that is reinforced, whether by accident or design, tends to reoccur or gain in strength, while behaviour that is not reinforced will tend to disappear. Behaviourists are concerned with observable behaviour. Thus their approach to classroom behaviour might involve such features as a behavioural analysis, a period of direct observation in the classroom and trying to assess what aspects of current teacher practice influence the pupils' behaviour. Such analysis might be followed by an intervention in which aspects of teacher behaviour might be modified with the aim of changing pupil behaviour, a process called behaviour modification.

Porter (2000) cites three behaviour-based approaches currently used in schools:

1   Limit-setting approaches such as 'Assertive Discipline' (Canter and Canter, 1992), which we have previously discussed. In this approach, a classroom discipline plan is devised by the teacher that includes a clear set of class rules, praise and rewards given to pupils who conform and a set of graded sanctions administered to pupils who choose not to conform. Advice is also given on whole school approaches.
2   Applied behaviour analysis, in which teachers are taught to attempt to analyse pupil behaviour by looking at the antecedents of the classroom behaviour, i.e. level of difficulty of work set or seating arrangements, and then the consequences of that same behaviour i.e. teacher or pupil attention. Teachers are trained to modify or change aspects of both the antecedents and the consequences in an attempt

to change or modify the pupils' behaviour. She cites Wheldall and Merrett's BATPACK (1988) as a good example of this approach.

3   Cognitive behaviourism which focuses on student self-management and also offers advice to teachers on managing their own thinking and hence their approach to teaching. The theory addresses pupils' attitudes to learning and behaviour and their ability to organise themselves and achieve certain standards of both work and behaviour. The aim is for pupils to become independent managers of their own behaviour rather than dependent on teachers to manage them. This approach has been used by a number of practitioners, including McNamara and Heard (1976) and Kaplan and Carter (1995) and is included in the approach of Rodgers (1998).

The strength of the behavioural approaches lies in their foundation in the basic principles of experimental psychology and as such their investigations have been subject to constant evaluation of their effectiveness.

Humanist

The third major theoretical model is that of humanistic psychology. This approach began as a reaction against the positivism of empirical sciences. It rejects 'mechanistic' explanations of human behaviour or generalisations about causal explanations. For humanists, the individual is unique and at the centre of the theoretical model. Therefore an individual's perception of themselves and the world around them is paramount.

The model has been applied in schools in the UK by Visser (1983). His approach is to consult students themselves over all issues around the organisation of the school and the way in which classes are run. The dialogue between students and teachers thus establishes an agreement on issues such as class rules and organisation. In the USA, the humanistic approach has been incorporated into the work of Glasser (1992), based on the assumptions that all children have basic needs of love, a sense of belonging, of power, freedom and fun. He argues that students will be motivated to produce high-quality work and behave responsibly if those needs can be met. Consequently, it follows that schools need to be democratic, the curricula relevant and children to be loved and their opinions valued. He suggests conflicts in schools are better resolved through problem solving than punishment or parental involvement.

Ecosystemic

This theoretical position was first proposed by Lewin (1935), based on the proposition that behaviour does not occur in isolation but is influenced by factors in the surrounding environment. It is the model that most easily fits with the work of Rutter et al. (1979), Mortimore et al. (1988) and Reynolds (1992) into school effectiveness.

Their research noted that schools varied widely in the outcomes for their pupils both in exam success and pupil behaviour. They related these varying outcomes to environmental factors within each school. These factors included not only how the school was managed but also other aspects such as the presence of graffiti, state of decoration and even whether there were potted plants in the corridors. Reynolds (1992) showed how by changing aspects of the school environment outcomes for pupils could improve. Cooper and Upton (1990) and Faupel (1990) also noted that difficult behaviour and poor results by some pupils may indicate that all is not well in any particular school and therefore changes need to take place at a whole school level in order for things to improve. This brings us to systems theory.

Systems theory

Systems theory draws heavily on work with families and, in particular, from solution-focused therapy. It takes the view that schools are like families. They can be extremely complex and it is impossible to consider one aspect of the family or school in isolation from the rest. Any individual part is but one small piece of one complex system that is interdependent on all other parts. Any system is invariably complex, with a number of competing variables interacting with one another; therefore inevitably there is more to any system than the sum of all its parts. Systems theory provides a framework for thinking about recurring problems in new ways. The theory conceptualises that behaviour problems arise when behaviour is mishandled or an attempted solution has not worked. Change can be affected by altering how behaviour is handled. Previous attempted solutions need to be identified and a different approach needs to be tried.

Davie (1980) used this approach to help teachers understand the processes at work in their school. This was later evaluated by Phillips *et al.* (1985) but only in terms of changes in teachers' understanding, not in terms of an evaluation of pupil behaviour. Miller (2003) uses such an approach to describe the psychosocial system of pupil behaviour in schools. He argues that individual and group behaviour in schools is influenced by a whole range of interdependent variables, but especially by leadership, policy and procedures, staff culture, pupil culture and both formal and informal groupings of staff and pupils. Miller's model has been used to help schools reflect on aspects of their functioning and hence to school improvement.

Labelling theory

Davie's final model shares with systems theory the idea that the behaviour of individuals or groups can never be viewed out of context. Labelling theory is usually attributed to an American sociologist, Becker (1963). He argued that what he called deviant behaviour is not intrinsic to the individual but created by society. Thus within any social system, e.g. a school, rules are set up and therefore expectations of behaviour. When rules are broken, deviancy is created and inevitably those who break the rules are labelled as deviants. In schools, the labels we give such children may vary, e.g. disaffected, 'EBD', maladjusted, disturbed. Whatever the label, Becker argues the effect will be the same. Once labelled, the group or individual's behaviour may well change in order to conform to the expectations of the label, e.g. pupils labelled 'EBD' will continue to behave badly. Second, the rest of society may well treat a labelled individual or group in a different fashion, thereby confirming the group's identity. In schools, this phenomenon has been noted by Henry (1989).

More general considerations

Labelling theory and indeed other humanist approaches are often described as phenomenological. Hargraves *et al.* (1975) have pointed out that phenomenological approaches are in stark contrast to the kinds of question asked by empirical scientists, who are much more interested in the collection of quantitative data and whose methods are described as positivism. The positivist paradigm assumes an objective world in which scientific methods are used together with measurement, seeking to predict and explain causal relationships among key variables.

The differences between phenomenological and positivistic approaches are apparent when a comparison is made between the various theories outlined earlier. Davie (1993) suggested that any comparison of theoretical explanations of classroom behaviour should be judged in terms of the insight they provide to teachers and the degree to which this insight leads to practical advice that can be incorporated into teaching practice.

While all the theories can claim to provide insight, they do vary in the extent to which teachers have been able to incorporate the ideas they generate into mainstream practice. They also vary in the extent to which the theories can be seen to be applicable to individual children or to whole classes. A good example is the psychodynamic approach, which has been used a great deal in terms of individual therapy, but has not generally been incorporated into general classroom practice. At the other end of the spectrum is systems theory, which, as Porter (2000) notes, has been concerned more with whole school approaches than with work with individuals or class-based interventions.

The theoretical approaches also differ in the extent to which their applications have led to an evidence base of their effectiveness. As O'Donohue and Krasner (1995) say, the evidence base for nearly all interventions based on the application of behaviourist theory is almost invariably more substantial than for non–behaviourist theories.

The focus of this book has been on the behaviour of pupils and teachers in classrooms and the impact that that can have on pupils' learning. A great deal of emphasis has been placed on empirical research and on the collection of quantitative data to provide evidence to support the practical advice being offered to teachers. The effectiveness of this advice has been further evaluated using robust empirical methods. As must be evident to the reader, we have been strongly influenced by the behaviourist/cognitive behavioural tradition and especially by applied behavioural analysis in which the behaviour of pupils is evaluated in terms of the effect of both antecedents and consequences surrounding that behaviour. The reader, however, may be also aware that there are aspects of other theoretical approaches evident in some of the interventions we have discussed. There are, for instance, strong 'humanist' influences in our advice on boosting self-esteem (Chapter 7) and strong ecosystemic influences on our approach to working on a whole school basis (Chapter 5).

Use of sanctions, punishments and 'telling off'

All schools and all teachers use sanctions of one sort or another on a daily basis. Sanctions vary from a simple admonishment or telling off to a whole range of punishments from lines, detention to temporary or permanent exclusion from school. Very little research has been carried out on the effectiveness of any sanctions or punishments. What we do know, however, can be summarised thus:

• As far as schools are concerned, those with higher exclusion rates tend to be the least successful, both in terms of the learning outcomes of their pupils and their pupils' behaviour (Rutter et al., 1979).

- As far as individual teachers are concerned, Swinson and Knight (2007) showed that teachers who over-relied on admonishments and other sanctions tended to be those with the least well-behaved classes.
- As far as the pupils are concerned, while they do not like being the subject of an admonishment, they can become immune to any effect it may have if they are repeatedly being 'told off' and, as Harrop and Williams (1992) have reported, pupils themselves feel being told off is not particularly effective.
- As far as local authorities are concerned, punishments by schools in the form of exclusions are not helpful. As Daniels (2011) has pointed out, on average an excluded pupil is without education for at least three months and for a sizable proportion (14 per cent), the wait is six months. Most of these excluded pupils are placed in what is called a pupil referral unit. The cost of keeping a pupil at such a unit is usually about five times that of any normal school place.

Given the limitations of admonishments one needs to consider why teachers, especially when faced with a particularly difficult class, persist in using them. The answer may lie in an apparent perceived effectiveness. The argument goes like this: the teacher hears 'Jonny' talking in class, he asks 'Jonny' to stop, which he does. Jolly good, thinks the teacher, telling off works. Four minutes later, however, he catches 'Jonny' talking again. 'Stop talking in class', he says and 'Jonny' stops. However, two minutes later 'Jonny' is at it again. Every time the teacher tells 'Jonny' to stop, he does stop, so the teacher feels the admonishment has worked. What the teacher has failed to notice is that every time he repeats a 'telling off', it becomes less effective and each successive 'telling off' results in less time without the annoying behaviour.

Generally speaking, any admonishment is bound to be ineffective because it tells the pupil what not to do, rather than what to do. Hence, to be effective, if an admonishment is given, it must be accompanied by a positive redirection as we have outlined in 'four essential steps' (see Chapter 3). What is key to appropriate behaviour, however, is getting the balance right between negative feedback and positive feedback. This will be discussed later in this chapter.

Before we move on, it is important to stress that we are not saying that all uses of admonishments and sanctions are valueless and are not a necessary part of the techniques needed by teachers to run a successful class. Indeed, we outline in the 'four essential steps' where and how these are sometimes needed in order for good discipline to be maintained. Certainly, in cases of serious assault of either fellow pupils, or indeed of the teacher themselves, there may be no alternative but to exclude a pupil from school. However, it remains the case that exclusion from school is a very serious sanction that can have little benefit for the child concerned and it is a sanction that has been overused by a small number of schools in the past.

Getting the right balance between positive and negative feedback

Some time ago, in the United Kingdom, Her Majesty's Inspectors of Schools (DES, 1988) carried out an exercise in which they examined their lesson observations from the previous three or four years and attempted to discover what it was that made some lessons successful, while others were less so. The results were, to some extent, predictable: well-planned lessons, enthusiastic and well-informed teachers, work that was sufficiently demanding for the pupils, a degree of differentiation for those pupils who might find the work difficult and some extension activities for the brightest. When they examined characteristics of the teachers' communication with the pupils, they found that the outstanding teachers praised their pupils three times more often than they told them off.

This ratio of 3:1, positive to negative, has been found to be important in many areas of life and appears to be the key not only to successful teaching but also to successful sports and business teams, successful appraisal, and to physical and mental health and well-being. This ratio would also appear to be a worldwide phenomenon with examples cited from South America to China (see Fredrickson and Losada, 2005).

In terms of physical well-being, the positive affect, as it is called, has been found to speed recovery from cardiovascular aftereffects (Fredrickson et al., 2000), to increase immune function (Davidson et al., 2003) and to lower levels of cortisol (Steptoe et al., 2005). In terms of mental health and psychological well-being, it has been associated with increased happiness (Fredrickson and Joiner, 2002), psychological growth and resilience to adversity (Fredrickson, Tugade, Waugh and Larkin, 2003).

Moreover, research in occupational psychology has shown that in appraisal exercises, the ratio of 3:1 is essential for positive outcomes. Anderson, (1985) and work by Losada (1999) and Losada and Heaphy (2004), has shown that high levels of positivity in business teams was associated with greater flexibility, resilience to adversity and optimal functioning.

Positive feedback has a huge impact on psychological functioning and has been shown to alter not only people's thinking about themselves but also to have an impact on their way of thinking in general. Investigations have shown that what is generally referred to as the 'induced positive affect', which is the result of positive feedback, can widen the scope of attention as well as broaden behavioural repertoires (Fredrickson and Branigan, 2005), increase intuition (Bolte et al., 2003) and increase creativity (Isen, Daubman and Nowicki, 1987). These are all characteristics that teachers would no doubt want to develop in their pupils.

The ideas behind this positive affect were developed by Barbara Fredrickson (1998) and generated what is known as the 'broaden and build theory'. This is a theory that asserts that positive emotions are evolved psychological adaptations that increased our human ancestors' odds of survival. An early ancestor who took a positive view of his likelihood of catching game was, according to this theory, more likely to succeed than his pessimistic brother and, therefore, of course, more likely to survive and have children.

Both positive and negative feedback are essential elements of the evolutionary process and appear to operate together to produce some startling natural phenomena. As Richard Dawkins points out in his elegant book, *The Blind Watchmaker* (1988), in nature negative feedback acts as a limiter on the development of variation, thus British mice show little variation from their uniform brown/grey colour so they can blend in with the background. By the same token, positive feedback that is apparent in aspects of sexual attraction rewards those who stand out from the crowd. This can lead to such amazing phenomena as the development of the peacock's magnificent tail or the fantastic colours of some tropical fish. Negative feedback can act to temporally suppress unwanted behaviour, but it is only positive feedback that can teach pupils new alternative behaviour and only positive feedback that can help pupils become the creative, imaginative writers, artistes, dancers and scientists that schools hope to produce.

The fact that Fredrickson and Losada's ratio of 3:1 is almost exactly the same as the ratio of 3:1 found by Her Majesty's Inspectors in their description of successful classrooms in British schools is food for thought. Moreover, in all our work we have found that positive feedback, both on an individual and group level, leads to successful outcomes for both teachers and for their pupils. Children have a right to be well-taught, by good teachers who are capable of inspiring their pupils to learn in safe environments that enhance and develop their physical, psychological and emotional well-being. We feel that these goals can be achieved if teachers not only employ the kinds of positive based strategy we have outlined in this book but, more fundamentally, if they adopt a positive philosophy in all aspects of their work in schools and in life.

The power of feedback

'The Power of Feedback' is the title of a paper by Hattie and Timperley (2007), who state unequivocally that: 'Feedback is one of the most powerful influences on learning and achievement.' They based that assertion on a major piece of research undertaken by Hattie himself. He examined the results of analyses of over 180,000 studies across the English-speaking world on the effects of feedback. He found the impact of feedback to be one of the most important variables affecting children's learning and achievement and to be a more important variable than their intellectual ability, economic background, size of class or amount of homework.

Feedback, of course, comes from more than one source. In this book, we have largely considered feedback from teachers, although it is evident that feedback in the classroom may come from a variety of sources. While teachers may be providing corrective information and encouragement, fellow pupils may be offering alternative feedback. A pupil who makes a joke, for example, may be very reinforced by the laughter (feedback) of the rest of the class, so that the behaviour is likely to be repeated.

Feedback from teachers is directed towards a number of goals that are not necessarily mutually exclusive. In general terms, these are instructional feedback, which is information relating to a specific learning task or to the process of learning, feedback about the pupil as a person and their motivation, and feedback directed towards self-regulation or behaviour. In practice, these types are feedback are often combined as in: 'Good boy, Chris [personal], you've got all those sums correct [task].'

The evidence from research, not only that of Hattie but also of a number of others (Lysakowski and Walberg, 1982; Walberg, 1982; Tenenbaum and Golding, 1989), makes the case that information about the correctness of any task has a substantial effect on learning outcomes. In fact, most teachers are intuitively aware of this because, as Airasian (1997) discovered, almost 90 per cent of teachers' questions are aimed at establishing pupils' level of understanding. However, as Winnie and Butler (1994) argue, the benefits of feedback about task is heavily dependent on attention to task, which brings us to feedback related to self-regulation and behaviour.

The role of feedback directed to the person has a much more mixed effect. An analysis by both Wilkinson (1981) and Kluger and Denisi (1998) found that positive feedback directed towards the person had little or no impact on pupils' achievement, although, as we have seen in the previous chapter, it may have a positive effect on other aspects of pupils' well-being. There are also differences in the way in which personal feedback is received, especially when considering older pupils. Sharp (1985), for example, reported that while 26 per cent of adolescents welcomed public praise, 64 per cent preferred it to be given quietly and privately and 10 per cent preferred it not to be given at all. Elwell and Tiberio (1994) and Burnett (2002) found that similar proportions of pupils preferred praise for effort rather than for achievement. Although most investigators using feedback about pupils' behaviour have not included any measure of learning outcomes, such studies were judged by Hattie (2009), on the basis of his survey, to be very effective ways of improving learning outcomes. Moreover, he noted that feedback became more effective the more information it carried.

Of all the studies we looked at, we could find very little evidence that negative feedback directed towards behaviour had any real effect on behaviour in the classroom. In practice, negative feedback on its own merely tells the pupil what not to do rather than what to do. Evidence we gathered in our study of very difficult pupils (Swinson and Knight, 2007) showed exactly this: high rates of negative feedback were associated with poorly behaved classes. If negative feedback worked, we would expect conformity and engaged pupils. We surmise that if teachers use only negative feedback as a means of directing a class, the more it is used, the less effective it becomes and the more the pupils become switched off.

As far as pupils' work is concerned, there is no doubt that positive feedback is extremely beneficial in boosting the amount of work completed and the quality of the work produced. Negative feedback, unless accompanied by more information to help the pupil understand what is expected, i.e. a redefining of the learning goal, has limited effect.

We have demonstrated in earlier chapters that using positive feedback directed towards specific behavioural goals is an effective strategy to use in order to achieve a well-run classroom. It would, however, be extremely naive to suggest that that is all that is needed to achieve a perfectly behaved class. Clearly, there will be times when pupils misbehave and have to be checked. The key to any successful intervention, as we have demonstrated earlier, is not the negative feedback itself, but the redirection that follows it. Lee Canter (Canter and Canter, 1992) advised: 'Never ignore disruptive behaviour.' He defined disruptive behaviour as behaviour that stops both class and individual from learning. This will include shouting out, talking to others, walking around the room and more serious disruption that will include name calling, refusal to follow the teacher instructions, open defiance and even fighting. These last incidents are rare in most schools, but they do happen and, as Canter advises, all teachers need a strategy for dealing with them if and when they arise.

Conclusion

As we have emphasised earlier in the text, the delivery of feedback in an appropriate manner is the key to successful teaching. In the previous sections, we have highlighted some of the important features that we feel teachers need to take note of and to adapt into their teaching repertoires. Good teachers are never completely satisfied with their performance, neither will they ever feel that they have got the balance exactly right, but we hope our comments will reinforce the central message of this book that it is the positive aspects of teacher feedback that all teachers need to concentrate on. All research both in the classroom, and with adults at work, in sports science, in health studies and, indeed, evolution itself shows that positive feedback increases confidence, emotional well-being, good health, enjoyment, diversity and creativity. Therefore we have every confidence in saying that no matter how difficult a child may appear both in terms of learning and behaviour, it is by looking for opportunities to praise him or her and by accentuating positive aspects of conduct that we can turn such children around. This is just as true for the individual child as it is for the very challenging class.

Comment/activity

At this point, you might be curious about the amounts of positive and negative feedback you yourself give to academic and social behaviour. If you haven't done so already, you could get a rough idea of the relative amounts if you just note each instance during a couple of short periods in your lessons. Alternatively, if you have a classroom assistant you could arrange to be observed more thoroughly. If you have difficulty deciding how to differentiate between academic and social behaviours you might find the following definitions we have used to be helpful:

- *Academic behaviour*: normal curriculum behaviours, reading, writing, listening, answering questions, i.e. performing prescribed activities.
- *Social behaviour*: behaviours indicative of classroom manners, following classroom rules and routines, e.g. settling down to work quietly, remaining seated when appropriate, putting hand up in answer to a general question to the class, lining up in an orderly manner when requested. They also include the converse behaviours of not settling down to work quietly, not remaining seated when appropriate, etc.

Comparing your results with those of the teachers in the tables in Chapter 2 should be of considerable interest to you, particularly when you reflect on the possible implications of the scores.

Chapter 9

A research basis

In the preceding chapters, there have been occasional references to relevant features of research, sometimes giving brief explanations of particular features of an investigation, but, in general, the references have been largely concerned with ways in which teachers can conduct investigations in their own classrooms without having to invest too much time and energy in setting up well-controlled investigations. It is, however, quite possible, given appropriate time for planning, for teachers to set up well-controlled investigations in their own classrooms, the results of which would be well worthy of publication in an academic journal. In this chapter, we aim to give you the necessary information to be able to undertake such a project. Less ambitious readers should find that reading through the chapter helps put our previous research comments into a more complete context.

The notion of a well-controlled investigation may be best illustrated by examining an early piece of research conducted and reported by the second author (Harrop, 1978). With hindsight, and with subsequent progress in experimental methods, it contains a number of features that can be profitably explored here. The work was undertaken, in collaboration with the author, by a teacher of some 10 years' experience, who had three particularly disruptive boys aged 14 to 15 in his class of boys and girls. The class was in a special school for pupils with learning difficulties and was taught by the same teacher for most of the day. The teacher, who had read a good deal about the success of some of the early investigations using positive psychology, was interested in finding out to what extent treating the difficult behaviour of one pupil would influence the behaviour of others in the class.

Briefly, the investigation unfolded and was reported as follows. The teacher described the disruptive behaviour of all three boys in terms of their being out of their seats, talking, blurting out and not paying attention. He defined these behaviours in what was considered to be easily observable terms. A student teacher acted as the primary observer and was seated as unobtrusively as possible at the back of the classroom. Since the class was quite accustomed to having student teachers in the room, it was assumed that the presence of the observer would create little disturbance.

Observations took place over several weeks, twice a week, but recording only took place for sessions of 21 minutes when the pupils were meant to be working at their desks. For the first six sessions, the observer practised recording using the teacher's definitions and consulted the teacher after each session to resolve any ambiguities in the definitions of behaviour and to develop observation categories. For the final three sessions, the teacher also observed the pupils' behaviour. In order to synchronise recording times, both the observer and the teacher took their timing from a classroom clock, complete with second hand, placed where each could conveniently see it. For the last of the six sessions, the agreement between the teacher and the observer was 86 per cent (the method of calculation follows later). After these six sessions, the final definitions of the behaviours were set out. These were:

1   Gross motor behaviour: getting out of seat, walking or running around the room without permission.
2   Talking: having a conversation with, or talking to, another pupil.
3   Blurting out: answering a question when not asked to do so, laughing, coughing loudly, making comments.
4   Not attending and disobeying, daydreaming, watching other pupils working, ignoring the teacher's directions or questions.

The observations were conducted on a rotational basis. In each 21-minute observation session one minute was spent observing Tom, one minute observing Dick and one minute observing Harry and so on (these are not, of course, their real names). In each minute the first 15 seconds was used for direct observation and the next 45 seconds were for recording and looking about the class generally so as to avoid making it obvious whose behaviour was being recorded. Each pupil was therefore observed for seven minutes per session. A record sheet for each pupil was constructed as shown in Table 9.1.

In the example given, it is seen that the pupil talked during the second and third 15-second intervals, showed non-attending/disobeying behaviour during the fifth interval and showed gross motor behaviour during the sixth and seventh intervals.

When the teacher recorded at the same times as the observer, the percentage agreement between the teacher and the observer was calculated based on intervals scored using the formula:

$$\text{Percentage agreement} = \frac{\text{Number of agreements}}{\text{Numbers of agreements} + \text{disagreements}} \times 100$$

An agreement was defined as an interval in which both teacher and observer noted the same (inappropriate) behaviour(s) occurring. Conversely, a disagreement was an interval in which the teacher and the observer did not see the same behaviour(s) occurring, so that, for example, if the observer recorded two different behaviours occurring in an interval (perhaps talking and gross motor) and the teacher recorded only one of those behaviours, the interval would be scored as a disagreement.

Table 9.1 Example record sheet for one observation session for one pupil

Gross motor behaviour						/	/
Talking		/	/				
Blurting out							
Not attending/disobeying					/		
Observation number	1	2	3	4	5	6	7

The agreement level of 86 per cent obtained between the recordings of the observer and teacher was regarded as good evidence that the categories of behaviour to be observed had been sufficiently defined.

The two main phases of the investigation

The baseline phase

To establish a baseline, the teacher continued to teach in his normal manner during four weeks and the behaviours were recorded by the observer for a further eight sessions, two per week. The teacher also recorded the pupils' behaviour during two of those observation sessions. After the baseline, one of the pupils, Tom, was selected for the intervention by, literally, 'drawing straws'.

The intervention phase

Because of the severity of Tom's inappropriate behaviour and because the teacher had previously had no success in improving Tom's behaviour, either by altering the curriculum or by the use of approval/attention to appropriate behaviour combined with an emphasis on rules, he decided that it was necessary to embark on more intrusive measures. He drew up a contract that specified clearly what Tom needed to do to qualify for some of the school activities that the pupils seemed to enjoy. For example, during language lessons, Tom had to produce at least 150 written words or answer 10 questions from a comprehension book and during maths lessons, he had to complete 15 sums or 10 problems in order to be allowed to play badminton at lunchtime on Mondays and Thursdays (an activity he was known to enjoy). If he was late for school, he had to make up for any work missed before he could play badminton. Tom readily agreed the contract. The teacher did not divulge the contract to other pupils.

Additionally, the teacher decided to increase the approval he gave to Tom when he behaved in an appropriate manner and to seek to give him pleasing tasks whenever his behaviour was particularly good. He also agreed to minimise his attention to Tom when he behaved inappropriately.

At the start of the intervention phase, the teacher devoted a lesson to discussing the classroom rules with the class, emphasising the undesirability of moving around the room when not working, talking, blurting out, etc. The intervention phase continued for five weeks, observations being made by the observer during 10 sessions and by the teacher during two of those sessions.

Results

The results showed that the mean number of intervals in which inappropriate behaviour was recorded for each pupil had diminished, as Table 9.2 shows.

The teacher recorded at the same time as the observer for sessions 3 and 4 in the baseline and 13 and 15 during the treatment phase. The average level of agreement between teacher and observer was 87 per cent.

While the average number of inappropriate incidents had diminished, it is possible that the overall time spent in inappropriate behaviour had not diminished, since there was no

Table 9.2 Mean number of intervals of inappropriate behaviour per observation session

	Baseline phase	Intervention phase
Tom	2.88	1.90
Dick	4.83	3.50
Harry	3.50	2.75

measure of the duration of the each incident. In the report, however, it was stated that both the teacher and the observer felt that there was no difference in the average length of the incidents in each phase of the investigation. As a consequence, it was concluded that treating and reducing the level of inappropriate behaviour of one pupil had had a beneficial effect not only on the one treated but also on the other two untreated pupils in the class.

An exploration of some of the features of the investigation

Key features worth exploring include defining behaviours in order to set up categories for observation, deciding when observations should be made, setting up a contract, the method of recording behaviour, the method of calculating observer agreement, the designs of investigations and the presentation and interpretation of the results.

Defining behaviours

The teacher described the disruptive behaviour of the three pupils and, because of his previous interest in earlier investigations, he was concerned to translate the behaviour of the pupils into observational terms. At that point it became the task of the observer to test out how useful these observational terms were and to develop from them some precise definitions of categories of behaviour that she felt she could accurately record. She then practised for three sessions, starting with the teacher's initial definitions, consulting him after each session and where necessary amending her definitions. Then she had the teacher record at the same time as her until she reached the level of 86 per cent agreement between the two sets of recordings. At that time it seemed to be universally accepted that anything over 80 per cent agreement was a good level to attain (see Harrop, 1983: p.66). The categories to be observed having been established, the investigation was begun with baseline observations.

(Note that it is essential that some independent checks are made from time to time on a single observer since, without such checks, we have no evidence of the observer's accuracy in recording.)

It is also worth mentioning here that time spent in refining categories for observation before the main phases of an investigation can have the additional benefit of allowing the pupils to become habituated to the presence of an observer in the class before the main parts of an investigation begin.

Deciding when observations should be made

Observations were made in the investigation for sessions of 21 minutes when the pupils were meant to be working at their desks. That was the teacher's decision, since that was when the pupils seemed to indulge in most of their inappropriate behaviour. That arrangement also helped ensure that when we compared baseline recordings with recordings taken during the intervention phase, we would be comparing like with like.

In other investigations, whole lessons have been used for observations. In one that you have already met in this volume, the numeracy hour was selected to fit the aim of the investigation (Chalk and Bizo, 2004).

Setting up a contract

Using a contract with a pupil is a strong intervention that should only be used if, as in this case, less intrusive measures have been unsuccessful. The main reason for that is that after the contract has brought about an improvement in the pupils concerned, the next stage is that the pupils should learn to behave as other pupils do, under the same conditions of feedback from the teacher, since, inevitably, the pupil will move on to other teachers. Consequently, a teacher needs to plan how to 'fade out' a contract once the appropriate behaviour has been established. Fortunately, circumstances can often help in that process, as the case of 'Bob' outlined in Chapter 1 illustrates.

With Tom, the reader will have noted that the contract was not the sole positive measure used. The use of teacher approval and the giving of pleasing tasks were part of the intervention from the start in order to help in an eventual fading out of the contract. In practice, what usually happens is that pupils' work improves and brings with it more approval. Very often the pupils who need such help have previously had little approval for their school work so that gaining approval for school work begins to act as a reward for them.

Finally, let us stress that making a contract with a pupil *before* less intrusive measures have been tried is akin to using a sledgehammer to crack a nut.

The method of interpreting and recording behaviour

The report of the investigation gave as its measure of success the statement that the average number of instances of inappropriate behaviour diminished. In retrospect, that was not the most useful way of presenting the results of the intervention. If we bear in mind the fact that inappropriate behaviour can increase immediately following an intervention, prior to decreasing, as in the case of Mavis recounted in Chapter 1, then average behaviour is not a useful measure of success. Moreover, it may take a while for the impact of an intervention to take effect, so that a more logical way of measuring success in interpreting results is to compare the level of the inappropriate behaviour at the end of the intervention phase with the baseline level.

The reader may have noted that while care was taken to define the inappropriate behaviour into four different categories, the results, as reported, did not differentiate between the four categories, which means that a good deal of information was lost and should have been reported. In fact, when the aim of the investigation is carefully considered there was little need to differentiate the inappropriate behaviour into different categories. It has to be admitted that that flaw was not noticed at the time.

If we turn our attention to the method of recording, we see that direct observations were made in the first 15 seconds of each interval of 1-minute duration. If an instance of behaviour occurred in the first 15 seconds, the interval was scored and the other 45 seconds were used for looking about the classroom. As was mentioned earlier, that meant that there was no measure of the duration of each instance of inappropriate behaviour. Since three pupils were observed in turn, each pupil had only 15 seconds' direct observation every three minutes and since each observation session took place for 21 minutes, each pupil was directly observed for 105 seconds (15 x 7) during each observation session. That was a relatively small sample of the behaviour of each of the three pupils. On the positive side, the observer had a good deal of time both to look about the classroom, so disguising her task, and to jot down her recordings.

With hindsight and the benefit of having conducted a number of similar investigations in the intervening years, we can indicate the way in which the method of observation could have been improved. First, however, it seems appropriate here to give a brief survey of commonly used methods of observation.

Methods of systematic observation

There are four methods of systematic observation that are generally used. Which method is selected depends on the observation task.

Frequency counting

In this method, the number of times an instance of behaviour occurs is counted. A good example is seen in the case of Tom, described in the opening chapter, in which his teacher, who was concerned about his 'pushing into the line,' used frequency counting to measure instances of the behaviour.

Duration recording

In this method, the total time spent in performing a behaviour is recorded. For example, a teacher may record the total time a pupil spends out of her seat when she is meant to be at her desk working.

Both of these methods have important weaknesses in general use because neither takes account of the information that the other one could obtain. Observing the frequency of a behaviour takes no account of the duration of individual acts and vice versa. Trying to observe both the frequency and the duration of behaviour is a task that is very difficult to carry out and one that makes the observer extremely narrowly focused. For those reasons and because observers typically want to observe more than one behaviour in a classroom, a method of time sampling is most often used in research. The two most commonly used of such methods are momentary time sampling and partial interval recording. Unlike the previous two methods, these are not methods a teacher could use while conducting lessons.

Momentary time sampling (MTS)

In this method, an observer records behaviour as occurring only if it occurs at a predetermined instant. For example, a pupil's on-task behaviour might be observed using MTS at 10 seconds. That means he would be watched by the observer and every 10th second the observer would record whether he was on-task or not at that instant. Provided the pupil was on task for long periods of time during the observation session, the MTS record would allow an accurate calculation of the total duration of the pupil's on-task behaviour.

(MTS is sometimes also known as 'instantaneous recording'.)

Partial interval recording (PIR)

Here, an observer watches a pupil for an interval of time and ticks off the interval if the behaviour occurs for any part of the interval. A teacher might use PIR in 10 second-intervals for observing a pupil who occasionally 'shouts out' in class. If the observation intervals followed one another the teacher wouldn't miss recording any of the pupil's shouting out behaviour. That gives the method an advantage over MTS. The drawback is that when examining the record afterwards the teacher would not know how many instances of 'shouting out' occurred or for how long 'shouting out' was taking place. (PIR is sometimes known as one zero recording.)

It is easy to appreciate how these two methods of time-sampling behaviour are applied but a few moments of reflection are needed to understand their inherent strengths and weaknesses. MTS, if done as frequently as every 10th second, can be quite a difficult vigilance task for an observer and it misses nine out of every 10 seconds. PIR used at its most intensive could involve using 10-second intervals following on from each other directly with the observer recording every interval in which a behaviour occurred. Done that way, PIR should not miss any occurrence of behaviour. Scoring intervals, however, means that an estimate of the duration for which a behaviour occurs cannot be calculated since an interval is scored whenever the behaviour occurs during the interval. MTS, although taking only a small sample of the behaviour occurring, does allow the duration to be calculated. For example, consider a 30-minute observation period of pupil 'on-task' behaviour with MTS every 10 seconds, so that 180 observations are taken. If the behaviour is recorded as having occurred 170 times it is quite reasonable to conclude that the behaviour occurred for 17/18 of the lesson, or 28 minutes 20 seconds of the 30 minutes. By way of contrast, had the behaviour only been recorded as occurring in 10 of the 180 observations then the data would be less likely to give a good estimate of duration unless, of course, those recordings were the result of one relatively long bout of behaviour.

As a consequence of such considerations, an observer using time sampling, who aims to record a number of behaviours at the same time, needs to make a careful choice of method. To simplify matters, if the behaviours to be recorded take place for relatively long periods of time, or for long bouts, then MTS is better than PIR. If behaviours are short and infrequent, then PIR is better, particularly if the aim is to reduce or increase behaviours, since research has shown that PIR is more sensitive than MTS to changes in rates and durations of behaviours. For further details, the reader might like to consult the work of Harrop et al. (1990).

In the investigation recounted earlier, the number of intervals in which inappropriate behaviour was recorded varied from a maximum of 4.83 to a minimum of 1.90 (see Table 9.2.). Unfortunately, we don't know for how long the inappropriate behaviour occurred during each interval so it would be rash to assume that the inappropriate behaviour was occurring for a large proportion of the recording time. Consequently, it looks as though it would be best to stay with PIR, which was the method employed. However, recording only for 15 seconds in every minute seems rather wasteful. It should be quite possible to record behaviour occurring for 15 seconds in every 30 seconds. That would still give the observer time to look around the class and it would double the number of observations made.

Observer agreement

As was noted earlier, more than one observer needs to be in operation, at least for part of the observation period, so that levels of agreement can be calculated if recordings are to be taken seriously. The calculation of observer agreement, however, is no simple task, neither is its interpretation.

Frequency counting and duration recording

In the case of an investigation using a frequency count or duration recording, the calculation itself is very simple.

For frequency counting, percentage observer agreement is calculated by dividing the smaller frequency obtained by the larger and multiplying the fraction by 100. As an illustration, if one observer records a behaviour as occurring 25 times in an observation session and the other records it as occurring 20 times then observer agreement is 80 per cent.

For duration recording, the calculation is similar. The smaller duration recorded is divided by the larger and the resulting fraction is multiplied by 100 to give the percentage agreement.

These percentages, however, are not very trustworthy, since even when 100 per cent agreement is obtained it doesn't necessarily mean that both observers see the same behaviours occurring at the same times. They might, for example, both record 20 instances of a behaviour occurring with no guarantee that they saw the same 20 instances.

Momentary time sampling and partial interval recording

For MTS and PIR, observer agreement can be calculated in the same way, on specific instances or intervals, which means that the observers are seeing the same behaviours occurring at the same time/during the same interval – which is a more rigorous way of looking at agreement.

For both MTS and PIR, percentage agreement is calculated by dividing the number of agreements by the total number of observations and multiplying by 100.

That sounds straightforward until you realise that there are different ways of deciding what constitutes an agreement. Examine the record sheet in Table 9.3, which shows the results obtained from two observers using partial interval recording.

Table 9.3 Record sheet of two observers who recorded whether a pupil was on-task (1) or off-task (0) for 10 intervals

Interval	1	2	3	4	5	6	7	8	9	10
Observer 1	1	1	1	1	0	0	0	0	1	0
Observer 2	1	1	0	1	1	0	1	0	1	0

By looking at the agreement between the two observers you might conclude that the observers agreed on the occurrence of the behaviour in four of seven intervals, giving 57 per cent observer agreement, if you only considered intervals in which the behaviour was seen as occurring, which was the method used in the investigation recounted.

Alternatively, however, you might see agreement as occurring for seven of the ten intervals, i.e. 70 per cent of the observation time, if you included intervals in which both observers agreed that the behaviour did not occur.

Which is the most appropriate measure of observer agreement? Before resolving that complication, look at Table 9.4, which shows a likely (one hopes) result from two observers recording pupil 'on-task' behaviour.

Using the two methods examined here, observer agreement would occur in either seven of nine intervals or in eight out of ten intervals, respectively, giving percentage agreement figures of either 78 per cent or 80 per cent. Both are reasonably high levels of agreement and, as mentioned before, texts used to recommend that investigators aim for at least 80 per cent agreement between observers, so that the former would have been seen to be too low and the latter would have been seen to be just satisfactory.

To avoid such complications, assume, as do most investigators, that an agreement occurs when both observers record the behaviour as occurring at the same time/ interval *and* when both observers record the behaviour as not occurring at the same time/interval. This is the most commonly used method at present.

Most investigators used to content themselves with that method of calculation and it was common to assert that observer agreement of 80 per cent or more was good evidence that observations were 'reliable'. More recently, however, it has become obvious to some of the more mathematically inclined investigators that if a behaviour is occurring either nearly all the time or, conversely, very seldom then observer agreement is likely to be very high by sheer chance alone. The implication of that is that it is very easy to get percentage agreement of 80 per cent or above if you are observing either a very frequently occurring behaviour or a rarely occurring behaviour. If, for example, two independent observers were recording a behaviour that was nearly always occurring, say 'pupil on-task behaviour in a well-ordered class, it would be very difficult to obtain a low percentage agreement.

As an illustration, consider the case when a behaviour is occurring 90 per cent of the time and two independent observers both record it as occurring in nine of the ten intervals observed. The percentage agreement between them purely by chance would be 82 per cent. Think about that! If you can't see why chance percentage agreement would be 82 per cent, don't worry (we have difficulty appreciating why that is so), a method for such calculations follows on. On the other hand, if the behaviour is

Table 9.4 More typical record sheet for two observers recording on-task behaviour (1) and off-task behaviour (0) for 10 intervals

Interval	1	2	3	4	5	6	7	8	9	10
Observer 1	1	1	1	1	1	1	1	0	1	1
Observer 2	1	1	1	1	0	0	1	0	1	1

occurring 50 per cent of the time and two observers record it as occurring in five of the ten intervals observed then the percentage agreement between them purely by chance would be 50 per cent. That means that the percentage agreement obtained between two observers is biased by chance and that chance agreement increases the more the pattern of behaviour observed departs from a situation of 50 per cent occurrence, 50 per cent non-occurrence. It was to eradicate this bias that Cohen (1960) invented the statistic commonly now known as Cohen's kappa.

Kappa

Kappa is a statistic that makes allowance for chance and yields a score between −1 and +1. A minus figure indicates observer agreement below chance, a positive figure indicates above chance. Just how high kappa needs to be is an open question, but a reasonable figure is +0.6 or above. An example of how kappa is calculated can be found in the appendix.

Designing investigations

There are a number of designs that can be used in investigations, most of which have already been met in early parts of this volume. The two that are very commonly met in educational research are the correlational design and the group design. Additional designs that are very appropriate for classroom investigations are the AB, the ABA and the multiple baseline. While the first two designs are used with groups of pupils the last three designs have the added benefit of being suitable for research aimed either at single pupils or with one class.

Correlational and group designs

A correlational design is used when an investigator seeks to find the relationship between two variables. In Chapter 2, for example, we described an investigation in which we measured various aspects of the feedback given by teachers to their pupils (variable 1) and at the same time we measured the on-task behaviour of the pupils (variable 2). In analysing the results, we were able to see a number of relationships, e.g. a positive relationship between positive feedback and on-task behaviour and a negative relationship between negative feedback and on-task behaviour. Moreover, as the appendix to Chapter 2 shows, we were able to assign numerical values to these relationships, the correlation between positive teacher verbal behaviour and pupil on-task behaviour being 0.31, whereas the correlation between negative teacher verbal behaviour and pupil on-task behaviour was −0.463. These results, while demonstrating a very strong link between teachers' verbal behaviour and pupils' on-task behaviour do not, however, allow us unequivocally to assert that the teachers' verbal behaviour caused the pupils' on-task behaviour, as we pointed out at the end of Chapter 2. We cannot rule out the alternative possibility that the pupils' on-task behaviour caused the teachers' verbal behaviour.

Group designs, unlike correlational designs, are concerned with *causes*. The investigation into improving reading attainment described in Chapter 6 is an example of a group study. In that investigation, the reading attainment levels of the pupils in two classes taught by the same teacher was measured. In one class (the experimental class), the pupils was given the promise of a favourable letter home if 'good progress' was made. In the other class (control class), the pupils were given no such promise. When the reading attainment of both classes was measured at the end of the investigation, the pupils who had been promised the favourable letter home showed far more gains in reading attainment than the other class. As a consequence, we were able to say that the promise of a favourable letter home had caused the large increase in reading attainment.

The purpose of the control class was to demonstrate what would have occurred without the promise of a letter home. Had there been no control class the increase in reading attainment achieved by the experimental class could have been ascribed to normal reading progress. Ideally, of course, control groups should be exactly the same as, or very similar in composition to, the experimental group. When the groups differ care has to be taken in setting up the investigation, as is noted in the 'research notes' in Chapter 6.

As previously noted, both of these designs are used traditionally in educational research and they have contributed in large measure to what we now know about class-room processes. They are, however, conducted with groups of pupils, so their findings are necessarily general rather than specific to individual pupils.

Interrupted time series designs

Despite the rather forbidding title, these designs are very simple in essence. Quite simply, a series of measurements is made before an intervention (which is the interruption) aimed at producing change is introduced. The investigations with individual pupils who are described in Chapter 1 and the one at the start of this chapter are all examples of one of the interrupted time series designs, the AB design. In each case, a series of observations of pupil behaviour was recorded as the 'baseline', an intervention was made and observations were continued to see whether the behaviour changed. There are three basic interrupted time series designs: the AB, the ABA and the multiple baseline. These designs were originally termed single subject designs because of their applicability with individuals. They can, however, equally be applied to groups of individuals, including school classes.

The AB design

The investigation recounted at the start of the chapter was based on an AB design. The design comprises two phases, the A phase being the baseline and the B representing the intervention (treatment) phase. The first phase is a measure of how the pupil normally behaves and the treatment phase shows the effects of whatever intervention is applied. Figure 9.1 shows the kind of recording that might be expected to be produced when an intervention reduces the inappropriate behaviour of a pupil.

The ABA design

This is an extension of the AB design. Following on from the baseline (A) phase and the intervention (B) phase, there follows a third phase (A), in which the intervention is

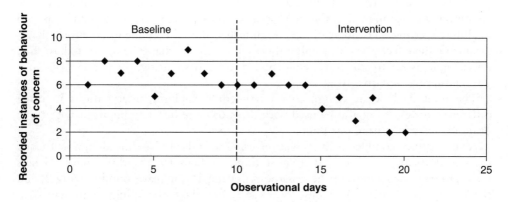

Figure 9.1 Day-by-day changes in a pupil's behaviour.

withdrawn. In other words, after the pupil has been treated by the intervention (in the B phase), the teacher reverts to their original way of treating the pupil. From an experimental point of view, the ABA design seems to be an improvement on the AB design since it appears to show more clearly that the intervention has had an effect. The logic is that if it is the intervention that has produced the improvement and not some other unidentifiable factor then that effect would be seen in the B phase and not in either of the A phases.

The ABA design is the one that was used in the early investigations undertaken in the USA. It isn't, however, a design we would use without very careful consideration, because, in practice it is not always desirable educationally to withdraw a treatment that is proving successful. From a theoretical point of view, the design is also suspect since it would be very difficult, if not impossible, for a teacher to revert to their original way of treating a pupil, if, for example, she had changed her verbal feedback and improved pupil on-task behaviour. By way of contrast, the design may well be appropriate when investigating the effectiveness of an innovative way of increasing academic performance. In Chapter 6, for example, the investigation into the effects of a self-management game on writing skills was examined using an extension of the ABA design, i.e. an ABAB design. The game was introduced after the baseline, removed and then reintroduced, and it was seen that output increased when the game was played and fell back when the game was removed, thus demonstrating the effectiveness of the game.

The multiple baseline design

The multiple baseline design is more complex than the other two. In its simplest form, it requires that in the first phase the investigator takes baseline observations of a pupil in three or more different settings, e.g. in class, in the playground and in the dining hall, and then introduces an intervention in each of the settings in sequence, so that for example, in the second phase, when the intervention (treatment) is applied in the first setting, the baseline conditions are maintained in the second and third settings. In the third phase, the treatment is applied in the first and second settings while baseline conditions are maintained in the third setting. In the final phase, treatment is applied in all three settings. The logic of the design is that, should it be the intervention that is producing the effect, the effect will only be observed on what is being treated, so that, for example, while treatment is being applied in the first setting, the pupil's behaviour should improve only in setting one, etc.

The multiple baseline design isn't restricted to applying interventions in three different settings; it can also be used with three or more different pupils or with three or more behaviours from one pupil.

A successfully conducted investigation using a multiple baseline design with one individual treated in three different settings, perhaps by awarding merit stickers for appropriate behaviour, in the classroom (setting 1), the playground (setting 2) and the dining hall (setting 3), would be expected to show recordings as presented in Figure 9.2, with behaviour in each setting improving only when the intervention is applied.

Like the ABA design, the multiple baseline design should demonstrate beyond reasonable doubt that it is the treatment and not some unknown factor that is causing the change in behaviour. Unlike the ABA design, the multiple baseline does not require any withdrawal of the intervention, which makes the design an attractive proposition for an investigator.

This design does need a word of warning, however, since, in practice, it can be difficult to set up a multiple baseline design, as became evident when the creative writing investigation described in Chapter 6 was conducted. Originally it had been intended that the investigation would follow a multiple baseline design, the three components of creativity, i.e. fluency, elaboration and flexibility, being the three behaviours to be focused on. However, when the teacher began the intervention phases by treating fluency alone, the results showed both of the other components began to improve as well as fluency. That meant the basis of the design was undermined, since it became evident that applying an intervention to any one of the behaviours would cause changes in the other behaviours. As a consequence, the investigation continued as a hybrid design, comprising three overlapping AB designs with a final A (removal of treatment) phase. In the final phase, when all treatment was removed, there was no improvement, but, importantly, no deterioration either, as might be expected when academic performance is concerned.

More generally, the interrupted time series designs are particularly suited for classroom investigations by a teacher since, unlike the more traditional correlational and group designs, they do not require large groups of pupils. They can be applied within one classroom and they do not require complex statistical analysis. They can be done with one pupil, or with one class of pupils, and the results of recording can be best interpreted by visual inspection of the recordings.

Concluding comments

We are aware that we have given a lot of detail on various aspects of the interrupted time series designs and that digesting such detail might be difficult prior to setting up an investigation. Consequently, we have supplied some guidelines to follow. More details can be found in an article by Harrop and Swinson (2007).

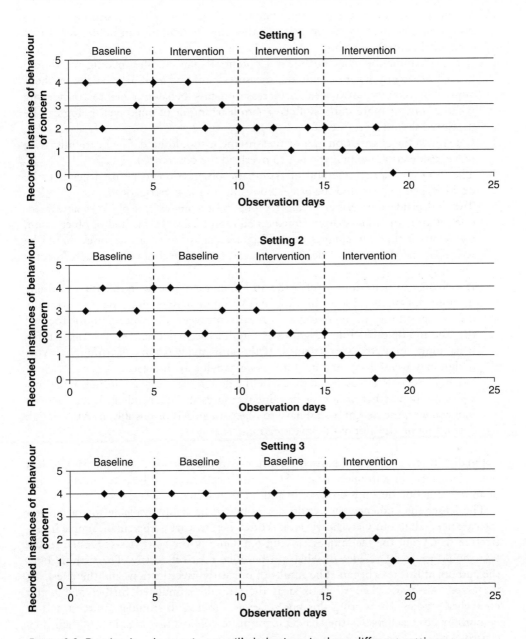

Figure 9.2 Day-by-day changes in a pupil's behaviour in three different settings.

1   Whatever the aim of the investigation, an examination of the classroom curriculum should be made to determine whether the curriculum can be delivered in a manner that meets the aim.

2   If that examination does not yield a potential solution, the investigator should consider carefully what behavioural measures could be used to meet the teacher's aims. The temptation to seek to increase on-task behaviour before considering whether one or more indices of classroom learning or of pupil well-being can be measured should be resisted.

3   Categories for observation and or measurement should be defined carefully with due consideration being given not to overload the observer(s).

4   The most appropriate method of systematic observation to be used needs to be decided, bearing in mind the projected results of the investigation.

5   Two independent observers should try out the categories and observer agreement calculated by the most stringent method allowed for by the method of observation, e.g. kappa if time sampling is used. If agreement is low, the categories should be redefined and the process repeated until a satisfactory level of observer agreement is obtained.

6   If a change in behaviour level is the aim it may be best to start with a multiple baseline design, because unlike the ABA design it does not have the ethically dubious possibility of removing a successful intervention. A limitation is the fact that the multiple baseline design does require the measurement of at least three behaviours, individuals or settings. If the aim involves pupil learning, an ABA design may well be appropriate, for reasons previously discussed.

7   When it is decided to use a multiple baseline design the initial recordings will show very rapidly whether or not the baseline measures are independent. If they are not independent, the design would have to revert to an AB or possibly an ABA design depending on the aim of the investigation.

Finally, it needs to be emphasised that, in classroom investigations, one should 'cut one's cloth according to one's means'. How much care needs to be taken in the design of an investigation depends on the aim and the prevailing circumstances.

The larger the audience the results are going to be made available to the greater the care needed. In our view, however, it is often best to start with a small, simple investigation to try out the techniques. Trying out some of the activities suggested in the text should give you an idea of what can be done relatively easily. That is how both the authors of this text began. The results of our early investigations and the questions we asked ourselves when we looked at their results stimulated further and better controlled studies. By writing this book, we are hoping to stimulate interest and to demonstrate to teachers that they have the means to conduct investigations in their own classrooms.

Appendix

This appendix is to help you with the calculation of kappa, so we start with the record sheets of two independent observers for the first 10 instances of 'inappropriate talking' in a classroom (1 = inappropriate talking, 0 = no inappropriate talking).

Table A9.1 Record sheet of two observers who recorded 'inappropriate talking' for 10 intervals

Instance	1	2	3	4	5	6	7	8	9	10
Observer 1	1	1	0	0	1	0	1	1	0	1
Observer 2	1	1	0	1	0	1	1	1	1	1

Stage 1. Observed agreement

Observed agreement = 60%   (6 agreements of 10 observations)

Stage 2. The calculation of percentage chance agreement

Percentage chance agreement is calculated by:

1   Multiplying the number of intervals/instances in which observer 1 records the behaviour as occurring by the number in which observer 2 records the behaviour as occurring.
2   Multiplying the number of intervals/instances in which observer 1 records the behaviour as not occurring by the number in which observer 2 records the behaviour as not occurring.
3   Adding the results of those multiplications together and dividing the result by the square of the number of intervals/instances observed.
4   The final figure obtained is multiplied by 100 to convert to a percentage.

Using the data in Table A9.1 the calculation is:

$$\text{Percentage agreement} = \frac{(6 \times 8)+(4 \times 2)}{100} \times 100$$
$$= 56\%$$

Note that the value of chance agreement is only slightly lower than that of observed agreement.

Stage 3. Kappa

Kappa = (observed agreement − chance agreement)/ (1 − chance agreement)
= (0.60 − 0.56)/(1 − 0.56)
= 0.04/0.44
= 0.09

This value of kappa is very small (which is what would be expected given that observer agreement is not very far above chance) and therefore little faith can be placed in the observations. Had kappa yielded a negative value, however, that would have meant that the observer agreement was even worse than chance.

Finally, there are some who criticise kappa as being itself a little erratic in its analysis of the results of recording (Harrop *et al.*, 1989), so it is a good idea to present raw data in a summarised form as shown here. If you examine Table A9.2, you will see it shows agreements on occurrences (5), agreement on non-occurrences (1) and disagreements (4). From these data, a reader can perform any calculations required. Be warned, it is not an easy table to read.

Again, looking at Table A9.2, you will see that all 10 recordings are accounted for. The 5 shows that there were five agreements on behaviour occurring, the 3 shows that observer 2 recorded three occurrences of the behaviour when observer 1 recorded non-occurrences, etc. Presenting data in this way gives any reader the opportunity of deciding on which, if any, statistic to apply.

Table A9.2 Raw data in summary form

	Observer 1: occurrences	*Observer 1: non-occurrences*
Observer 2: occurrences	5	3
Observer 2: non-occurrences	1	1

Critical comments and conclusions

In this final chapter, we will first look at some of the questions and criticisms that are commonly raised about the use of the positive approach in classrooms. We have tried to put these questions in a logical sequence but that hasn't always been possible, so we apologise if the early part of the chapter seems a little fragmented.

Does applying positive psychology work equally well in the infant, primary and secondary school?

We can see why that question is posed since there are evident differences in the three kinds of school along a number of dimensions, most obviously in the age of the pupils, the school organisation and the amount of daily contact teachers have with individual pupils. The simple answer to the question, however, in our opinion, is that the principles are equally applicable in the three kinds of school, although the way in which these principles are applied will necessarily vary.

The basic principle underlying the positive approach is that of reward. We know that the vast majority of children and young people like to be told positive things about themselves, they like to be praised. It makes them feel good about themselves and it gives them information that what they are doing is the right thing. Behaviour that is rewarded tends to be maintained or increased. If a pupil continually chats with another pupil, ignoring the teacher who is talking to the class, it is evident that the pupil is being rewarded for that talking behaviour and is not being rewarded for listening to the teacher. A pupil who keeps behaving inappropriately in class, despite the teacher's frequent disapproval, may well be being rewarded by the teacher's attention as well as by the attention of other pupils.

The principle of rewarding behaviour the teacher wants and removing rewards from unwanted behaviour remains constant across the various levels of schooling. Usually, in our experience, teachers' positive feedback (approval) is sufficient with young children and for many children at secondary level. Approval from teachers whom the pupils like and respect is likely to be rewarding but approval from certain other teachers may not be received in the same way. Pupils tend to respect teachers who keep good order and let them get on with the work (see Raymond, 1987). We are well aware that the results of our own investigation, when we gave teachers a short course that raised their approval levels, showed teachers from all three levels achieving the same success with their pupils. That certainly demonstrated that the approach worked equally across the levels but it needs to be borne in mind that we were dealing with volunteer teachers, whose approval was likely to be rewarding to their pupils.

In Chapter 2, we described an investigation in which we looked at various aspects of verbal feedback given by teachers to their pupils. It will have been noted that there were some striking similarities between the three levels of schooling when we examined the data for positive and negative feedback to academic and social behaviour (Table 2.2). It should, however, be mentioned that listening to the tape recordings of the teachers it was noticeable there were clear differences in what was actually said as feedback and in the tone of voice used at the different levels. Moreover, when we looked more closely at that feedback, we noted, among other findings, that infants were given considerably more description with negative feedback than juniors and secondary pupils and that secondary teachers used pupils' names with negative feedback much less than did infant and junior school teachers. These findings are readily explicable in terms of the age of the pupils and the frequency with which individual pupils are taught at the various levels. The point we want to emphasise here, however, is that although the approach is equally applicable at all three levels there are undoubtedly minor variations within the practice.

The school structure also plays a part in that secondary schools tend to have a stronger departmental structure than primary schools. You may recall that in the investigation recounted in Chapter 3, we noted that the secondary school teachers had time to discuss what they were doing with others in their department. Compared with primary schools, secondary schools usually have that extra layer of organisation, and if teachers in a department are to work in harmony, it is important that they keep their colleagues informed of any changes in their teaching.

There is also the fact that secondary school teachers see their pupils less frequently than their infant and junior school counterparts. Some classes may be taught once a day, others only once or twice a week. Consequently, it takes longer for secondary school teachers to get to know their pupils and for their pupils to get to know them. That should not, however, prevent them from using the same general principles of approval for appropriate behaviour and minimising attention to inappropriate behaviour in their teaching. If, however, they wish to improve the behaviour of a particular pupil, a group of pupils or a whole class then the process is likely to take longer than if they were teaching in a primary school.

Identifying pupils whose inappropriate behaviours are at such levels that they would benefit from the application of positive psychology is a less complicated task for primary school teachers than for secondary school teachers because they are normally with the pupils for most of each day. Secondary school teachers, who each see many more pupils for much less time than their primary school counterparts, may well take a long time to notice such pupils. As a specific example, we have in mind a teacher on one of our early in-service courses who identified a pupil in her junior school class who seldom communicated. He would only give single word replies if spoken to, he never initiated a conversation and would never raise his hand to ask for assistance or ask a question. For this pupil, the inappropriate behaviour was, somewhat paradoxically, a lack of the behaviour of communication. It was certainly inappropriate, however, because it was interfering with his own learning. While some of the teachers on the course jokingly said that they wished all their pupils were like that, the selection of this pupil came as a valuable addition to the course and the realisation that when we think of inappropriate pupil behaviour we tend to focus on those pupils who disturb others in the class. Moreover, when we thought back to our own classroom teaching experiences in secondary schools we realised that we had indeed been guilty of ignoring such pupils. Had we been teaching in a primary school, we would have been less likely to miss them because we would have been seeing them for much longer periods of time. Although that is a rather extreme example we hope it illustrates the fact that identification of pupils who need help is more straightforward in the primary school than in the secondary school. For more information on such a case, see Harrop (1977).

To reiterate our earlier comment, in our view applying the principles of positive psychology can work equally well in infant, junior and secondary schools but the practice differs in some respects according to circumstances.

I don't see how applying positive psychology in the classroom is any different from what good teachers normally do

We have to agree with that comment in general terms. Good teachers apply positive psychology in the classrooms without having ever heard the term. They make positive comments to their pupils for appropriate behaviour, they give disapproval for inappropriate behaviour, describing what is inappropriate and explaining what the pupil ought to be doing, and so on. That, of course, is only part of what good teachers do. They have a good grasp of the curriculum material that they are able to present in a way that rewards pupils; they have an understanding of children's thinking so that they can tailor the work to the pupils' cognitive level; they have a good understanding of the diversity of the abilities and personalities of their pupils, etc.

Over the years we have worked with many teachers in their schools and on in-service courses. What has struck us forcibly is that the teachers who volunteer to try out the techniques are almost invariably good teachers. When we have worked with all the staff at a school we have noticed that it is the good teachers who understand our message more quickly than the rest and quickly apply our techniques. Average teachers also improve to become good teachers and even teachers who are slow to understand our message eventually discover that when they apply positive techniques their classes improve. A brief anecdote may illustrate the point about good teachers volunteering. Many years ago one of us went into a school at the request of a teacher to help him improve the behaviour of one of his pupils. The head teacher of the school, when consulted about the work, professed amazement that the teacher should seek help, since, in his opinion, the teacher was so proficient that he needed none.

Nevertheless, the study went ahead and the pupil's behaviour was improved. The lesson we learned from that, and from subsequent work with teachers, is that good teachers can improve. We don't want to speculate too much about how that occurs but it seems evident that, their attention becomes focused on their good practice, which they are then able to extend. If we focus for a moment on the training course described in Chapter 3, we can see that the elements used in the course are all aspects of good practice in schools. What applying positive psychology seems to be doing is to sensitise teachers to what is effective and what is not.

In answer to the question put, therefore, we can sum up by saying that we agree that good teachers do use the practices that positive psychology advocates but that even good teachers can improve their applications.

There is an old saying that teachers are born not made. Are you saying that the use of positive psychology can turn anyone into a good teacher?

It is certainly true that some entrants to teaching have in-built advantages. From a positive psychology viewpoint, this is most evident during first teaching practices in those student teachers who stand out as having personalities that their pupils enjoy and respect. For want of a better word, the pupils seem to see them as charismatic. The pupils are usually eager to please such individuals and they will follow their instructions willingly. In positive psychology terms, these student teachers find it very easy to reward their pupils by their approval. As a consequence, the pupils respond positively to the student teachers and this positive pupil feedback rewards the teacher so that the whole tenor of the classroom becomes positive.

When these student teachers combine their natural rewarding value with a good knowledge of the curriculum, seeking to impart their material to their pupils in a way that is in itself rewarding to the pupils, outsiders looking at the teaching would be tempted to say that they are observing 'born teachers'. But, of course, they are not 'born' teachers because they have many other facets of good teaching to learn, such as, for example, appropriate ways of delivering the curriculum, developing an understanding of children's thinking etc., before they can achieve their teaching aims.

Coming back to the question posed, there is no doubt that individuals enter the teaching profession with a range of different characteristics, some being apparently more suited to teaching than others. The task of teacher training, both initial and in-service, is to build on what individuals possess and to help them achieve their full potential. No one, in our view, enters 'ready made'. When we consider all that teachers have to know in order to function well the role of positive psychology is relatively minor, but we would assert, very important. That assertion is made on the basis of the evidence presented in the earlier chapters, showing that when applied properly, positive psychology can have a strong impact on the way teachers respond to their pupils and, as a consequence, on the way in which the pupils respond to their teachers.

Thus lessons become mutually enjoyable and a reciprocal relationship is established. The pupils enjoy being taught by a positive teacher who rewards them for behaving well and getting on with the work. The teachers enjoy teaching the group because lessons are trouble free and they have the confidence to try more imaginative and exciting lessons. This type of lesson, in which everyone is engaged in the lesson and real learning is taking place, has been described by one of the leading exponents of positive psychology, Csikszentmihalyi (2002), as being in a state of 'flow'. Flow is a state where everything seems to be going right and the participants don't have to think about what to do next, they are so absorbed in the current.

Are there any dangers associated with teachers using the techniques associated with positive psychology in the classroom?

Yes, there are most certainly some dangers associated with the use of the techniques of positive psychology in the classroom. Perhaps the greatest danger is that teachers could use the techniques in the absence of an appropriate curriculum. In other words, teachers could be using the practices of positive psychology to give their pupils a poor or even misleading academic diet. The use of positive psychology is no more immune to misuse than such human advances as drugs, television and the internet. To try to ensure that abuse does not occur, any procedures used need to be discussed, to be open, publicised and scrutinised.

Another danger lies in the use of the principles by a teacher who has only an incomplete understanding. When we reported on our research, summarised in Chapter 3, in which we trained teachers to be more positive, numerous articles appeared in the press. In an attempt to catch the readers' attention, a number of journalists strayed well beyond the facts of what was done. Most gave the impression that it was praising pupils that caused their improved behaviour. They completely missed the point that it was approval selectively given to appropriate behaviour and not just indiscriminate praise that was the key. Any teacher who tried to improve pupils' behaviour by increasing praise or approval in an indiscriminate manner would be very unlikely to be successful and might well produce a deterioration in behaviour.

Despite the dangers of abuse, in fact *because* of these very dangers, it is important that teachers have a thorough understanding of the principles and procedures involved. Indeed, one way to protect against the abuse of positive psychology is for members of the teaching profession to be able to apply positive psychology expertly in appropriate situations for the advantage of their pupils, as we have shown in this book. It is teachers who over-rely on sanctions and admonishments who do the damage, not those who are positive.

Some of the procedures used by positive psychology seem to be based on bribing pupils to behave

When the straightforward procedures involving approval and disapproval and emphasising classroom rules do not improve pupils' behaviour, teachers have to look for more powerful rewards. That is when such features as contracts and allowing pupils to earn extra time in favoured lessons can come into play. Now, it is easy to see how making a contract with a pupil such that a certain amount of school work completed per lesson leads to the pupil's being allowed to play badminton in the school hall at lunchtime can be regarded as bribery, provided one doesn't look closely at what the word 'bribery' actually means.

A moment of reflection on how bribery operates should, however, help to dispel this interpretation. When bribes are given it is the intention of the bribers that they will gain advantages from the bribe. Bribes are not given in order to gain advantages for the person bribed. There is something pejorative about the word bribe but there is nothing pejorative about rewarding someone in order to help them to do something in their best interests. We don't say that teachers are bribed by receiving salaries for their work in school; neither should we say that children are bribed by being rewarded for working well in class.

Why should children who misbehave in class be given extra rewards when the other hard-working pupils do not get such rewards?

This is a criticism sometimes raised by teachers who feel that there is a certain injustice in giving special treatment to pupils who behave inappropriately. It stems, we think, from a view that the pupils involved are 'difficult children' and that the inappropriate behaviour is the pupils' fault, without appreciating that such pupils are really 'children with difficulties'. It is a view that can have the unfortunate consequence of stopping teachers from trying to help such pupils.

As former teachers, we know very well how easy it is to slip into that way of thinking and, in fact, we often use the term 'difficult children' ourselves when we really mean 'children with difficulties'. In our view, however, pupils who behave inappropriately in classrooms have learned to behave in that inappropriate way as a consequence of their previous learning environments. They have been rewarded for their inappropriate behaviour and not for their appropriate behaviour.

Our opinion is that it is the teachers' duty to help those pupils to learn to behave appropriately and this is best achieved by rewarding the pupils' appropriate behaviour and removing rewards from their inappropriate behaviour. With many pupils, that can be achieved through the teachers' use of positive feedback, but for some pupils stronger interventions are needed, at least initially.

How can we get children to behave appropriately in school when they are allowed to do as they please at home?

This question suggests that schools can have little influence on the behaviour of pupils and we can understand teachers who are exasperated by the behaviour of their pupils giving voice to such a question. Moreover, in our teaching careers, we have heard that question voiced much more strongly, by teachers who have gone into detail about how they think their pupils are chastised at home and contrasting that with mere 'telling off'.

There is, however, strong evidence to the contrary. If we observe pupils' behaviour in school, we see large differences in the way they behave with different teachers. That is particularly obvious in secondary schools where the same class is taught by a number of teachers each day. It is evident that there is considerable variation in the extent to which pupils behave appropriately for their teachers.

It may be more difficult for some pupils to learn appropriate behaviour in school than it is for others, because of what they have learned at home. Nevertheless, children do learn to discriminate between home and school and consequently they can learn to behave appropriately in school. The only children who cannot learn to behave appropriately in school are those who are in the wrong school setting. For all other children, to say that they cannot learn to behave appropriately because of their home environment is an abdication of teachers' responsibility.

If we reflect on how long pupils spend in schools, it seems very unlikely that schools don't have a strong influence. It was estimated by Michael Rutter and his colleagues that pupils spend 15,000 hours in school between the ages of 11 and 15, (Rutter *et al.*, 1979) and we presume a similar length of time in primary school. That surely gives long enough for pupils to differentiate between home and school.

What else does a teacher need to do in the classroom apart from giving positive feedback for appropriate behaviour and trying to minimise feedback for inappropriate behaviour?

A full answer to that question could fill several textbooks but we can at least answer by noting one feature that seems to us to be of prime importance. As we have mentioned earlier in the text, the curriculum is really at the heart of teaching. If every pupil in a class were engrossed, motivated and learning the material presented by the teacher, life in school would be a delight for all. The pupils would feel rewarded by working with the curriculum material and the teachers would feel rewarded by the pupils' obvious engagement with the material. Sadly, because of individual differences between the pupils, it is very difficult for a teacher to arrange such a situation. Nevertheless, presenting the curriculum in a way that enables as many pupils in the class as possible to learn while feeling rewarded by the material is what most teachers continually strive for.

Delivering the curriculum, however, isn't just a matter of presenting appropriate material to the pupils. It involves such functions as the way in which teachers talk to the pupils, the way they use questions, the way in which they respond to pupils' questions, their use of illustrations, experiments, the way in which pupils are seated and so on. Moreover, in order to perform these functions well, teachers also need a good understanding of their pupils' characteristics, which takes us into the realm of cognitive, personal and social development, as well as into such aspects as gender and ethnicity. To give advice on all of these and other relevant aspects of the teacher's role would be well beyond the scope of this text.

Shouldn't the applications of positive psychology be one of the main features of initial teacher training?

We have to give an unequivocal yes to that question. That response does, however, need to be tempered by the realisation that the training given to graduates during the PGCE year takes place in a very limited time and even the time devoted to education in BEd degree programmes is limited by many other demands. The teacher-in-training has a good deal of material to assimilate about the curriculum, about children, about classrooms and schools, etc., not to forget the time spent in schools on teaching practice. Nevertheless, we do feel that it is important that the teacher-in-training receives a good grounding in the principles of positive psychology.

We see, however, the applications of positive psychology as best suited to in-service training for teachers. We mentioned previously that our training courses have tended to attract good teachers and that in our view, based on the evidence, such courses have helped these teachers to become even better. There has been a lot of research into 'expertise in teaching' and the results have shown that expert teachers are far better at analysing the dynamics of classroom situations than are less expert teachers. It seems therefore likely to us that good teachers, because of their expertise, are able to analyse more carefully than others what is taking place in their classrooms and, as a consequence, they will be able to apply the principles of positive psychology to maximum advantage. This is not to say, of course, that only good teachers can benefit. It does, however, give support to the idea of making in-service courses the main focus for positive psychology training since it is serving teachers who will gain the most benefit from such courses.

Is it the teachers not the pupils who need to change their behaviour?

The simple answer to this question is yes. It is, we hope, clear from what we have written that in order for the pupils' to change their attitude, behaviour, learning, motivation or indeed feelings of self-worth, it is incumbent on teachers to change the way in which *they* respond to and engage with their pupils. Teachers cannot expect to bring about change in children without changing the way that they themselves behave. As the adults, it is up to teachers to take the lead.

It is far too easy for teachers to blame children or young people for being badly behaved or for being unmotivated. It is the responsibility of teachers to provide the structure and reinforcement in lessons to ensure good behaviour and to make lessons interesting so as to motivate their pupils. Incidentally, teachers aren't the only ones who tend to blame the pupils. Certainly politicians have been known to refer to 'out-of-control feral kids'. Others tend to be more subtle in their approach; social workers, psychiatrists and indeed even psychologists are prone to describe young people as 'disturbed', 'maladjusted' or 'socially disadvantaged'. The implication in such labels is the notion that such children are unteachable or at best difficult to teach and require specialist treatment. We hope we have demonstrated in this book that all children, no matter what label they are given, if dealt with in the right way, are capable of behaving well and learning.

A brief recapitulation of what positive psychology has to offer to teachers

The easiest way of highlighting what positive psychology has to offer is to look briefly at the seven chapters in this text that address applications in schools.

In Chapter 1, we set the scene. We described the origins of the positive psychology approach, moving from work with individual pupils to work with whole classes.

That was followed in Chapter 2 by a discussion of the results of our work with 50 teachers in which we found that there was a positive relationship between teachers' use of positive feedback and pupil on-task behaviour and a negative relationship between teachers' use of negative feedback and pupil on-task behaviour. We found that the teachers gave positive feedback predominantly to pupils' academic (school work) behaviour and predominantly negative feedback to pupils' social behaviour. Less than half of teachers' feedback carried a description of why feedback was given. Pupils' names were seldom used with positive feedback but were used more than four times as frequently with negative feedback. Around 30 per cent of negative feedback explained what the pupil ought to be doing (redirection). More positive than negative feedback was given to individuals while the reverse was the case for groups. In general, we found a remarkable similarity between teachers' verbal behaviour in all three types of school. Moreover, pupil mean on-task rates in the three types of school were extremely close, averaging around 80 per cent.

In Chapter 3, we gave an account of a half-day training programme during which 19 teachers were trained to alter the pattern of their verbal feedback to pupils in accordance with aspects of positive psychology. Observations of the teachers taken before and after training showed the teachers had been able to alter their verbal feedback, to become more positive and that their pupils' on-task behaviour had increased considerably following that alteration.

Chapter 4 was concerned with pupils of differing ability levels, race and gender, and with pupils who are especially difficult, i.e. those pupils for whom teachers' verbal behaviour seems to be insufficient to enable them to behave appropriately. We discussed more intrusive techniques. In particular, we discussed 'individual behaviour plans', 'fair pairs', 'on report', 'self-report', 'behavioural contracts' and 'motivational interviewing'.

In Chapter 5, we moved our focus from the individual and the class to that of the whole school. Here we gave an account of the successful use of positive psychology with the staff of a comprehensive school, the various stages leading to implementation and the evaluation being outlined. It was emphasised that the approach was not a straight application of techniques but rather that it emerged from considered consultation and was 'tailor-made' for that particular school.

Chapter 6 marked a departure from examining ways in which pupils' classroom behaviour could be improved to considering how teachers can use positive psychology to meet their learning objectives. Some examples, taken from the teaching of English and of mathematics were given as illustrations.

In Chapter 7, we looked at the way in which positive psychology can be applied to pupils' well-being. We considered how pupils' self-concepts might be influenced by applications of positive psychology together with a discussion of influences of teacher expectations on pupil expectations.

More generally, these first seven chapters were aimed at showing the breadth of applications that positive psychology has to offer teachers. Along one dimension, we looked at work first with individuals, then with classes, with specific groups of pupils within classes (ability levels, race, gender), and finally with schools. On another dimension, we considered work with pupils who had difficulties in ordinary classes and then with pupils who had more extreme difficulties. On yet another dimension, we looked first at how inappropriate classroom behaviour might be tackled, and later at how teachers can be helped to achieve their learning objectives and how pupils' well-being might be improved.

Chapters 8 and 9, which were not aimed directly at applications of positive psychology in schools, were concerned, respectively, with more theoretical issues and with how to conduct well-controlled investigations in schools using positive psychology.

We hope we have demonstrated the power of the positive psychological approach, while emphasising positive feedback. Benefits have been produced in many areas of life including employment, physical health, sport, emotional well-being, psychological health and in our specialist area of education. The approach has the capacity to change the lives of children for the good and, as we have seen, transform even the most difficult classes into ones that teachers enjoy teaching and in which children enjoy learning.

Where does positive psychology go from here?

From our point of view, we would like to see applications of positive psychology become more widespread in schools and the best way to achieve that is by introducing the principles during initial training and by the use of in-service training courses with serving teachers.

So far as investigative work is concerned, the reader will probably have gathered that those investigations that have so far been undertaken have sprung from the initiative of relatively few investigators, the present authors included. If we consider first the applications that we have written about in this text, it seems reasonable to conclude that so far a good deal of work has been done on improving the appropriate behaviour of pupils in normal classrooms. Considerably more work needs to be done however in a number of areas, in particular:

1   Further investigating approaches to be used with pupils who have relatively severe difficulties.
2   Working with whole schools.
3   Helping teachers achieve their learning objectives.
4   Increasing pupils' well-being.
5   Examining the relationship between classroom discipline and pupil learning.

   If we try to look beyond what we have covered in this text, there are five particular areas of investigation we see that haven't as yet, so far as we know, been systematically investigated. These are:

1   The written (or word-processed) feedback that teachers provide to their pupils on their work. The reader might recall one brief example, that of the teacher of creative writing (Chapter 6) who adjusted her feedback to make it what she considered to be more easily comprehended by her pupils.
2   The role of non-verbal feedback. This very important kind of feedback has not been researched in any depth, largely, we think, because of the difficulty involved in measuring non-verbal behaviour in such a way that investigators could feel confident about the accuracy of measurement.
3   The role of positive psychology in the use of information technology. With so many ways of communication opening up, there must be considerable scope for investigation. After all, the success of much modern media lies in their instant feedback.
4   Examining the role of other adults, particularly teaching assistants, in the classroom.
5   Involving parents in their children's education. We know from working in schools how difficult it is to open up dialogues with more than a few parents, as the low level of returns of questionnaires sent to parents demonstrates. The use of positive psychology to improve the involvement of parents in the education of their children is, we think, another very fruitful potential avenue of investigation.

Bibliography

Aaron, R. and Powell, G. (1982) Feedback practices as a function of teacher and pupil race. *Journal of Negro Education*, 51: 50–59.

Airasian, P. (1997) *Classroom Assessment* (3rd edn). New York: McGraw-Hill.

Alvidrez, J. and Weinstein, R.S. (1999) Early teacher perceptions and later student academic achievement. *Journal of Educational Psychology* 91: 732–746.

Anderson, G.C. (1985) *Performance Appraisal*, Glasgow: Strathclyde Business School.

Andrews, L. and Kozma, S. (1990) Increasing praise and altering its distribution. *Canadian Journal of Behaviour Science* 22(2): 110–120.

Apter, B., Arnold, C. and Swinson, J. (2010) A mass observation study of student and teacher behaviour in British primary classrooms. *Educational Psychology in Practice* 26(2): 151–171.

Bandura, A. (1977) *Social Learning Theory*. Englewood Cliffs, NJ: Prentice Hall.

Barnes, W. (1978) Student–teacher dyadic interaction in desegregated high school classrooms. *Western Journal of Black Studies* 2: 132–137.

Beady, C. and Hansell, S. (1981) Teacher race and expectations for student achievement. *American Educational Research Journal* 18: 191–206.

Beauman, R. and Wheldall, K. (2000) Teachers' use of approval and disapproval in classrooms. *Educational Psychology* 20(4): 431–446.

Becker, P. (1963) *Outsiders: Studies in the Sociology of Deviance*. New York: Free Press.

Bennett, S.N. (1976) *Teaching Styles and Pupil Progress*: London: Open Books.

Bennett, S.N. (1978) Recent research on teaching: a dream, a belief and a model. *Educational Psychology* 48: 127–147.

Berg, I. and Shilts, L. (2004) *Classroom Solutions: WWW Approach*. Milwaukee, WI: BFTC Press.

Berg, I. and Shilts, L. (2005) *Classroom Solutions: WWW Coaching*. Milwaukee, WI: BFTC Press.

Bijou, S.W. (1965) Experimental Studies of Child Behaviour, Normal and Deviant. In L. Kasner and L. Ullman (eds), *Research in Behaviour Modification*: New York: Holt, Rinehart & Winston.

Blyth, E. and Milner, J. (1996) Black Boys Excluded from School: Race or Masculinity Issues? In E. Blythe and J. Milner, *Exclusions from School: Interprofessional Issues for Policy and Practice*. London: Routledge.

Bolte, A., Goschke, T. and Kuhl, J. (2003) Emotion and intuition: effects of positive and negative mood on implicit judgments of semantic coherence. *Psychological Science* 14: 416–421.

Breen, M. and Littlejohn, A. (2000) *Classroom Decision Making: Negation and Process Syllabuses in Practice*. Cambridge: Cambridge University Press.

Brophy, J. (1981) Teacher praise: a functional analysis. *Review of Educational Research* S1: 5–32.

Brown, D. and Pedder, J. (1979). *Introduction to Psychotherapy*. London: Tavistock Publications.

Burden, R. (1998) Assessing children's perceptions of themselves as learners and problem solvers. *School Psychology International* 19: 291–305.

Burnett, P. (2002) Teacher praise and feedback and students' perceptions of the classroom environment. *Educational Psychology* 22(1): 1–16.

Byers, P. and Byers, H. (1972) Non-verbal Communication in the Education of Children. In C. Cazder, V. John and D. Hymes (eds) *Functions of Language in the Classroom*. New York: Teachers College.

Canter, L. and Canter, M. (1992) *Assertive Discipline: Positive Behaviour Management for Today's Classrooms*. Santa Monica, CA: Lee Canter Associates.

Chalk, K. and Bizo, K. (2004) Specific praise improves on-task behaviour and numeracy enjoyment: a study of year four pupils engaged in the numeracy hour. *Educational Psychology in Practice* 20(4): 335–351.

Charlton, T., Lovemore, T., Essex, C. and Crowie, B. (1995) Naturalistic rates of teacher approval and disapproval and on-task behaviour in first and middle school classrooms in St Helena. *Journal of Social Behaviour and Personality* 10: 817–826.

Clarricoates, K. (1980) The Importance of being Ernest . . . Emma . . . Tom . . . In M. Galton, L. Hargreaves, D. Wall, C. Comber and A. Pell, *Inside the Classroom: 20 Years On*. London: Routledge.

Cohen, J. (1960) A coefficient of agreement for nominal scales. *Educational and Psychological Measurement* 20: 37–46.

Cohen, J. (1993) *The World Tonight*, BBC Radio 4, 11 June.

Connolly, P. (1995) Racism, masculine peer-group relations and schooling of African/Caribbean infant boys. *British Journal of Sociology of Education* 16: 1–22.

Cooper, J.O., Heron, T.L. and Heward, W.L. (1987) *Applied Behaviour Analysis*. Columbus, OH: Merrill.

Cooper, P. and Upton, G. (1990) An ecosystemic approach to emotional and behavioural difficulties in school. *Educational Psychology* 10(4): 301–321.

Corabieth, C. and Korth, W. (1980) Teacher perceptions and teacher–student interactions in integrated classrooms. *Journal of Experimental Education* 48: 259–263.

Corrie, L. (1997) The interaction between teachers' knowledge and skills when managing a troublesome classroom behaviour. *Cambridge Journal of Education* 27(1): 93–105.

Croll, P. (1985) Teacher interaction with individual male and female pupils in junior-age classrooms. *Educational Research* 27(3): 220–230.

Csikszentmihalyi, M. (2002) *Flow: The Classic Work on How to Achieve Happiness*. London: Rider

Daniels, H. (2011) Exclusions from school and its consequences. *Psychological Science and Education* 1: 38–50.

Davidson, R., Kabat-Zinn, J., Schumacher, J., Rosenkranz, M., Miller, D., Santerelli, S. *et al.* (2003) Alteration in brain and immune function produced by mindfulness mediation. *Psychosomatic Medicine* 65: 564–570.

Davie, R. (1980) Behaviour problems in schools and school-based in-service training. In G. Upton and A. Gobell (eds), *Behaviour Problems in the Comprehensive School*. Cardiff: Faculty of Education, University College.

Davie, R. (1993) Assessing and understanding children's behaviour. In T. Charlton and K. David (eds), *Managing Misbehaviour in Schools*. London: Routledge.

Davie, R. and Galloway, D. (eds) (1996) *Listening to Children in Education*. London: David Fulton.

Davies, J. (2008) Differential teacher positive and negative interactions with male and female pupils in a primary school setting. *Educational and Child Psychology* 25(1): 17–26.

Dawkins, R. (1988) *The Blind Watchmaker*. London: Penguin Books.

Dencrombe, M. (1980) Keeping 'em Quiet: The Significance of Noise for the Practical Activity of Teaching. In P. Woods (ed.), *Teacher Strategies*. London: Croom Helm.

Department for Education (DfE) (1994) *Pupils with Problems*. London: DfE (Circulars 8–13/94).

Department of Education and Science (DES) (1988) *Secondary Schools: An Appraisal by HMI*. London: HMSO.

Department for Education and Science (DfES) (1989) *Discipline in Schools (Elton Report)*. London: HMSO.

Department for Education and Science (DfES) (2003) *Every Child Matters*. London: DfES.

Dinkmeyer, D. and Dreikurs, R. (1963) *Encouraging Children to Learn: The Encouragement Process*. Englewood Cliffs, NJ: Prentice Hall.

Dweck, C., Davidson, W., Nelson, S. and Enna, B. (1978) Sex differences in learned helplessness. In *Developmental Psychology* (14th edn).

Eaton, M. and Hansen, C. (1978) Classroom Organisation and Management. In N. Haring, T. Lovitt, M. Eaton and C. Hansen (eds) *The Fourth R: Research in the Classroom*. Columbus, OH: Merrill.

Eaves, R. (1975) Teacher race, student race and the behaviour problems checklist. *Journal of Abnormal Child Psychology* 1: 1–9.

Elwell, W. and Tiberio, J. (1994) Teacher praise: what students want. *Journal of Instructional Psychology* 21(4): 322–328.

Faupel, A.W. (1990) A model response to emotional and behavioural development in schools. *Educational Psychology in Practice* 5(4): 172–182.

Fitz-Gibbon, C.T. and Clark, K.S. (1982) Time variables in classroom research: a study of eight urban secondary school mathematics classes. *British Journal of Educational Psychology* 52: 301–316.

Flanders, N. and Havumaki, S. (1960) The effect of teacher-pupil contact involving praise. *Journal of Educational Psychology* 51(2): 65–68.

Frankland, S., Pitchford, Y. and Pitchford, M. (1985) The use of video recording to provide repeated monitoring of the successful use of rules, praise and ignoring. *Behavioural Approaches with Children* 9: 67–68.

Fredrickson, B. (1998) What good are positive emotions? *Review of General Psychology* 2: 300–319.

Fredrickson, B. and Joiner, T. (2002) Positive emotions trigger upward spirals toward emotional well being. *Psychological Science* 13: 172–175.

Fredrickson, B. and Branigan, C. (2005) Positive emotions broaden the scope of attention and thought-action repertoires. *Cognition and Emotion* 19: 313–332.

Fredrickson, B. and Losada, M. (2005) Positive affect and the complex dynamics of human flourishing. *American Psychologist* 60(7): 678–686.

Fredrickson, B., Manusco, R., Branigan, C. and Tugade, M. (2000) The undoing effect of positive emotions. *Motivation and Emotion* 24: 237–258.

Fredrickson, B., Tugade, M., Waugh, C. and Larkin, G. (2003) What good are positive emotions in crises? *Journal of Personality and Social Psychology* 84: 365–376.

Fredrickson, N. (2002) Evidence-based practice and educational psychology. *Educational and Child Psychology* 19(3): 96–111.

French, J. and French, P. (1984) Gender imbalances in the primary classroom: an interactional account. *Educational Research* 26(2): 127–136.

Fry, P.S. (1983) Process measures of problem and non-problem children's classroom behaviour: the influence of teacher behaviour variables. *British Journal of Educational Psychology* 53: 79–88.

Galton, M., Simon, B. and Croll, P. (1980) *Inside the Primary Classroom*. London: Routledge & Kegan Paul.

Galton, M., Hargreaves, L., Wall, D., Comber, C. and Pell, A. (1999) *Inside the Primary Classroom: 20 Years On*. London: Routledge.

Galvin, P., Mercer, S. and Costa, P. (1990) *Building a Better Behaved School*. York: Longman.

Georgiades, N. and Phillimore, L. (1975) The myth of the hero innovator. In C. Kiernan and P. Woodford (eds), *Behaviour Modification with the Severely Retarded*. Amsterdam: Associated Scientific Publishers.

Gilcrist, E.P. (1916) The extent to which praise and reproof affect a pupil's work. *School Society* 4: 872–874.

Gilham, W.E.C. (1981) *Problem Behaviour in Secondary Schools*. London: Croom Helm.

Gillborn, O. and Gibbs, C. (1996) *Recent Research on the Achievement of Ethnic Minority Pupils*. London: HMSO.

Glasser, W. (1992) *The Quality School: Managing Students without Coercion* (2nd edn). New York: Harper Perennial.

Goleman, D. (2005) *Emotional Intelligence* (10th anniversary edn). New York: Bantam Books.

Gottlieb, D. (1964) Teacher and students: the views of negro and white teachers. *Sociology of Education* 37: 345–353.

Gray, J. and Sime, J. (1988) Findings from National Survey of Teachers in England and Wales. In *Elton Report Discipline in School*. London: DES.

Hammersley, M. (1990) An evaluation of two studies of gender imbalance in primary classrooms. *British Journal of Educational Psychology* 70(4): 473–484.

Hanko, G. (1993) The right to teach – but what are Lee Canter's children learning? *British Journal of Special Education* 20(2): 71–85.

Hargraves, D.H., Hester, S.K. and Mellor, F.J. (1975) *Deviance in Classrooms*. London: Routledge.

Harris, A. and Kaphe, R.C. (1978) Problems of quality control in the development and use of behavioural change techniques in public school settings. *Education and Treatment of Children* 1: 43–51.

Harrop, A. (1974) A behavioural workshop for the management of classroom behaviour. *British Journal of In-Service Education* 1(1): 47–50.

Harrop, A. (1977) The vanishing problem. *Quarterly Bulletin of the British Association for Behavioural Psychotherapy* 5(3): 51–55.

Harrop, A. (1978) Another gain for the modifiers? *Special Education: Forward Trends* 5(4): 15–17.

Harrop, A. (1980) Behaviour modification in schools: a time for caution. *Bulletin of the British Psychological Society* 33: 158–160.

Harrop, A. (1983) *Behaviour Modification in the Classroom*. London: Hodder & Stoughton.

Harrop, A. and McCann, C. (1983) Behaviour modification and reading attainment in the comprehensive school. *Educational Research* 25: 191–195.

Harrop, A. and McCann, C. (1984) Modifying 'creative writing' in the classroom. *British Journal of Educational Psychology* 54: 62–72.

Harrop, A. and Williams, T. (1992) Rewards and punishments in the primary school: pupils' perceptions and teachers' usage. *Educational Psychology in Practice* 7(4): 211–215.

Harrop, A. and Holmes, M. (1993) Teachers' perceptions of their pupils' views on rewards and punishments. *Pastoral Care* 11(1): 30–35.

Harrop, A. and Swinson, J. (2000) Natural rates of approval and disapproval in British infant, junior and secondary classrooms. *British Journal of Educational Psychology* 70: 473–483.

Harrop, A. and Swinson, J. (2003) Teachers' questions in the infant, junior and secondary school. *Educational Studies* 29(1): 49–57.

Harrop, A. and Swinson, J. (2007) The behavioural approach in schools: a time for caution revisited. *Educational Studies* 33(1): 41–52.

Harrop, A. and Swinson, J. (2011) Comparison of teacher talk directed to boys and girls and its relationship to their behaviour in secondary and primary schools. *Educational Studies* 37(1): 115–125.

Harrop, A., Foulkes, C. and Daniels, M. (1989) Observer agreement calculations: the role of primary data in reducing obfuscation. *British Journal of Psychology* 80: 181–189.

Harrop, A., Daniels, M. and Foulkes, C. (1990) The use of momentary time sampling and partial interval recording. *Behavioural Psychotherapy* 16: 121–127.

Hathiwala-Ward, H. and Swinson, J. (1999) Teachers' verbal responses in a multi-racial primary school. *Educational & Child Psychology* 16(3): 37–43.

Hattie, J. (2009) *Visual Learning*. London: Routledge.

Hattie, J. and Timperley, H. (2007) The power of feedback. *Review of Education* 77(1): 81–112.

Heller, M. and White, M. (1975) Rates of teacher approval and disapproval to higher and lower ability classes. *Journal of Educational Psychology* 67: 796–800.

Henry, S. (ed.) (1989) *Degrees of Deviance: Student Accounts of their Deviant Behaviour*. Aldershot: Gower

Hillman, S. and Davenport, G. (1978) Teacher–student interactions in desegregated schools. *Journal of Educational Psychology* 70: 545–553.

Houghton, S., Wheldall, K., Jukes, R. and Sharpe, A. (1990) The effects of limited private reprimands and increased private praise on classroom behaviour in four British secondary school classes. *British Journal of Educational Psychology* 60: 255–256.

Irvine, J. (1985) Teacher communication patterns as related to race and sex of student. *Journal of Educational Research* 78(6): 338–345.

Isen, A., Daubman, K. and Nowicki, G. (1987) Positive affect facilitates creative problem solving. *Journal of Personality and Social Psychology* 52: 1122–1131.

Jolly, M. and McNamara, E. (1992) *Pupil Behaviour Schedule*. Ainsdale, UK: Positive Behaviour Management.

Jones, S. and Dinda, K. (2004) A meta analytical perspective on sex equality in the classroom. *Review of Educational Research* 74(4): 443–471.

Kanfer, F. and Spates, C. (1977) Self-monitoring, self-evaluation and self-reinforcement in children's learning. *Behaviour Therapy* 8: 17–23.

Kaplan, J.S. and Carter, J. (1995) *Beyond Behaviour Modification: A Cognitive Behavioural Approach to Behaviour Management in the School*. Austin, TX: Pro-Ed.

Kelly, A. (1988) Sex stereotypes and school science. A three year follow up. *Educational Studies* 14: 151–163.

Kluger, A. and Denisi, A. (1996) Feedback interventions: towards the understanding of a double-edged sword. *Current Directions in Psychological Science* 7: 67–72.

Kounin, J.S. (1970) *Discipline and Group Management in Classrooms*. New York: Rinehart & Winston.

Kounin, J.S. and Gump, P. (1958) The ripple effect in discipline. *Elementary School Journal* 59: 158–162.

Kounin, J.S., Gump, P.V. and Ryan, J.J. (1961) Explorations in classroom management. *Journal of Teacher Education* 12: 235–247.

Kyriacou, C. (1986) *Effective Teaching in Schools*. Oxford: Basil Blackwell.

Lepper, M.R. and Green, D. (1978) *The Hidden Costs of Reward*. Morriston, NJ: Lawrence Erlbaum.

Lepper, M.R., Green, D. and Nesbitt, R.E. (1973) Understanding children's intrinsic interest with extrinsic reward. *Journal of Personality and Social Psychology* 28: 129–137.

Levy, R. (1977) Relationship of an overt commitment to task compliance in behaviour therapy. *Journal of Behaviour Therapy and Experimental Psychiatry* 8: 25–29.

Lewin, K. (1935) *Dynamic Theory of Personality. Selected Papers*. New York: McGraw-Hill.

Lewis, A. and Lindsay, G. (eds) (2000) *Researching Children's Perspectives*. Buckingham: Open University Press.

Losada, M. (1999) The complex dynamic of high performance teams. *Mathematical and Computer Modelling* 30(9–10): 179–192.

Losada, M. and Heaphy, E. (2004) The role of positivity and connectivity in the performance of business teams. *American Behavioural Scientist* 47(6): 740–765.

Lysakowski, R. and Walberg, H. (1982) Instruction effects of cues, participation and corrective feedback. *American Educational Research Journal* 19: 559–578.

McAllister, L.W., Stachowakia, J.G., Bear, D.M. and Conderman, L. (1969). The application of operant conditioning techniques in a secondary classroom. *Journal of Applied Behaviour Analysis* 2: 277–285.

Macbeath, J., Demetriou, H., Ruddock, J. and Myers, K. (2003) *Consulting Pupils: A Toolkit for Teachers*. Cambridge: Pearson.

McColl, L. and Farrell, P. (1990) Method used by educational psychologists to assess children with emotional and behavioural difficulties. *Educational Psychology in Practice* 9(3): 164–169.

McCormick, S.L. (1985) Students' off-task behaviour and assertive discipline. *Dissertation Abstracts International* 46: 1880A.

McNamara, E. (1999) *Positive Pupil Management and Motivation*. London: David Fulton.

McNamara, E. (ed.) (2009) *Motivational Interviewing*. Ainsdale, UK: Positive Behaviour Management.

McNamara, E. and Heard, A. (1976) Self-control through self-recording. *Special Education: Forward Trends* 3: 157–168.

McNamara, E., Evans, M. and Hill, W. (1986) The reduction of disruptive behaviour in two secondary school classes. *British Journal of Educational Psychology* 56: 209–215.

Madsen, C.H., Becker, W.C. and Thomas, D.R. (1968) Rules, praise and ignoring elements of elementary classroom control. *Journal of Applied Behaviour Analysis* 1(2): 139–50.

Mageean, B. (2002) The evidence of psychology in action. *Educational and Child Psychology* 19(3): 22–31.

Makins, V. (1991) Five steps to peace in the classroom. *Times Educational Supplement* 1–11–91.

Marzillier, J. (2004) The myth of evidence-based psychotherapy. *The Psychologist* 17(7): 392–395.

Mayer, G.R. (1995) Preventing anti-social behaviour in the schools. *Journal of Applied Behaviour Analysis* 28: 467–478.

Mayer, G.R. and Butterworth, T. (1979) A preventative approach to school violence and vandalism: an experimental study. *Personal and Guidance Journal* 57: 436–441.

Mayer, G.R., Butterworth, T., Nafpaktitis, M. and Sulzer-Azaroff, B. (1983) Preventing school vandalism and improving discipline: a three-year study. *Journal of Applied Behavioural Analysis* 16: 355–369.

Merrett, F. and Blundell, D. (1982) Self-recording as a means of improving classroom behaviour in secondary school. *Educational Psychology* 2: 145–157.

Merrett, F. and Wheldall, K. (1986) Observing pupils and teachers in classrooms (OPTIC): a behavioural observation schedule for use in schools. *Educational Psychology* 6: 57–70.

Merrett, F. and Wheldall, K. (1987) Natural rates of teacher approval and disapproval in British primary and middle school classrooms. *British Journal of Educational Psychology* 57: 95–103.

Merrett, F. and Wheldall, K. (1992) Teachers' use of praise and reprimands to boys and girls. *Educational Review* 44(1): 73–79.

Merrett, F., Jackson, P. and Fitzpatrick, A. (1991) The effect of changes in teacher response ratios on pupils' behaviour. *Positive Teaching* 2 (2): 79–91.

Meyer, W. and Lindstrom, D. (1969) *The Distribution of Teacher Approval and Disapproval of Head Start Children*. Washington, DC: US Office of Economic Opportunity.

Miller, A. (2003) *Teachers, Parents and Classroom Behaviour. A Psychosocial Approach*. Maidenhead: Open University Press.

Miller, W. and Rollnick, S. (eds) 1991 *Motivational Interviewing: Preparing People for Change*. New York: Guilford Press.

Mortimore, P., Sammons, P., Stoll, L., Lewis, D. and Ecob, R. (1988) *School Matters*. Wells, Somerset: Open Books.

Myhill, D. (2002) Patterns of interactions and responses in whole class teaching. *British Education Research Journal* 28(3): 1–13.

Nafpaktitis, M., Mayer, G.R. and Butterworth, T. (1985) Natural rates of teacher approval and disapproval and their relation to student behaviour in intermediate school classrooms. *Journal of Educational Psychology* 77: 363–367.

Nau, P.A., Van Hoten, R. and O'Neil, A. (1981) The effects of feedback and a principal-mediated time-out procedure on the disruptive behaviour of junior high school students. *Education and Treatment of Children* 4(2): 101–113.

Nichols, D. and Houghton, S. (1995) The effect of Canter's assertive discipline programme on teacher and student behaviour. *British Journal of Educational Psychology* 65: 197–210.

O'Donohue, W. and Krasner, L. (1995) *Theories of Behaviour Therapy*. Washington, DC: American Psychological Association.

Office for Standards in Education (Ofsted) (1996) *Exclusions from Secondary Schools 1995–1996*. London: The Stationery Office.

O'Leary, K.D. and O'Leary, S.G. (1972) *Classroom Management: The Successful Use of Behaviour Modification*. Oxford: Pergamon Press.

Osler, A. (1997) *Exclusions from Schools and Racial Equality*. London: Commission for Racial Equality.

Osler, A. (2000) Children's rights, responsibilities and understandings of school discipline. *Research Papers in Education* 15(1): 49–67.

Panagopoulou-Stamatelatou, A. and Merrett, F. (2000) Promoting independence and fluent writing through behavioural self-management. *British Journal of Educational Psychology* 70: 603–622.

Paterson, G.R. and Reid, J.B. (1971) Reciprocity and Coercion: Two Facets of Social Systems. In C. Neuringer and J. Michael (eds) *Behaviour Modification in Clinical Psychology*. New York: Appleton Century Crofts.

Pearce, N. and Hallgarten, J. (eds) (2000) *Tomorrow's Citizens*. London: Institute of Public Policy Research.

Peters, T. and Waterman, R. (2004) *In Search of Excellence*. London: Profile Books.

Peterson, C. (2008) *A Primer in Positive Psychology*. Oxford: Oxford University Press.

Phillips, D., Davie, R. and Callely, E. (1985) Pathway to institutional developments in secondary schools. In D. Reynolds (ed.), *Studying School Effectiveness*. London: Falmer.

Porter, L. (2000) *Behaviour in Schools Theory and Practice for Teachers*. Buckingham: Open University Press.

Raymond, J. (1987) An educational psychologist's interaction with a class of disruptive pupils. *Educational Psychology in Practice* 3(2): 16–22.

Read, J. (2005) *Toward Zero Exclusions: An Action Plan for School and Policy Makers*. London: Institute for Public Policy Research and Centre for British Teachers.

Rees, C., Farrell, P. and Rees, P. (2003) Coping with complexity: how do educational psychologists assess students with emotional and behavioural difficulties? *Educational Psychology in Practice* 19(1): 35–64.

Reynolds, D. (1992) School Effectiveness and School Improvement: An Updated Review of British Literature. In D. Reynolds and P. Cattance (eds), *School Effectiveness: Research, Policy and Practice*. London: Cassell.

Rhodes, J. (1993) The use of solution-focus brief therapy in school. *Educational Psychology in Practice* 9(1): 27–34.

Rodgers, B. (1998) *You Know the Fair Rule*. Melbourne: ACER.

Rodgers, T.A. and Iwata, B.A. (1991) An analysis of error-correction procedures during discrimination training. *Journal of Applied Behaviour Analysis* 24: 775–782.

Rosenshine, B. (1971) *Teaching Behaviours and Student Achievement*. Slough: NFER.

Rosenthal, R. and Jacobson, L. (1968) *Pygmalion in the Classroom: Teacher Expectation and Pupils' Intellectual Development*. New York: Rinehart & Winston.

Rowe, D. (2006) Take responsibility: school behaviour policies in England, moral development and implications for citizenship education. *Journal of Moral Education* 35(4): 519–531.

Rubie-Davies, C.M. (2007) Classroom interactions: exploring the practices of high and low expectation teachers. *British Journal of Educational Psychology* 77: 289–306.

Rubie-Davies C.M. (2010) Teacher expectations and perceptions of student attributes: is there a relationship? *British Journal of Educational Psychology* 80: 121–135.

Russell, A. and Lin, L.G. (1977) Teacher attention and classroom behaviour. *The Exceptional Child* 24: 148–155.

Rutter, M., Maughan, B., Mortimore, P. and Ouston, J. (1979) *Fifteen Thousand Hours: Secondary Schools and Their Effects on Children*. London: Open Books.

Schwieso, J. and Hastings, N. (1987) Teachers' use of approval. In N. Hastings and J. Schwieso (eds), *New Directions in Educational Psychology, Vol. 2: Behaviour and Motivation in the Classroom*. London: Falmer.

Scott, L., McNamara, E. and McPherson, E. (1986) The use of behaviour modification in a secondary school: a further development. *Educational and Child Psychology* 3: 4–20.

Sharp, P. (1985) Behaviour modification in the secondary school: a survey of students' attitudes towards rewards and praise. *Behavioural Approaches with Children* 9: 109–112.

Sharp, S. and Thompson, D. (1994) The role of whole-school approaches in tackling bullying behaviour in schools. In P. Smith and S. Sharp (eds), *School Bullying: Insights and Perspectives*. London: Routledge.

Sherman, T.M. and Cormier, W.H. (1974) An investigation of the influence of student behaviour on teacher behaviour. *Journal of Applied Behaviour Analysis* 7: 11–21.

Skinner, B.F. (1953) *Science and Human Behaviour*. New York: Macmillan.

Skinner, B.F. (1968) *The Technology of Teaching*. New York: Appleton Century Crofts.

Sommer, R. and Sommer, B. (2002) *A Practical Guide to Behavioural Research* (5th edn). Oxford: Oxford University Press.

Spender, D. (1982) *Invisible Women: The Schooling Scandal*. London: Writers and Readers Pub. Cooperative Society.

Squires, G. (2001) Using cognitive behavioural psychology with groups of pupils to improve self-control of behaviour. *Educational Psychology in Practice* 17(4): 317–336.

Steptoe, A., Wardle, J. and Marmot, M. (2005) Positive affect and health-related neuroendocrine and inflammatory responses. *Proceedings of the National Academy of Sciences, USA* 102: 6508-6512.

Stoiber, K.C. and Waas, G.A. (2002) A contextual and methodological perspective on the evidence-based intervention movement with school psychology in the United States. *Educational and Child Psychology* 9(3): 7–21.

Strain, P.S., Lambert, D.L., Kerr, M.M., Stagg, V. and Lenker, D.A. (1983) Naturalistic assessment of children's compliance to teachers' requests and consequences for compliance. *Journal of Applied Behaviour Analysis* 16: 243–249.

Stuart, R.B. (1971) Behavioural contracting within the families of delinquents. *Journal of Behaviour Therapy & Experimental Psychiatry* 2: 1–11.

Swinson, J. (1990) Improving behaviour: a whole-class approach using pupil perceptions and social skills training. *Educational Psychology in Practice* 6(2): 82–89.

Swinson, J. and Melling, R. (1995) Assertive discipline – four wheels on this wagon – a reply to Robinson and Maines. *Educational Psychology in Practice* 11(3): 1–8.

Swinson, J. and Cording, M. (2002) Assertive discipline in a school for pupils with emotional and behavioural difficulties. *British Journal of Special Education* 29(3): 72–75.

Swinson, J. and Harrop, A. (2002) The differential effects of teacher approval and disapproval in junior and infant classrooms. *Educational Psychology in Practice* 17(2): 157–167.

Swinson, J. and Harrop, A. (2005) An examination of the effects of a short course aimed at enabling teachers in infant, junior and secondary schools to alter the verbal feedback given to pupils. *Educational Studies* 31(2): 115–129.

Swinson, J. and Knight, R. (2007) Teacher verbal feedback directed towards secondary pupils with challenging behaviour and its relationship to their behaviour. *Educational Psychology in Practice* 23(3): 241–255.

Swinson, J. and Harrop, A. (2009) Teacher talk to boys and girls and its relationship to their behaviour. *Educational Studies* 35(5): 515–524.

Swinson, J., Woolf, C. and Melling, R. (2003) Including emotional and behavioural difficulties pupils in mainstream comprehensives. *Educational Psychology in Practice* 19(1): 65–75.

Tenenbaum, G. and Golding, E. (1989) A meta analysis of the effects of enhanced instructions. *Journal of Research and Development in Education* 22: 53–64.

Tharp, R.G. and Wetzel, R.J. (1969) *Behaviour Modification in the Natural Environment*. New York: Academic Press.

Thomas, J.D., Presland, I.E., Grant, M.D. and Glynn, T. (1978) Natural rates of teacher approval and disapproval in grade 7 classrooms. *Journal of Applied Behaviour Analysis* 11(1): 91–94.

Thorndyke, E.L. (1898) Animal intelligence. *Psychological Review Monogram*, Supplement No. 2.

Topping, K. (1980) *Educational Systems for Disruptive Adolescents*. London: Croom Helm.

Torgerson, D. and Torgerson, J. (2008) Randomised controlled trials in educational research. *British Journal of Educational Studies* 49(3): 13–25.

Tunstall, P. and Gibbs, C. (1996) How does your teacher help you to make your work better? Children's understanding of formative assessment. *The Curriculum Journal* 7(2): 185–203.

Van Bilsen, H. (1991) Motivational interviewing: perspectives from the Netherlands. In W. Miller and S. Rollnick (eds), *Motivational Interviewing: Preparing People for Change*. New York: Guilford Press.

Verma, G.K. (1986) *Ethnicity and Educational Achievement in British Schools*. Basingstoke: Macmillan.

Visser, J. (1983) The humanistic approach. In G. Upton and A. Gobell (eds), *Behaviour Problems in a Comprehensive School*. Cardiff: University College Faculty of Education.

Walberg, H. (1982) What makes schooling effective? *Contemporary Education Review* 1: 1–34.

Ward, L. (1984) The effectiveness of assertive discipline as a means to reduce classroom disruptions. *Dissertation Abstracts International* 44: 2323A.

Webster-Stratton, C. and Hammond, M. (1997) Treating children with early-onset conduct problems. *Journal of Consulting and Clinical Psychology* 65(1): 93–109.

Webster-Stratton, C. and Reid, J. (2004) Strengthening social and emotional competence in young children. *Infant and Young Children* 17(2): 96–113.

Wheldall, K. and Austin, R. (1980) Successful behaviour modification in the secondary school – a reply to McNamara and Harrop. *British Psychology Society Division of Educational & Child Psychology Occasional Papers* 4(3): 3–9.

Wheldall, K. and Beaman, R. (1994) An evaluation of the WINS (Working Ideas for Need Satisfaction) training package. *Collected Original Resources in Education* 18(1): fich4E01.

Wheldall, K. and Merrett, F. (1986) Reducing troublesome classroom behaviour in the secondary school. *Maladjusted and Therapeutic Education* 3(2): 37–46.

Wheldall, K. and Lam, J. (1987) Rows versus tables II: the effects of two classroom seating arrangements. *Educational Psychology* 8: 303–312.

Wheldall, K. and Merrett, F. (1987) What is the behavioural approach to teaching? In N. Hartings and J. Schwiesco (eds), *New Directions in Educational Psychology II: Behaviour and Motivation in the Classroom*. London: Falmer.

Wheldall, K. and Merrett, F. (1988) Packages for training teachers in behaviour management. BATPACK, BATSAC and the positive teaching packages. *Support for Learning* 3: 86–92.

Wheldall, K., Merrett, F. and Borg, M. (1985) The behavioural approach to teaching package (BATPACK) and experimental evaluation. *British Journal of Educational Psychology* 55: 65–75.

Wheldall, K., Houghton, S. and Merrett, F. (1989a) Natural rates of teacher approval and disapproval in British secondary school classrooms. *British Journal of Educational Psychology* 59: 38–48.

Wheldall, K., Houghton, S., Merrett, F. and Badderley, A. (1989b) The behavioural approach to teaching secondary aged children (BATSAC). Two behavioural evaluations of a training package for secondary school teachers in classroom behavioural management. *Educational Psychology* 9(3): 185–196.

White, M.A. (1975) Natural rates of teacher approval and disapproval in the classroom. *Journal of Applied Behaviour Analysis* 3: 367–372.

White, O. and Haring, N. (1980) *Exceptional Teaching* (2nd edn). Columbus, OH: Merrill.

Wilkinson, S. (1981) The relationship of teacher praise and student achievement. *Dissertation Abstracts International* 41(9-A): 3998.

Williams, H. (2012) Fair pairs and three part praise – developing the sustained use of differential reinforcement of incompatible behaviour. *Educational Psychology in Practice* (in press).

Winnicott, G.K. (1971) *Therapeutic Consultation in Child Psychiatry*. London: Hogarth.

Winnie, P. and Butler, D. (1994) Student cognition in learning and teaching. In T. Husen and T. Postlewaite (eds) *International Encyclopedia of Education* (2nd edn). Oxford: Pergamon.

Winter, S. (1990) Teacher approval and disapproval in Hong Kong secondary school classrooms. *British Journal of Educational Psychology* 60: 88–92.

Wolf, M.M., Giles, D.K. and Hall, V.R. (1968) Experiments with token reinforcement in a remedial classroom. *Behaviour Research and Therapy* 6: 51–64.

Woods, S., Hodges, C. and Aljunied, M. (1996) The effectiveness of assertive discipline training: look before you leap off this wagon. *Educational Psychology in Practice* 12(3): 175–181.

Woolfolk, A., Hughes, M. and Walkup, V. (2008) *Psychology in Education*. Harlow: Pearson.

Wyatt, W.J. and Hawkins, R.P. (1987) Rates of teachers' verbal approval and disapproval. *Behaviour Modification* II(1): 27–51.

Index